797,885 Books
are available to read at

www.ForgottenBooks.com

Forgotten Books' App
Available for mobile, tablet & eReader

ISBN 978-1-330-32188-1
PIBN 10026661

This book is a reproduction of an important historical work. Forgotten Books uses state-of-the-art technology to digitally reconstruct the work, preserving the original format whilst repairing imperfections present in the aged copy. In rare cases, an imperfection in the original, such as a blemish or missing page, may be replicated in our edition. We do, however, repair the vast majority of imperfections successfully; any imperfections that remain are intentionally left to preserve the state of such historical works.

Forgotten Books is a registered trademark of FB &c Ltd.
Copyright © 2015 FB &c Ltd.
FB &c Ltd, Dalton House, 60 Windsor Avenue, London, SW19 2RR.
Company number 08720141. Registered in England and Wales.

For support please visit www.forgottenbooks.com

1 MONTH OF FREE READING

at

www.ForgottenBooks.com

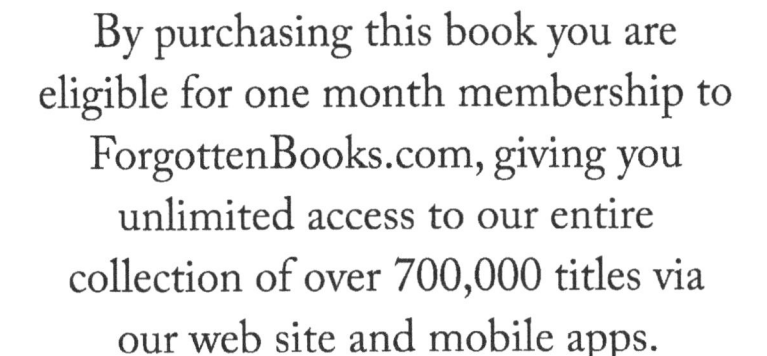

By purchasing this book you are eligible for one month membership to ForgottenBooks.com, giving you unlimited access to our entire collection of over 700,000 titles via our web site and mobile apps.

To claim your free month visit: www.forgottenbooks.com/free26661

* Offer is valid for 45 days from date of purchase. Terms and conditions apply.

Similar Books Are Available from
www.forgottenbooks.com

An Account of the Manners and Customs of the Modern Egyptians, Vol. 1 of 2
by Edward William Lane

Cults, Customs and Superstitions of India
by John Campbell Oman

Primitive Manners and Customs
by James Anson Farrer

Etiquette for Gentlemen
Or, Short Rules and Reflections for Conduct in Society, by A Gentleman

Totem and Taboo
Resemblances Between the Psychic Lives of Savages and Neurotics, by Sigmund Freud

The Sun and the Serpent
A Contribution to the History of Serpent-Worship, by C. F. Oldham

Etiquette for Americans
by A Woman Of Fashion

An Account of the Manners and Customs of Italy
With Observations, by Giuseppe Marco Antonio Baretti

The Aztecs
Their History, Manners, and Customs, by Lucien Biart

The Bell
Its Origin, History, and Uses, by Alfred Gatty

Bible Manners and Customs
by G. M. Mackie

Chinese Life and Customs
by Paul Carus

Cumberland & Westmorland, Ancient and Modern
The People, Dialect, Superstitions and Customs, by J. Sullivan

Customs and Traditions of Palestine
Illustrating the Manners of the Ancient Hebrews, by Ermete Pierotti

Oriental Customs
by Samuel Burder

Wedding Customs
Then and Now, by Carl Holliday

Dramatic Traditions of the Dark Ages
by Joseph S. Tunison

Hindu Manners, Customs and Ceremonies
by Abbe J. A. Dubois

The Kachins
Their Customs and Traditions, by O. Hanson

Manners, Customs, and Antiquities of the Indians of North and South America
by Samuel G. Goodrich

Indo-China and its Primitive People... By Captain Henry Baudesson. Translated by E. Appleby Holt.

With 48 Illustrations from photographs. : : : :

LONDON: HUTCHINSON & CO.
PATERNOSTER ROW

TO
PROFESSOR ANTOINE CABATON
TOKEN OF REVERENCE AND AFFECTION

GN
635
I6 B3813

CONTENTS

BOOK I
AMONG THE MOÏ

CHAPTER I
AMONG THE MOI
General characteristics of the Moï—A legend as to their selection of a home—The part played by ocean currents in the distribution of races—Had primitive peoples a sense of direction ?—Features of daily life—The hut—The village—Clothing and ornaments—A primitive method of kindling a fire . . . . *p.* 3

CHAPTER II
INDUSTRIES AND OCCUPATIONS
Agriculture—Industries—Weaving, iron and copper mining—Commerce and industrial products—Food supplies—Fishing—How we once fished with dynamite—Hunting—Various methods of big-game hunting—My first elephant hunt—Some useful hints to big-game hunters—Poisons—Arms and weapons of defence—The tiger, a dangerous neighbour—A bathing tragedy . . . . . *p.* 18

CHAPTER III
FAMILY LIFE
Diseases and their cure—Betrothal and marriage—Adultery—Divorce—A Moï wedding—Birth—Childhood—The game of Pig-Snatcher *p.* 52

CHAPTER IV
SOCIAL LIFE
Property—Slavery—Utilitarian morals—A bashful race—The Levirate—Law and custom—An amateur arbitrator—Principles and practice of the Ordeal . . . . *p.* 75

CHAPTER V
RELIGIOUS BELIEFS AND RITES
Similarity between the philosophical conceptions of uncivilized races—Most of the ritual derived from magic—Dualism—Private and public talismans—The Pi—The Legend of the Dog-King—Totemism—Sorcery—Rebel Moï . . . . *p.* 98

CONTENTS

CHAPTER VI
RITES AND SUPERSTITIONS (*continued*)

Tribal and proprietary signs—Tattooing and mutilation—Principles and practice of the taboo—Its survival in modern Europe—The incarnation of Spirits in stones, trees and animals—Belief in the magic powers of the tiger—Animal poison—Bones as a charm—A protecting ear—Ex-votos offered to the Spirit of the tiger—Superstitions about monkeys —Hunting rites . . . . *p.* 116

CHAPTER VII
RITES AND SUPERSTITIONS (*continued*)

Agrarian rites—How Me-Sao, King of the Moï, opens the jar—Rites of initiation and "coming of age" . . . . . *p.* 137

CHAPTER VIII
BELIEFS AND RITES

The origin and observance of funeral rites—The ceremony of the Commemoration of the Dead—Burial rites and various methods *p.* 161

CHAPTER IX
ART AND CULTURE

The relation between the evolution of artistic expression and social development as illustrated by the Moï and the Laotians—The intimate connection between Music, Dance and Stage—A Moï orchestra and war dance—Deficiencies in the sense of sound due to lack of artistic education—The effect of a gramophone—Predominance of the analytical over the synthetic faculty—Exaggerated respect for form—Impression produced by the stereoscope—Decorative arts—Sports, fêtes, and public amusements—Extensive use of marks for ritual and other purposes . . . . *p.* 177

CHAPTER X
INTELLECTUAL LIFE

The relations between the development of language and social evolution—An enigmatic system of writing—Knotted cords, notches in sticks and their accessories—The evolution of literature among primitive races—Length of memory among races that have no written records—Historical value of legends transmitted by oral tradition—Nature of the more usual alterations to be met with in documentary folklore—The most general legends, fables and proverbs of the Moï *p.* 193

BOOK II
THE CHAM

CHAPTER I
THE CHAM

General characteristics of the Cham—A Mohammedan group—Its place among ancient civilizations—Social life—Dress and ornaments—The calendar—Rites accompanying the construction of a house, a cart, and a junk—Agriculture and industry—Medicines—The use of narcotics by criminals to stupefy their victims . . . . *p.* 225

CHAPTER II
SOCIAL AND FAMILY LIFE
Traces of the matriarchal system in the conception of the family—The "Karoh"—Circumcision—Precautions against seduction—Rites incidental to betrothal, marriage, birth and infancy . . *p.* 248

CHAPTER III
RITES AND SUPERSTITIONS
The beginnings of Islam in Indo-China—Rites which accompany initiation into the priestly caste—The gods of Cham—Temples—Resemblance between the architecture of the Cham and that of the Kmer—Phallic rites—A visit to a royal sepulchre . . . . *p.* 266

CHAPTER IV
RITES AND SUPERSTITIONS (*continued*)
Agrarian rites—Tabooed ricefields—Secret ploughing—Sleeping rice—Various uses of eaglewood—How the Cham procure it—Public festivals and holy days . . . . *p.* 297

CHAPTER V
RITES AND SUPERSTITIONS (*continued*)
Burial rites—Philology—Legends and fables . . . *p.* 310
BIBLIOGRAPHY . . . . *p.* 325

LIST OF ILLUSTRATIONS

The Tomb of a Rade Chief.	*Frontispiece*	
A Moï Maiden with enlarged Ears	*Facing page*	16
A Cham Chief and his Daughter .	,,	16
Laotian Barque under full sail		17
A Moï Farmer at work		17
Fishing with Dynamite		26
A Floating Village		26
A Typical Village in Laos .		27
Primitive Irrigation in Laos.		27
Birth Ceremonies		54
The Wife of a Moï Chief		55
A Little Moï Family .		55
A Sorcerer performing the Marriage Ceremony		64

LIST OF ILLUSTRATIONS

Children scrambling over the Remains of the Marriage Feast	*Facing page*	65
A Little Kha		78
Our Native Prisoners		78
The Village Musician serenading a Young Couple		79
A Hut of Propitiation		100
Tombs fenced with Bamboo and decorated with Elephants' Tusks		100
Woven Bamboo Baskets used to carry Offerings to the Priests		101
Memorial Stone erected to a Tiger		130
A Hunting Party		131
An Elephant and his Driver		131
The Festival of the Dead: carrying home the Sacrificial Buffalo		160
The Festival of the Dead: Poles erected for the Celebration		161
Funeral Rites: the Body in a Coffin made from the Hollowed Trunk of a Tree		174
Funeral Rites: the Body by its weight has indicated its wish to be buried in this spot		175
A Medical Examination		186
Looking through the Stereoscope		186
Three Boys of our Native Guard		187
A Court of Trial on an Annamese Stage		204
A Group of Amateur Actors in Annam		205
A Mandarin of Annam		205
Royal Elephants in Cambodia		250
A Buddhist Procession		251
Image of a Departed Saint in a Phallic Temple		272
Statues erected to the Dead in Laos		272
Shrine of a Laotian Priest		273
The Interior of the Shrine		273
Statue of an Ancient King of Cambodia		288
Statue of an Ancient Queen of Cambodia		288
An Old Cham Temple in a Cambodian Forest		288
The House of a Cham Aristocrat		289
A Cottage Home in Cambodia		289
Cremation in Cambodia: the Head of the Procession		312
A Catafalque upon which several Bodies are carried away for Cremation		312
The Hearse and Bearers at an Annamese Funeral		313
The Altar of his Ancestors, which accompanies the Deceased		313

FOREWORD

No nation which desires worthily to fulfil the rôle of Protector to the barbarous races on whom it proposes to confer the benefits of civilization can afford to remain ignorant of their ways of life and thought. The interchange of ideas is as essential to successful colonization as the exchange of commodities. Unfortunately the path to knowledge is beset with difficulties. In the first place the savage or semi-savage is unable to apply the method of synthesis to those of his institutions which seem founded on custom. He cannot tell us which of his usages have been borrowed or imposed from outside. Further, as a rule, it seems impossible to find any medium of communication between his language and ours, so that any attempt at cross-examination is met by the sorry pretence that our questions " make his head ache."

During the period covered by the geodetical and topographical surveys which preceded the construction of the Trans-Indo-Chinese railway, the members of the mission to which I was attached lived for years among the natives upon terms of the greatest familiarity. We saw them in their homes, at their work and recreations, and we can at least claim that we obtained our knowledge at first hand.

I have not hesitated throughout this book to record the conclusions of my colleagues and to compare or contrast them with my own for the sake of the light they may throw upon each other.

I have analysed the rites and superstitions which came to my notice with a mind unhampered by obsession or prejudice. If I have seemed to dwell too fondly on analogous ceremonies among other peoples and in other days it is only because I wish to arrive at the broad principles which seem to me to underly all these phenomena, principles which are as immutable as human nature itself.

BOOK I
AMONG THE MOÏ

People

CHAPTER I

AMONG THE MOI

General characteristics of the Moi—A legend as to their selection of a home—The part played by ocean currents in the distribution of races—Had primitive peoples a sense of direction?—Features of daily life—The hut—The village—Clothing and ornaments—A primitive method of kindling a fire.

THE half-civilized races who inhabit the mountains and uplands of Indo-China are known by different names among their neighbours. The Birmans call them " Karens," the Laotians, " Kha," the Cambodians, " Stieng," or " Pnong," the Annamites, " Man," or " Moï." " Moï," which can be translated by " savage," is perhaps the most convenient label for the whole complex of these primitive folk.

Their number is not capable of exact computation but probably approaches 400,000, divided between tribes of different names. They are to be found scattered between the eleventh and the twentieth

Indo-China and its Primitive People

CHAPTER I

AMONG THE MOI

General characteristics of the Moï—A legend as to their selection of a home—The part played by ocean currents in the distribution of races—Had primitive peoples a sense of direction ?—Features of daily life—The hut—The village—Clothing and ornaments—A primitive method of kindling a fire.

THE half-civilized races who inhabit the mountains and uplands of Indo-China are known by different names among their neighbours. The Birmans call them " Karens," the Laotians, " Kha," the Cambodians, " Stieng," or " Pnong," the Annamites, " Man," or " Moï." " Moï," which can be translated by " savage," is perhaps the most convenient label for the whole complex of these primitive folk.

Their number is not capable of exact computation but probably approaches 400,000, divided between tribes of different names. They are to be found scattered between the eleventh and the twentieth degrees of latitude, from the frontiers of China to the boundaries of Cambodia and Cochin-China.

From the earliest times they have made their homes in the wooded uplands at an altitude which secures them from the fear of inundation. Their love of mountain and forest is a primitive and unchangeable instinct and all attempts to acclimatize them to the plains have ended in failure. Further, this instinct is reinforced by their religious beliefs and their respect for ancestral tradition. According to a charming legend this domain was the gift of Eve herself.

"The first human family had offspring so numerous that the land of their birth could no longer sustain them. The mother resolved that they should scatter to people other portions of the earth. Before the separation she called them all together for the last time and made a great feast in their honour. All did credit to her bounty with the exception of one, who took nothing but some red pimento.

"This self-restraint was not lost on Eve. She recommended those of her sons who appreciated good cheer to share the fertile plains, and giving a bow and arrows to her sober guest, promised him the kingdom of the mountains where the beasts rove the forests.

"He was the father of the Moï. His descendants share his frugality, and, like his, their wants are few."

These characteristics distinguish them to-day. Our first discovery on arrival among them was that the use of money is unknown. They value an empty bottle more highly than a piastre, and if by chance they accept some such coin it is only to cut it in pieces for an ornament. Though their disposition is generally peaceful, some tribes are extremely jealous of their independence and receive an intruder, however innocent, with showers of arrows. In this, as in all other respects, the people reflect the character of their surroundings.

As the national costume consists of the absence of it there is no obstacle to the observation of their physical forms. The European on his first arrival in this country will think himself in a museum of classical statuary! Simplicity, harmony, virility and grace are all exhibited in perfect combination.

An average figure measures five feet five inches in height. Few of the natives are more than five feet nine inches, or less than five feet one inch. The torso is faultless, the line of the loins elegant. Sometimes the lower limbs are rather frail. The big toe, while preserving its prehensile faculty (the feature of all races of the far East), is not detached from the other toes. In this respect the Moï differ from the Annamites, who have gained the nickname of " Giao-Chi " (detached toe).

The adipose tissue is so fine that obesity is rare. Generally speaking the skin is of the colour of earth and varies between reddish brown and dark yellow. It has a characteristic odour resembling that of a wild beast in good condition. There is an abundance of coarse black hair, which is generally rolled up in a knot at the back and fastened with a comb or band of stuff. In case of illness the patient lets his hair fall loose to conceal his face. The forehead is low and narrow and sometimes terminates in a point. The expression of the eyes, which are frequently oblique, is one of fearless frankness. The thick chin is the characteristic prognathous feature. The lips are fleshy and colourless. The prominence of the cheek-bones give the face the appearance of a pentagon with the chin as its apex. The long and narrow skull places the type among the dolichocephalic races.* These are the broad characteristics of all branches of the Indonesian race and are especially to be remarked among the peoples of the Asiatic archipelago, the Battaks of Sumatra, the Dyaks of Borneo and the Alfurs of the Celebes, who show the least alteration from the original type.

It is well known that these primitive peoples were aware of the existence of ocean currents and used them for their own purposes. No other theory can account for the distribution of the Malayo-Polynesian races among the swarm of islands, some of them hundreds of leagues apart. It demonstrates beyond doubt the importance of the influence of currents on the dispersion of the human race over the surface of the globe.

* According to the measurements of Dr. Noel Bernard the cephalic index of the living male is 76. The transverse nasal index varies between 84 and 95.

The existence of a large number of legends common to the two peoples reinforces the physiological resemblance between the Moï and the primitive races of the Malay Archipelago. The folklore of all of them speaks of the existence of human beings reputed to have had a tail like a monkey's, and, what is even more extraordinary, a razor-edged membrane on the forearm which was used to cut down branches obstructing their path.

Curiously enough Borneo possesses a people, the Murut, who habitually wear the skin of a long-tailed monkey. At a distance this appendage seems to belong to the wearer rather than to the garment.

In the same way it may be that the custom of carrying a wooden knife, practised by forest-roving peoples, is responsible for the illusion which confuses the weapon with the arm which wields it.

The Moï have a wonderful memory for places and a marked sense of direction. The latter faculty is attributed mainly to a peculiarly highly-developed sensibility to physical contact. Like all peoples who spend most of their time in the open air they are constantly noting the direction of the wind. They know the exact hour at which, according to the season, the wind will rise or fall. However light, a breeze will induce a sensation of freshness immediately recorded by their bodies, especially when moist with exertion. As they walk or run they note carefully every movement which obstacles oblige them to make. According to Doctor Ouzilleau, this sixth sense is localized in the ampullæ of the semicircular canals. A movement of the head causes the displacement of the endolymph which acts on the auditory nerves.

Further, the Moï possess keen vision and a highly-developed sense of smell which bring to their notice objects which would remain unobserved by Europeans. A small drop of blood is on a leaf. It is the evacuation of a wild boar whose lair is close at hand.

As is well known, instinct prompts almost all the actions of the semi-savage. Accordingly the psychology of the Moï is not easy to describe. Is he capable of altruism, pity, or gratitude ? With few exceptions these virtues are almost completely unknown. But he will learn them, like anyone else, as soon as civilization has given him more favourable conditions than under his present precarious existence. To-day he falls an easy victim to injustice, intrigue and exaction. So if Europeans arrive in force they are treated as an enemy to be feared and therefore worthy of respect, but a casual foreigner may easily pay for his rashness with his life.

Like all men of weak character, the Moï is very revengeful and awaits with patience the day of redress. Months and years may pass without effacing the least detail of his wrong. I was frequently called upon to compose their quarrels and it was seldom that the injury was not one of long standing.

" But why," I asked, " wait so long before taking action ? "

" I had other things to do," came the answer

" What other things, you idler ? "

" Oh, invitations to share a flask of spirits of rice or a fat pig."

Nothing, not even the most imperious necessity, can overcome their inveterate laziness.

I shall never forget the curious impression produced on me by my first entry into a Moï village. The village in question was Dran on the Da-Nhim, whose narrow valley marks the outposts of the great Annamite chain. Five or six straw huts had been erected on stakes some ten feet above the earth, less to avoid dampness than to secure immunity from the raids of wild beasts.

Some women were pounding paddy (a preparation of rice) for the evening meal in mortars of ironwood. The measured beat of a metronome and the regular thuds of the pestles set the time for the wailing chant with which the women beguiled their work. On seeing me they looked up startled. A single piece of flimsy cloth draped from the waist to the knee revealed the outline of many a full and graceful thigh and emphasized rather than concealed their sinuous movements. The children played around or pretended to help in lifting the heavy pestles

At the top of a pole a rude figure had been carved of the genius of the village armed with a murderous looking crossbow. He was the tutelary deity of the place.

The supports of the houses are built of ironwood,

the other portions being of plaited bamboo sticks. The roof is open to the sky and overhangs both the farmyard and the pigsty. We had no difficulty in conjuring up the discomforts that awaited us should we ever be compelled to lodge in such a place. The thin wattled walls would not spare us the least noise nor the slightest odour.

My unwonted appearance still continued to excite demonstrations of alarm, but it seems my beard was mainly responsible for the indiscriminate flight which ensued. One old woman only was brave enough to remain seated in her doorway. I asked her for permission to inspect her dwelling, accompanying my request with a gift of a large packet of tobacco. She acceded, not without hesitation and a look of infinite distrust in her eyes. A rude wooden approach with apologies for steps led up to the interior. The rooms, one of which is assigned to each distinct family, were about the size of a horse-box, but a special apartment was reserved for strangers and solemn occasions such as a general reunion. The hearth, raised a few inches above the level of the floor, consisted of a platform on which three fires were burning and an appetizing and harmonious murmur proceeded from three pots in which rice, the evening meal, and the food for the pigs were being prepared. There was no chimney, for the duty of the smoke is to keep off the mosquitoes, which are such a plague in these regions. Accordingly every object in the place was covered with a thick layer of soot, and no window was to be seen.

The inhabitants of this particular village were poor and the huts were very small, but in some of the more fortunate villages the houses sometimes attain a length of two hundred yards.

Huge blocks of wood served as beds to a people usually too tired to be critical. The walls of the partitions were hung with a medley of gongs, tom-toms, weapons and domestic utensils. The spirit flask, without which no family celebration is complete, was suspended from a post adorned with rude carving.

The frightened inhabitants eyed us askance and behaved like whipped curs. The children squalled and hid under any convenient object, nor could I gain their confidence by emptying my pockets of all the tempting trifles I had brought with me for the purpose.

Seen from a distance there was nothing to point to the presence of a village. It was perched on the side of a ravine with the forest behind it, and thick brushwood in front protected it from the gaze of the inquisitive. The only entrance, known to the initiated alone, was that furnished by two narrow passages. Even when the entrance has been found, another dark passage has to be traversed which is designed for easy defence in case of attack. A small number of determined warriors would be quite sufficient to repel invaders.

The open space in the centre of the village was adorned with two public buildings, a large hut reserved for the boys who had just attained the age of puberty and another which contained the last harvest. The door of this public granary was secured in a manner which demonstrated to perfection the naïve simplicity of these folk. The lock consisted of a rattan thread passed through an empty egg-shell. Of course it was impossible to touch the thread without breaking the shell, and as all are equally interested in the preservation of the precious grain supply, each man thus became policeman to his neighbour.

The Moï is not nomadic by nature, but moves his habitation periodically as soon as he has exhausted the natural resources of the soil he occupies. Other causes of this periodical exodus are serious misfortunes, such as a fire, an epidemic, or unpleasantly frequent raids by the tiger. Such mishaps are invariably attributed by the Moï to the evil influence of the genius of the place. To dispute the possession of the ground with so powerful a divinity would be sheer madness, and accordingly he yields with grace and betakes himself elsewhere without regret.

The choice of the next habitation is not a mere matter of chance. The Geomancer is called in to consult the omens, and no selection is made until after ripe reflection.

But I am forgetting the mild adventure which was the occasion for these general observations. After some time I became aware that my visit could not be prolonged without a breach of etiquette and that I was trespassing on the time of my hostess.

She herself recalled me to good manners by resuming her multifarious household duties. Accordingly I bade her farewell and left her surrounded by a crowd of the feathered tribe who assembled in answer to her guttural cry of " loc-loc," the usual signal for a generous distribution of maize.

The national costume is marked by an almost evangelical simplicity. The men may truly be described as clothed in sunbeams, for a flimsy piece of cloth draping the waist can hardly be dignified with the name of dress. A knife in a leather or wooden sheath is the only weapon carried, though another small knife is frequently fastened in. the hair, which is twisted into a knot and secured by a comb. The women have a clinging skirt, which does full justice to their graceful figures. The bust is seldom covered at all, but in cold weather a large piece of cloth is draped round the waist. Both sexes sometimes wear a rough cloak trimmed at the edge with a variegated fringe, but in spite of such precautions they are very liable to affections of the throat.

The chief peculiarity, however, which distinguishes them from the other groups of Indo-China is their inordinate love ot personal decoration. The passion for finery gives rise to the most embittered rivalry among the women, and takes many curious forms, such as the artificial elongation of the lobe of the ear, in which various ornaments are introduced. This painful process begins in infancy, when the ears are pierced with a sharpened bamboo rod. A wooden ring is inserted in the hole thus made, and weights hung from it, at first small, then increasing in size. The lobe, unnaturally distended, sometimes reaches the shoulder, in which case it is accounted a feature of the greatest beauty, and a husband with every talent and virtue is assured to its fortunate possessor. But it is of prime importance that the ear should remain unbroken. Should the skin give way, the two hanging pieces will be an eternal reproach. No husband will want a woman thus degraded, and a hopeless spinsterhood will be her lot in life.

The men are addicted to the same practice, but with rather more discretion. They confined themselves to filling the holes in their ears with our champagne corks, which were quite at a premium on the market and shared the honours with our boxes of Swedish matches. Sometimes, too, their taste turned to an ivory serviette ring or even a simple drawing pencil. Another fashionable masculine ornament is a brass collar, consisting of a number of spiral rings. We never satisfied ourselves as to whether this was pure decoration or served some ulterior purpose, such as protection against affections of the throat.

Copper and brass bangles adorned the wrists and ankles, but he who wished to touch the supreme height of fashion wrapped his head in one of the towels with which we rewarded our more industrious coolies.

I brought from Paris a supply of beads, in the hope

of finding them useful as a medium of exchange.
To my surprise the natives took no interest in them
at all and they proved almost worthless. The Moï,
like the European, follows the caprice of fashion,
and our beads, it seemed, were too heavy and not
gay enough for his taste. Besides, they were not
the mode of the moment.

It was thus sufficiently demonstrated that the
wearing of clothes is not even essential for the display
of feminine vanity and coquetry. Artifice can
dispense with clothing, and if the sexes in this strange
land attract each other by means that seem curious
and unaccountable to us, the end in view is always
and among all peoples the same, the continuance
of the race.

It must be remembered, too, that the development of a fashion is similar to the development of
a living organism. A certain form of dress or style
of decoration undergoes successive transformations,
the stages being generally exaggeration, diminution
and ultimate disappearance. For illustration we
need go no further afield than the recent vagaries
of fashion in Europe which seem to oscillate between
the bell and the asparagus, but perhaps a more
striking example is the long, pointed shoes of the
Middle Ages. At first the points were quite reasonably short. Then little by little each man tried to
sort himself out of the common ruck of his neighbours
by having longer points, and after about a century
the fashion culminated in the absurd extravagance

of the shoe with points long enough to be drawn upwards and fastened to the knee. The mode first saw the light in the middle of the thirteenth century and disappeared abruptly in 1428. The same evolution can be traced in the progress of the ruff of the fifteenth century and the crinoline of the nineteenth.

It is at least open to belief that ethnical transformations are governed by similar laws. This distension of the lobe must be traced to the practice of continually adding to the number of ornaments with which the ear was overloaded.

Every individual tends to overrate the feature which is considered the characteristic of his race. " Le beau pour le crapaud c'est sa crapaude," said Voltaire, and the natural instinct of the savage is to exaggerate what he regards as the most worthy of admiration. This instinct is indubitably responsible for most of the mutilation practised by primitive peoples. Thus the negresses of Africa produce an artificial elongation of the nipple by the sting of a certain insect, and the platyrrhine Malays make their flat noses even flatter, while the Persians take the most elaborate pains to induce an extreme hook on a nose already aquiline. This theory of exaggeration inherent in our nature can alone explain certain customs which are otherwise unaccountable.

I ought perhaps, before leaving the subject, to enumerate three other methods of decoration practised by the leaders of fashion among the Moï.

A Moï Maiden with Enlarged Ears.

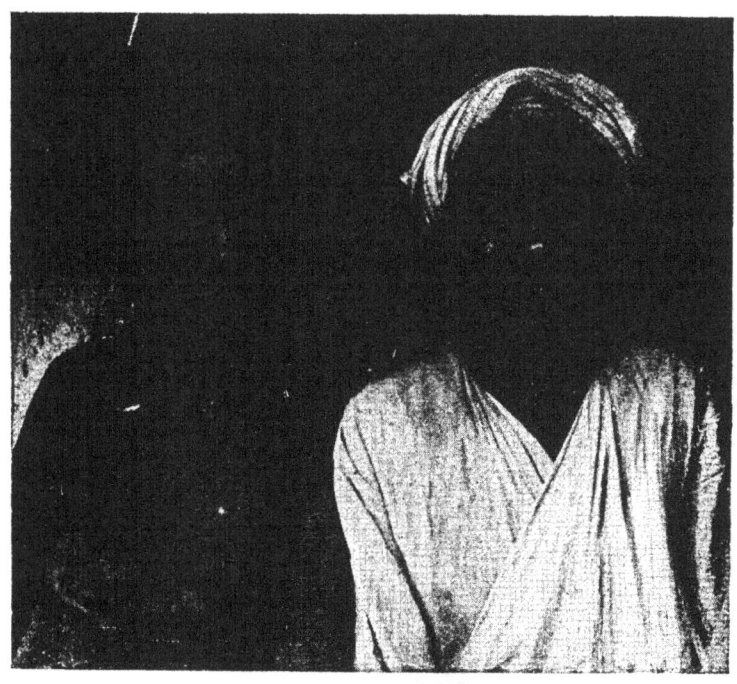

A Cham Chief and his Daughter.

Laotian Barque under Full Sail.

A Moi Farmer at work.

[To face

The women powder their hair with an odorous substance obtained from the berries of the vetiver. Both men and women smear their teeth with a kind of lacquer to protect the enamel from the action of lime, the principal ingredient of the betel leaf.

Finally the society ladies dye their nails a vivid vermilion with the sap of the plant " Semrang."

As I said above, our matches soon went to a premium as a medium of exchange, but the Moï already employed two methods of kindling a fire. One was by striking a flint against a piece of pyrite of iron, the other by simply rubbing together two pieces of wood. The process is as follows. A very dry bamboo is split at one end for about five inches of its length. The two sections are kept apart by the insertion of a wooden wedge. In this way a rude ventilating chimney is made under which the operator piles up some dead leaves, bamboo cuttings and moss. He now passes a long cane under the apparatus (which he keeps steady with his foot) and rubs it rapidly backwards and forwards until a spark appears, which is usually within a minute. The movement closely resembles that of sawing.

This last method is only practised in the bush, for in the villages the fires are carefully preserved under the ashes and seldom allowed to go out. This preservation of fire is a phenomenon which characterizes all primitive peoples in every clime.

CHAPTER II

INDUSTRIES AND OCCUPATIONS

Agriculture—Industries—Weaving, iron and copper-mining—Commerce and industrial products—Food supplies—Fishing—How we once fished with dynamite—Hunting—Various methods of big-game hunting—My first elephant hunt—Some useful hints to big-game hunters—Poisons—Arms and weapons of defence—The tiger, a dangerous neighbour—A bathing tragedy.

THE principal industry of the Moï is the cultivation of rice. The method adopted, however, is unlike that of the Annamites of the plains. Instead of cultivating a ricefield by continuous irrigation which produces three crops a year, the Moï wait until November, the end of the rainy season. They then clear a portion of the forest large enough to raise a crop for the entire population of the village. In April they set fire to the fallen trunks which the sun has dried. For several days the whole mountain is illuminated by these immense braziers and the crackling of the timbers can be heard for miles around. Finally the ground is covered with a layer of fine ashes, which are washed into the soil by the first rains. Then begins the sowing.

INDUSTRIES AND OCCUPATIONS

Armed with a pointed stick the women hollow trenches in the soil and throw in the seed. The rains first and then the soil itself complete their work. The baskets are soon full and the public granaries stocked with the precious cereal. Good as a harvest may be, however, it is seldom that a crop is sufficient to support the population till the next. More often the supply runs short and the tribe has to subsist for several weeks on bamboo shoots and forest roots.

Several times during my visit I tried to inculcate in the natives some elementary notions of thrift and foresight. A " Pholy," or village chief, once showed me in a word the weak point of my counsels. " If I were to start putting by a store," he gravely told me, " my elder brother, the white warrior, would take it from me to feed his escort."

I vigorously denied in the name of my kind any such evil intentions.

" In that case," he continued, " my younger brothers in the neighbourhood would seize it. So I am prudent and keep no store at all."

Now what answer could I have returned to that ?

However, whether the Moï blames civilization or his very human neighbours, it is certain that he is happy-go-lucky by nature and lives from hand to mouth. His ignorance of economy may be ascribed to two causes, one that he possesses nothing of his own, since all property is held in common by the tribe, the other that Nature is so bountiful as to render foresight generally unnecessary.

Quite otherwise is the character of the Annamite, who spares no pains over the cultivation and improvement of his ricefields. His barn is never empty. The Emperor of Annam himself sets the example and takes part each year in sowing the grain which is destined for religious sacrifices. By a long series of proclamations the Government has raised the status of the tiller of the soil, for it is generally accepted that the prosperity of the country depends more on its agriculture than on the expansion of its commerce. As for the profession of arms, it has long been regarded as a relic of ancient barbarism.

Here is an example of one of these proclamations:

"The tiller of the soil is a man of worth. The police shall never molest him. But he who bears arms is a brigand and my sbires will treat him as such."

This is no doubt the origin of the popular scorn of the military profession. A parallel is offered by France in the time of Sully, when the interests of agriculture were the special concern of the legislature.

Throughout the territories occupied by the Moï the cultivation of rice is carried on alternatively with that of maize. In the fertile soil this latter grows to an enormous size. On the plateau of Langbian it is quite usual to find stalks thirteen to seventeen feet high.

Every household grows its own tobacco. Cigarettes

INDUSTRIES AND OCCUPATIONS

are made by rolling up tobacco in the dried leaves of the banana tree. In shape they resemble an extended cone of which the small end is put in the mouth. The pipes are of copper and have a long stem. An inner shell of bamboo fibres is attached to the bottom of the bowl and the more this is impregnated with nicotine the more it becomes an object of desire, especially to the women. Even the babies play their part in this little comedy, for they compete eagerly for a suck at the stick which serves their fathers as a pipe-cleaner.

Industry is in its infancy and is confined to the manufacture of simple objects of daily use, such as stout wicker baskets and glazed pottery. These vessels are not baked in a furnace but dried in the sun, and are consequently very brittle. Another staple manufacture is the three-foot chandelier, surmounted by a torch of resin. The women weave various coarse cloths of cotton. Their sole implement is a weaving frame consisting of two pieces of wood between which are stretched two sets of threads. The shuttle is worked by hand with a fair degree of skill.

Without professing any great knowledge of the art of dyeing the women are quite familiar with the properties of certain substances, of which they take full advantage. Thus indigo furnishes black as well as two shades of blue, a colour more highly esteemed. Yellow is obtained from the saffron. Alum and filtered cinders are put to a similar use.

Cotton is bleached by soaking the material in a concoction of rice-water boiled for several hours.

The needles which we bestowed on the most skilful of the housewives were accepted and preserved by them as precious objects of art. These ladies, as guardians of the ancient traditions, remained faithful to ancestral custom and preferred to use a blunt brass pin, which dispenses with the necessity for a thimble, the manipulation of which passes their understanding.

Iron, though found almost everywhere in its natural state, is worked by only a few tribes which have specialized in the industry. The anvil consists either of a huge stone or of a block of metal encased in a wooden armature. The hammer is fairly long and has a bamboo handle. Bamboo cylinders convey the draught to the furnace. This rudimentary equipment produces lances and knives of the greatest efficacy.

The extraction of iron is carried on by the Catalan method. The mineral in its natural state is first mixed with a large quantity of charcoal and then covered over with clay and collected into a kind of circular bin made of bricks. The mixture is then stirred vigorously for twenty-four hours, at the end of which it liquefies and falls into three layers. The lower part is composed of iron of a very poor quality, the upper mainly of ashes. The middle layer alone is of the desired temper and can be prepared for all purposes by a vigorous hammering.

INDUSTRIES AND OCCUPATIONS

All these operations are accompanied by a series of religious sacrifices, for the genii of the mine must be propitiated, and copious libations alone can humour their caprice. A special day, the fourth of the month, is devoted to an annual festival in their honour.

A few groups manufacture gongs of copper, which is found just below the surface of the soil. It seems to be the practice among these tribes, as soon as copper-bearing lands have been discovered, to secure seclusion and freedom from interference by expelling all the inhabitants of the country around. This is certainly one explanation of the weird stories which the evicted competitors tell of their successful rivals. If the vanquished are to be believed, the industry is carried on by the women, who live alone except for one annual visit to their husbands. These women are not merely unnatural wives, but also unnatural mothers, for they slay all their male children, keeping only the girls. Their other characteristics are hardly less formidable. They wield the lance with a skill and vigour of which any man might be envious. They are always accompanied by dogs, and finally (for a touch of the supernatural is inevitable), the legend runs that their spinal column terminates in a short tail.

I was extremely curious to make the acquaintance of these Amazons, but my informant invariably took refuge in silence when I pressed him for information of their whereabouts.

Whatever may be the value of these stories, it is well known that in this country, where money is unknown, gongs, pots and jars serve as the medium of exchange. The measure of value is the antiquity of the particular object. If it has several centuries behind it, its price reaches a truly fantastic figure.

Perhaps the Moï recognize that the arts are on the decline and that modern productions, if more attractive, are far less beautiful than those of bygone ages. It is very unlikely, for their æsthetic sense is still in an early stage of development.

The value of a red earthenware jar three feet in height and two hundred years old is equal to that of thirty buffaloes. Another vessel known as "The Mother and Child," which is composed of two jars of different sizes joined after the manner of the Siamese twins, is worth fifty buffaloes. At the top of the scale stands a vase worth one hundred buffaloes, partly because it enjoys the reputation of being unique and partly because it is adorned with the figure of a shapeless and mysterious human being.

The same curious standards of taste are revealed in the sets of gongs and tom-toms. These instruments are designed to give three or five concords, by the blending of which every variant of the Moï scale may be produced.

There is also a flourishing industry in the cultivation of cinnamon, both for the home market and for export to China, which is the largest customer for that product.

The hunters make long journeys for the purpose of exchanging elephants' tusks and feet and rhinoceros horn. A horn of the latter animal is ordinarily worth ten buffaloes among the Moï, but one which is new and flawless has been known to fetch the enormous sum of five hundred piastres, or fifty pounds in English money. The Annamites are the most successful hunters and dealers. Every power aiming at colonial expansion should concentrate its efforts on developing commercial relations with the natives. Trade is the most potent agent of conquest and the only one which brings prosperity and security in its train.

We found fishing with dynamite another means of peaceful penetration into these regions, though available only in places watered by a stream or river. We made a point of inviting all the inhabitants of the villages in the neighbourhood of our camp and it was seldom that the audience was not large and representative, so great was the interest roused by this operation. Judging by the horde of women which issued from every hamlet and the enormous baskets brought by the children we might have been setting out to clear the river of every living creature in it. The men, who fish both for food and sport, showed themselves very willing to indicate the favourite haunts of our prey.

Curiosity was roused to the highest pitch by the preparation of the charge and the Bickford train was an object of interest almost approaching reverence. I fired a few inches of this and astonishment knew no bounds. The younger members of my audience spoke openly of sorcery, while the elder smiled in a knowing manner but kept at a safe distance.

At length the charge was ready. I fired the end of the train and threw the infernal machine, weighted with a stone, into the middle of the water. The stone described a long parabola and fell into the dark depths carrying the instrument of destruction after it. For some seconds there was a deathly silence. Then a terrific explosion rent the air and a column of smoke and steam rose from the surface of the water to the height of the highest trees. There was a whirr of wings as the birds scattered from the branches. The Moï gaped at each other in amazement and prostrated themselves on the ground. Screams of fear from the children announced their conviction that the genius of the river, enraged at this intrusion on his dominions, was coming to carry them off.

Soon the cloud vanished, transformed into a shower of refreshing rain. Calm replaced the storm. The startled doves cautiously returned to their nests. The stream flowed on, unruffled, forgetful. Suddenly a few white specks appeared on the surface, vanished and reappeared in ever-increasing numbers until the waters seemed alive. These were the fish, their air-bladders burst by the force of the explosion and now floundering helplessly at the mercy of the swift current. The crowning moment had arrived. With one accord the spectators dived into the stream to secure their easy prey. The

Fishing with Dynamite: After the Explosion.

A Floating Village.

[To face p

A Typical Village in Laos.

Primitive Irrigation in Laos.

[*To face p.*

more wary had armed themselves with a *liane*, to which they fastened their victims by the gills. The booty was then easily towed between their teeth.

The women and children were in the very forefront of the fray, and there are few more entertaining spectacles than that of all these babies racing each other amid screams of delight. In a few moments the water was cleared of its shouting, struggling invaders, whose bronze skins glistened beneath a silver film of pearly drops. One by one, after adjusting their simple garb, they advanced to lay their booty in a large basket at my feet, then withdrew with a delightful affectation of indifference as to my intentions. Then began the ceremony of distribution. The basket raised on a mound of earth became the centre of a circle. The children advanced in single file, the youngest first. At the head of the procession was a youngster of less than six years of age, who had no difficulty in selecting the largest fish, which he dragged away by the tail stammering with excitement. The mothers followed, more modest in their desires. In a few moments I was left alone, a dismal survival of the merry throng.

Fish is the favourite food of the people in these regions and every river contains an apparently inexhaustible supply of it. The three current methods of fishing are with line, net, and spear. The nets are spread across the narrow channel, which is always left in the middle of the bamboo dams. The bait consists of the stalks of certain weeds and plants,

INDUSTRIES AND OCCUPATIONS

which are treated to form a soft paste. When a haul has been particularly successful the fish is smoked and preserved for several months. For this purpose it is pounded with salt and pimento and stored in bamboo tubes. In this state it is a favourite condiment.

There is little change of diet, for the food supply is virtually restricted to the products of fishing and hunting. Domestic animals are never used for food except upon special occasions such as religious sacrifices.

Traps are preferred to weapons for keeping down the wild beasts which swarm in the forests. Both in devising and constructing snares the natives display a high degree of invention and skill. We found apparatus of different kinds all over the country, its form being apparently determined by the seasons of the year and the particular region. For example, the following method is employed in a thickly-wooded country where the presence of beasts of prey is only known by the tracks leading to their watering-places.

The hunters select a young tree, supple but yet sufficiently strong for their purpose. The top is forced over and secured to the ground by means of a tough fibre in which a noose is made. The long grass conceals all these traces of human intervention. Now the monster, tiger or panther, approaches. It cannot pass the spot without disturbing the simple mechanism which the least shock would set in motion. The sapling, suddenly released, flies back, and the unfortunate captive finds its neck or paw firmly gripped by the noose. The more it struggles the tighter becomes the knot, and if not actually strangled, it soon becomes exhausted by its agonized efforts to escape, and hangs, a miserable object, on this improvised gallows.

Another method is to dig a pit in a track the course of which has been carefully noted. Animals have fixed habits according to the season of the year. Shortly before nightfall they emerge from their lairs on an expedition to secure an evening meal. The pit must be both narrow and deep, and its dimensions calculated so nicely that the movements of the prisoner will be hampered in every direction. This object is further secured by driving stakes into the ground at the bottom so that the mere act of falling in will inflict the most severe injuries. The place is then concealed by a layer of branches, a part of the operation which needs the greatest care if the trap is not to be detected. A little earth from the excavation lying on the ground at the side is quite enough to warn some animals of the presence of danger and the condition of the grass and branches, which quickly decay, is in itself a suspicious circumstance. The tiger is one of the most wary and observant of beasts and is seldom captured in this manner, except when being pursued, when it has not the time to take its usual precautions. Deer, on the other hand, seem much less suspicious and frequently fall a victim to this particular wile.

There is another trap which requires equal care in construction, and closely resembles the eel traps which are common in Europe. It is a cage, circumscribed by a double row of bamboos as a palisade. The beast has to penetrate a hedge of bamboos to find the entrance which leads to an open space where a pig or goat rewards its curiosity. Once inside, however, its retreat is cut off, for the bamboos spring back to their natural position, thus closing up the entrance, and the palisade is quite strong enough to resist attack, however fierce.

It will be recognized that the construction of these snares calls for a degree of skill and experience to which few Europeans can attain. Sometimes the pits were so cunningly dug that it was almost impossible to detect their presence and we were in serious danger of falling in ourselves. As a rule the natives indicate the proximity of a trap by some signal such as a broken branch, a spear driven into a tree, or a stalk twisted in a certain manner; but, of course, the purport of these signs is known only to the initiated, and at the beginning of our expedition we had much more to fear from the tiger-traps than from the chances of an encounter with the beast for which they were intended.

It must not be imagined that the Moï confine themselves to the destruction of wild beasts only, or merely those which threaten their safety.

Elephants are slaughtered ruthlessly for the sake of their ivory. The elephants haunt the damp and sandy regions of this country. During the dry season from November to March herds consisting of anything from ten to twenty beasts make their way to the forests both for shelter from the heat and for the pools which have not yet dried up. It is generally at watering-time that the creature makes itself heard with loud trumpetings which are audible at an immense distance and betray ist presence to its human enemy. When the elephant is undisturbed its progress is sedate and leisurely and it stops every now and then to pluck a branch either for recreation or to serve as a fly-swish.

It is this last habit, well known to the native hunter, which betrays it and leads to its down fall. The first time I took part in an elephant-hunt I was amazed to see that the native who was guiding me kept his eyes fixed upwards all the time. I should have thought it was obvious that we needed no other guide than the enormous footprints left by the unwieldy beasts, and told him so. I was not long left in error. Without relaxing his efforts he soon showed me that these tracks were very unreliable, that they frequently pointed different ways, cut across each other, and sometimes, in fact, disappeared altogether. He told me also that the evacuations of the creature are liable to be misleading unless quite fresh, still viscous, and unaffected by insects. A trail in a forest must then be sought not on the ground but in the branches of the trees. It is by the broken branches, the appearance of the severed ends, and the consistency of the gum which escapes, that the experienced hunter can deduce the more or less recent passage of a herd.

I smile now when I think of the succession of surprises I experienced on that first hunting adventure and the ignorance I must have exhibited. We came to some swampy ground where my guide stopped short before some tracks that seemed to him the most fresh we had yet encountered. He carefully made some fresh tracks at the side with his feet and then lay at full length on the ground to compare the two sets of footprints. After a most minute examination of their respective appearances he calculated that less than half an hour had elapsed since the animals had passed by and went on his way without comment.

We had started out at sunrise, which is the orthodox and best time. To set out earlier is to court failure, for it is impossible to be sure of the traces in the darkness. At first we had directed ourselves by the pools, and on reaching a third pond were overjoyed to observe some traces obviously quite fresh. It is usually hopeless to start on a trail which is several days old, for a track made only the previous evening may easily take one much farther than is agreeable. Hunters who say that they have tracked elephants for weeks show more perseverance than intelligence. As it was, my companion lost the trail several times, but never took a short cut in the wild hope of picking it up farther on. He might as well have started hunting for shadows. Every time this mishap occurred he retraced his steps to the point of departure and looked again. He was not to be deflected from his purpose even by the trumpetings of the elephants themselves, though these were quite audible at times.

"Ong Bioi (Mr. Elephant) would make a liar of me," he explained in his picturesque jargon.

He was quite right, for in tracking these monsters the only safe rule is to follow the trail and leave short cuts severely alone. Besides, this hunting sense, if I may so call it, is only a practical application of that sense of direction of which I have spoken before, and which seems almost to be an instinct with some people. It is something analogous to the sense of danger which is found in certain specially constituted individuals who can foretell the presence of a danger by the twitching of the muscles of the back.

Soon, without any apparent reason, my guide signalled to me to relieve myself, and as I did not comply at once, he repeated his order with a gesture that left no doubt as to his wishes. He knew from long experience of big-game hunting how dangerous a nervous contraction, such as that of an overcharged bladder, can be at a moment when the accuracy of a shot may make all the difference between life and death.

He then took off my colonial helmet, which in all its khaki glory was a somewhat conspicuous object, and replaced it by his own head-gear, a muddy-coloured turban, quite unnameable, which certainly harmonized better with our surroundings. I was dressed in a suit of Chinese linen, slate grey in colour, which seemed to meet with his approval, while, for himself, he carried his whole wardrobe, consisting of a thin woollen cloth, lightly wrapped round his waist.

He then picked up a handful of dust and threw it up in the air to observe the direction of the wind. This is the most indispensable precaution, for if the elephant is not blessed with keen sight, its hearing is extremely acute and can detect an unwonted sound at a great distance. It must be approached, therefore, against the wind.

During the hottest part of the day the elephant either stands with its trunk wound round the lower branch of a tree, or else lies down, sometimes with its legs folded under it and sometimes at full length on its side, just like a horse. In none of these positions does it need the assistance of a mound of earth or a tree trunk to rise, though some travellers would have us believe it. In spite of its immense bulk it can get up unaided at the first hint of danger. M. Millet, of the Woods and Forests Department of Indo-China, who was also a member of our party was a specialist in this form of sport, and gave me the benefit of his fifteen years' experience.

It must be understood that though the preliminary stalking is usually done by the natives the honour of executing the sentence of death is reserved for the European. This would naturally seem the easiest part of the operations, for it would appear impossible to miss so vast an object at short range. The uninitiated always fall into the error of underrating the difficulties involved in killing these creatures, but the error rarely survives the first experience.

To begin with, the hunter who wishes to kill with the first shot must have a considerable knowledge of the beast's anatomy. Otherwise he exposes himself to a furious charge or to the mortification of seeing his bullet reach a non-vital spot and his prey vanish into the forest unharmed. A knowledge of the structure of the skull is, in fact, indispensable, for a miss by a hair's-breadth in that region will change a wound that might have been mortal into an insignificant scratch. The natives are notoriously ignorant of such matters, and, in consequence, usually aim at the shoulder and lose half the animals they hunt.

The vulnerable spot to which all experienced shots direct their attention is the temple, or rather a spot about one third of an inch above the ear-hole. If the hunter can find some eminence which puts him at the level of this vital place his bullet will pass straight through the brain and out at the other ear. Death occurs instantaneously. The creature sinks down, its fore legs bent under him, its back legs stretched out, while its head and body remain rigid.

The same result is obtained by aiming behind the ear. On the other hand it is almost useless to fire straight into the advancing creature or hit it at the base of the trunk, especially with rifles of small bore.

It was this last shot that I attempted on this first elephant hunt when I was still in the depths of ignorance. The creature uttered a roar of agony, raised its trunk in the air and charged straight at me, covering thirty yards in a flash. I thought myself lost, but when almost on me it suddenly made a half turn on its haunches with as much agility as a circus pony and dashed off at a tangent smashing every obstacle in its path. My tracker had also fired with his Laotian rifle, and both shots were, in fact, mortal, though quite incapable of arresting its mad career. Only next day we came upon its carcase, already in a state of putrefaction and half devoured by white ants.

No less important for big-game hunting of this character is the choice of a rifle.

Fired by an expert a Winchester bullet not more than seven millimetres in diameter and fourteen grammes in weight is quite sufficient for all purposes, but a beginner should never start with anything less than ten millimetres in diameter and nineteen grammes in weight when hunting the tiger or any larger animal. Such a ball, projected at an initial velocity of 650 metres to the second, will stop any animal if it strikes either the shoulder or the breast. The Moï, of course, are not armed with our modern rifles. In fact, few of them possess a rifle at all, but the more fortunate among them buy the rustic Laotian rifles, a kind of blunderbuss which kicks and not infrequently knocks them down. The projectile used is not a bullet but a poisoned arrow made from an extremely hard wood.

Among the Moï the sorcerers alone know the secret processes which are employed in the manufacture of two extremely powerful cardiac poisons, antiarin and strophanthin, though these are also in use among the Dyaks of Borneo. No one else is allowed to be present when their preparation is taking place, but fortunately one of my compatriots in the mission, M. Odera, who was in the Woods and Forests Departments and had thirty elephants killed or captured to his credit, was once honoured by an invitation to be present at the ceremony.

A moonlight night is chosen. The novice first invokes the genii of the forest and then cuts a portion of the creeper *strophantus giganteus*, strips off the bark, grinds it up in a mortar and boils it over a fire until it attains the consistency of gum. This operation takes place at a great distance from the village, for the fumes are supposed to be noxious. To ascertain whether the required strength has been attained they cut off part of a lizard's tail and put a drop of the concoction on the severed end. Death ought to be immediate.

The second poison is obtained from the *antiaris*

toxicaria without any special preparation. An incision is made in the bark of the tree. In some regions the arrows are poisoned by the simple expedient of sticking them into the trunk of the poison-bearing tree and leaving them in this novel pincushion until required.

It is a curious fact that game killed by poisoned arrows is perfectly wholesome if the wound is carefully washed at once. The young plants also of the *antiaris toxicaria* supply an absorbent poison. Their sap is not as powerful as that of the full-grown trees, but on the other hand has neither its bitterness nor repulsive smell.

Both the *strophantus giganteus* and the *antiaris* are found all over the Indo-Chinese and Malay peninsulas. The effect of *antiaris* is the same whether introduced into the digestive organs or applied to the cellular tissue, but in the former case the dose must be considerably stronger to produce the same result. It is pleasant to record that there is little data on which to base observations on the effect of the Moï poisons on human beings. Our own experience furnished one or two illustrations, however. While we were in Nhe-An, a province of Annam, one of our captains was wounded by two arrows and, though they were taken out at once, he died twenty-two days later in fearful agony. Another officer was struck by a poisoned missile and after a few minutes went mad and committed suicide. The danger of attack by the rebellious Moï was always

INDUSTRIES AND OCCUPATIONS

present to our minds during the expedition. Two officers, MM. Canivey and Barbu, were wounded by several arrows. As there was no post where medical assistance could be obtained within several days' march and no doctor among us, I undertook a rational cure. All the symptoms pointed to poison. The nervous tremours, the alternating phases of excitement and lethargy, the dilation of the pupil, the feeble voice and the subnormal temperature left no doubt as to the nature of the malady. For a long time it seemed that recovery was impossible, for the arrow heads had not been immediately extracted; but events took a happier turn and in four weeks' they were both well again. I can only conclude that the poison cannot have been fresh and consequently had lost much of its strength. The natives treat a patient for poison by first making the wound bleed, then washing it in water impregnated with sea salt and calcined alum, and finally inducing a heavy perspiration by making him drink an infusion of mulberry leaves.

Most of the Moï arm themselves with the crossbow, which is a deadly weapon at a range of not more than forty yards. At half that distance the arrow will easily penetrate through two inches of the hardest wood. The arrow head is made of iron or wood, around which is wound a thread impregnated with the poisonous substance. It is fashioned with a notch at the base to make its extraction from a wound difficult, if not impossible.

The manipulation of the cross-bow requires no little strength. The bowman props the cross against his body and holds the bow firm on the ground with his foot. The strain of fixing the arrow is so great that it has been known to burst the bladder.

When the Moï goes to war with his neighbours he generally swathes his body in a multitude of thick wrappings to give him protection against such weapons as knives and daggers. His shield is of stout cane or buffalo hide and usually ornamented with the insignia of his tribe. Finally his panoply is completed by a spear with a handle of mahogany or sometimes by a two-handed sword. He is also ingenious at constructing subsidiary defences. On the outbreak of hostilities the neighbourhood of a village is thickly studded with small bamboo javelins, which are extremely difficult to distinguish from the grass and brushwood. Some of our party received grievous wounds from these concealed weapons.

The forests we encountered during our topographical survey are the home of a certain kind of buffalo of immense size. This species, which is very rare and not found elsewhere, is no other than the Aurochs, which are called "Con-minh" by the Annamites and "Co-bay" by the Moï. These animals are bay in colour and have a short and scanty coat, with the longest hairs under the belly and at the throat. They have white spots on all four feet, and resemble the wild buffalo in not being dewlapped. They are formidable foes and never wait to be attacked, but charge with lowered head at a prodigious speed. The tiger seems to have no terrors for them and many are the stories of their triumphs over the king of the forest himself.

Now, as a rule, a tiger is not dangerous unless it takes the initiative itself, which it seldom fails to do in these regions, where its supremacy has hardly yet been seriously challenged. Hence the saying which experience has abundantly justified: "In Indo-China the tiger is the hunter and man the hunted."

Of course, it is very unusual to meet this ferocious creature by daylight, even in regions where its ravages are the most frequent. Every traveller will pass by its lair in the bamboo groves, but it is quite exceptional to see the beast itself, except at nightfall, when it comes forth to seek its prey. Once a tiger has tasted human flesh it prefers it to all other food. Accordingly, the natives live in a state of chronic fear of the man-eater and will willingly abandon their villages rather than make the least effort to rid themselves of the pest. As I shall show later, they endow their enemy with human qualities and frequently refuse to destroy it when at their mercy for fear of arousing the vengeance of the whole species.

One of our party once witnessed the following scene. A tiger had fallen into a pit which had been laid for some deer. It had not been wounded, but the space was so cramped that it was quite unable to move. The natives were terrified lest it should die, in which case its spirit would never cease to molest them; so they decided to set it free. They made a cage without a floor, lowered it into the pit and then raised it up again by means of ropes passed under the creature. Perched on the neighbouring trees they pulled away the prison and let the captive go, offering it their humble apologies for having already detained it so long! Our representative had been compelled to promise his acquiescence, and, lest he should repent and show fight, his rifle was carefully left behind in the village.

I myself saw tigers on several occasions and often under circumstances when I wished them at the bottom of the deepest pit that human ingenuity could devise. One such occasion has left so vivid an impression on my mind by reason of its tragic outcome that I shall relate it here.

It was during the hot season when Sergeant Valutioni and I were in charge of a reconnoitring party sent forward to report on a region which he assured me was infested with tigers. In fact on the day in question he had gone so far as to bet me that we would meet a man-eater before nightfall. Now during the whole of my ten months' residence in Annam I had frequently passed through alleged tiger-stricken provinces but had never seen a single tiger, though at every station I was literally shot through and through with stories of their wholesale depredations. According to my colleagues every step was accompanied by the probability of immediate destruction. I became more and more sceptical and finally persuaded myself that the fearsome tales were spread by the old colonists with a view to discouraging newcomers. Accordingly I dismissed Valutioni's sinister predictions with a knowing smile.

Our way led through a magnificent forest. The sun grew hotter with every step, the ground harder as the carpet of moss and ferns dried up and withered. The trees became more stunted and their branches, almost denuded of leaves, took on strange fantastic shapes. Such foliage as there was seemed burnt up and ready to fall at the first breath of wind. Now and then a huge ant-heap broke the level sky-line and blended bewitchingly with the reddening trunks. A deathlike silence reigned, unchallenged even by a bird, over this realm of ill-omen.

Sao, the nephew of the chief of our escort, was walking a few yards ahead of me carrying my rifle. He was an intelligent boy about twelve years of age, with a peculiarly frank and pleasant expression, and I had had considerable hesitation in bringing him with us on an expedition which was bound to be long and trying, if not actually dangerous. His urgent request to join the party, however, overcame my reluctance, and I was also tempted by the knowledge that the young Moï is more tough and reliable than his elders.

He busied himself with cutting down the low projecting branches which impeded my progress and enlivened our march by humming a plaintive native melody in honour of the great Spirit who keeps watch and ward over the tigers. About midday we found a thick bamboo grove which offered welcome shelter against the torrid heat. Sao now took on the duties of scullion and rendered invaluable aid to my boy in preparing our bushman's lunch.

Valutioni lost no time in attacking a consommé of parrakeet, while a salmi of rat met with universal approval, and this sumptuous feast was crowned with a cup of mocha in St. Galmier water, which accompanies every expedition, as the forest pools are both few and foul.

Meanwhile our Moï escort were preparing and taking their more frugal meal. They made a fire and cooked a kind of pancake, of which rice is the chief constituent. The thick paste swells up rapidly looking like a piece of bread soaked in water. Sao made a hearty meal, showing a healthy contempt of European delicacies.

When we resumed our journey the sun was more cruel than ever. Not a breath of wind stirred the parched air, which almost burnt our nostrils. The bearers were hindered in their march by a thick carpet of dried branches and the necessity of stopping at frequent intervals to remove the thorns from their feet.

These delays were particularly aggravating, as we had resolved to make our night quarters at Song-Phan, where the river promised us a welcome bathe

INDUSTRIES AND OCCUPATIONS 45

and an ideal spot for a camp. Also the horses, tormented by the flies, became so restive as to be almost unmanageable.

At length the sound of the torrent broke the silence, and presently a sheet of water gleaming like burnished steel appeared between two gaunt bluffs. In a few minutes our men had felled two large trunks to serve as a bridge from one bank to the other, and in a few more the fires were burning brightly. Valutioni insisted on my taking some precautions against the attacks of wild beasts and I issued an order that no one should go to find water without some escort.

One who has never experienced the pangs of a tropical thirst cannot imagine the delirious delight of a " bushman " when a chance is presented of a drink of pure water. How much greater is his ecstasy when the opportunity of a bathe is added! We threw prudence to the winds and took to the water like ducks in spite of Valutioni's solemn warning that the hour was late and none other than that selected by the tiger for its evening work.

Soon night came down, unheralded by twilight, and shrouded the earth in a thick mantle of darkness. We felt somewhat awed and dressed ourselves in silence. The way back to the camp took us by a narrow path cut in an impenetrable bamboo thicket. A party of water-carriers passed us, Sao bringing up the rear swinging his heavy gourd and singing the same melancholy chant. He looked so happy that

I could not resist giving him a friendly pat on the cheek as he went by.

I had not advanced five yards when a heart-rending scream made me turn round sharply just in time to see the boy in the grip of a huge tiger and still struggling feebly. I snatched my rifle, raised it and took aim. At what? With one bound the monster had cleared the stream, bearing its prey in its fearful jaws, and vanished into the jungle.

A hoarse roar of horror and dismay broke the silence. All the Moï of our escort were screaming frantically as if suddenly stricken with madness.

"The Lord Tiger," they yelled, waving their long bamboo poles in the air.

My companion and I gazed at each other dumbfounded. What was to be done? The night was now black, the jungle impenetrable. Pursuit under such circumstances would be the height of folly. Realizing that we must wait for daylight and raging at our impotence, we returned to the camp fires thinking of the ghastly tragedy that was being enacted behind that barricade of brambles, perhaps only a few yards away.

I called up the unhappy uncle to offer what consolation I could. He was almost dumb with weeping, but managed to inform me amid his tears that the same evil fate had befallen both the father and mother of the poor boy.

"My brother should know," he added gravely, "that the spirits of my relations who never received

INDUSTRIES AND OCCUPATIONS 47

burial nor the rites that were their due have long demanded another companion."

At that time I was profoundly ignorant of beliefs and superstitions which came to my notice later, and I attributed his words to the raving of a madman. Valutioni soon enlightened me, however, and showed me that not only the Moï but most of the Annamites also entertain the most curious beliefs on this subject.

They believe that the spirit of a tiger's victim is compelled to ride on the back of his murderer and guide it. Accordingly, when a trap is being laid the natives are careful to sprinkle a quantity of roasted maize around the place. When the monster approaches the spirit smells the grain, is warned of the impending danger, and leaps off in time to avoid falling with the tiger into the snare.

The story may raise an incredulous smile but is not so fanciful as it sounds. The attacks of the tiger on the Moï are so frequent, ruthless, and calculated that a savage naturally ascribes them to the direct instigation and assistance of some supernatural power. All Europeans will testify to the ferocious malevolence of the creatures, and many a traveller has paid for his ignorance or carelessness with his life. It was probably pure chance that Sao's evil fate did not befall my companion or myself.

It was evident that while we were enjoying our reckless bathe the tiger must have been watching us from the thicket, awaiting a favourable moment to spring. With its usual cunning it selected the weakest for its prey, and neither rifles nor knives would have barred its path. The slightest wound from its paw filled with putrefying matter is calculated to bring tetanus and an agonizing death.

Such was the course of our melancholy reflections when our attention was aroused to the presence of a new danger by the voices of a number of coolies who were arguing in undertones. We pretended to be asleep but listened carefully. They were talking of flight.

Someone was seeming reluctant, suggesting that the country was strange, the tigers at large. The whites had angered the spirits and brought all this evil upon them. It would be better to wait till the morning and steal away at daybreak.

We realized that vigorous measures were called for to avert a crisis. The nearest station was more than a hundred miles away and the country was absolutely without resources. If our escort fled we should have to give up the expedition. Fortunately the chief remained faithful to us. I ordered him to collect all the identification cards which every coolie carries with him in accordance with the regulations. Each card recites the length of the finger-joints of its owner and is stamped with each of his finger-prints.

Deprived of their cards, our men became as meek as sheep. The prospect before them was not inviting. They would have to pay the native equivalent of three piastres and produce satisfactory evidence of

INDUSTRIES AND OCCUPATIONS 49

identity in the capital of the province before a duplicate would be supplied, and happily a coolie with three piastres is a rare phenomenon.

This danger disposed of, we attempted to sleep, but all in vain. The dog trembled and whined as if scenting evil. The tiger must have been watching us!

At dawn we beat out the thickets and at length came upon the tiger's lair where, among a mass of unrecognizable remains, we distinguished the corpse of the last victim. Not a fragment of flesh was to be seen on the skull which looked like an ivory ball. The animal's rough tongue had literally scraped it clean. A few paces away was a path, access to which was barred by the fallen trunk of an immense banian struck by lightning. It was plain that persons using this path had been unable to pass this obstacle and had been compelled to make a detour through the thicket. Hidden behind its bamboo barrier the tiger had watched them threading their way, and fallen upon them at the moment they presented their backs to it. We saw several fragments of human clothing and many bones to prove, if proof were needed, that we were on the site of a veritable man-trap.

We proceeded to give the poor boy as decent a burial as time and the circumstances permitted. His corpse was reverently laid in a shroud of latania leaves and buried in a grave at the very spot on which he had met his death. His uncle asked me for a piece of drawing paper, on which he traced the rude figure of a tiger with a pencil. He then drew three figures on the tiger's back. He explained to me that as the boy's parents were both very big, only a small place remained on the beast's back, quite near the tail.

"That is the reason," he added, "that my brother, the White Mandarin, has not been devoured. The tiger loves the flesh of a white man far more than that of my countrymen, and if there had been room he would doubtless have taken my brother for his victim."

I could say nothing to turn him from this conviction, and indeed I knew that my imprudence in bathing at so dangerous a time might very well have proved fatal.

The old man finished his drawing and then solemnly burnt it, scattering the fine ashes over the tomb to the accompaniment of many prayers. When the soil had all been returned the gravediggers strode several times round the grave crying to the High and Mighty One to seek no more victims.

The moral effect of this tragedy was so great on the Moï of our escort that it seemed to me wiser to suspend the expedition with a view to avenging the boy's death and restoring confidence. Unfortunately the Moï were even more terrified at this suggestion and spared no efforts to dissuade me. They feared the vengeance of the tiger, but I was not to be turned from my purpose.

I took up my station in a tree and secured a fine young roebuck as bait. For fourteen nights I waited for the tiger to come within range, but it never came. It ravaged the neighbourhood frequently, startling the forest with its roars, but we never had a glimpse of it. At the end of the period the escort became restive and I acceded to the general desire to strike our camp and retreat before the enemy.

A few months later Lieutenant Gautier, another member of the mission, was devoured on the same spot.

CHAPTER III

FAMILY LIFE

Diseases and their cure—Betrothal and marriage—Adultery—Divorce—
A Moï wedding—Birth—Childhood—The game of Pig-Snatcher.

NO one with the least experience of the savage, no matter to what race he may belong, will deny that the best way to win his friendship is to cure his ailments.

Speaking for myself I habitually relied on my medical knowledge as a passport to the approval of the Moï, and I was rarely disappointed, for invalids of all sorts and conditions came daily to invoke the aid of my medicine chest. Most of them suffered from ailments caused by sudden changes of temperature, and their scanty clothing is a prolific source of bronchial affections. They always came up with their hair in disorder, hiding their faces as a sign of distress, putting out their tongues, and striking themselves on the breast to draw my attention to the seat of all their woe. They could hardly contain their glee when I painted the affected part with iodine. Their bronzed skins assumed a violet hue, then turned to browny red, assisted by their vigorous scratching.

Some came from immense distances for auscultation, and my patients included a large number of women, inspired, I think, more by curiosity than any immediate necessity, for I usually presented a mirror to each new patient. A few brought me their aged parents, under-the impression that I was quite capable of restoring them to youth. A man with one arm came to ask for another, a man with one eye seemed astounded when I repeated my refusal to get him a new one. I remember once a patient appearing who was shivering with fever. I gave him a few grains of quinine and a glass of water to wash it down.

" Now whistle, my boy."

He whistled at once under the impression that this musical exercise was part of the treatment, whereas in truth my only object was to make sure that the drug had really been swallowed. Its bitterness had no deterrent effect whatever, for he stretched out his hands, accompanying the movement with a wink which means in all languages ; " I can do with as much as you like."

In another case a chronic bronchitis demanded treatment by wet-cupping. A thick plank which happened to be handy took the place of an operating-table, while an empty Madeira glass had to perform the functions of the cupping-glasses of which I was destitute.

Lack of cleanliness and ordinary precautions is mainly responsible for the fatal outcome of so many of the more serious complaints. Even the most trifling ailments last an abnormal time, but I soon proved that with reasonable treatment the adult Moï easily shakes off quite virulent diseases. The race is, in fact, submitted to a process of strict selection by the mortality among the infants, which is very high. Only the hardiest specimens survive their childhood and are all the more fitted to resist the attacks of disease.

Infants are fed in the most ignorant and reckless manner, hence the prevalence of gastro-enteritis and rickets. On the other hand, the Moï suffer considerably less from malaria than the Annamites and the Chinese. Tuberculosis is uncommon and where found carries off its victims with incredible rapidity.

The use of simples is not unknown and some of the less complicated ailments have been successfully treated by this method. In general, however, all diseases are attributed to the displeasure of the Spirits, a superstition which the Sorcerer habitually turns to his own advantage.

At first we had the greatest difficulty in inducing the natives to submit to vaccination. The story was busily circulated that the mark left by inoculation was a badge of servitude, and it was some time before we succeeded in exposing the fallacy.

Among certain Moï groups, such as the Sedang, Djarai and Rognao of the lower lakes, it is usual for the boys to sleep in a special hut after puberty has

Birth Ceremonies: Carrying Fuel to a Young Mother.

[*To face p.* 54

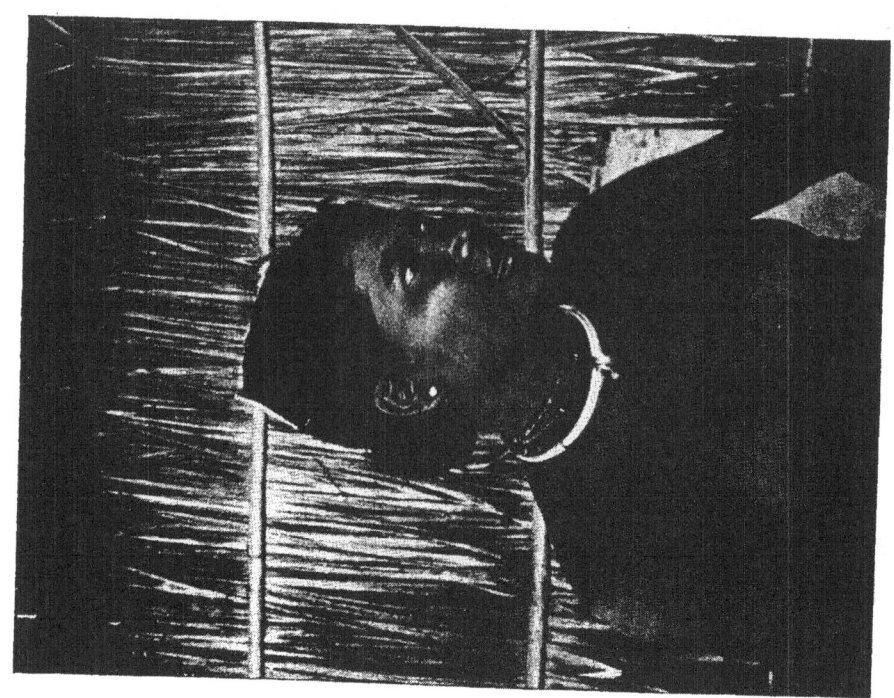

The Wife of a Moï Chief.

been reached. The primary purpose of this custom is to prevent sexual intercourse before marriage, but it is quite ineffectual to prevent the girls from meeting their lovers on the sly. The usual result is that the mother generally kills her firstborn, as no one comes forward to claim the fatherhood.

It is not too much to say that the Moï seems to attach no importance to feminine chastity. Marriage is only the consecration of a cohabitation of long standing, and sometimes there are several children of the union before either party thinks of putting it on a legal footing.

As a rule, a man must take his wife from the same group, or, in other words, endogamy is *de rigueur*. The only connecting links with other groups are the alliances with female slaves, to which the woman need not be a consenting party. The consequence is that all the inhabitants of a region are related. We have often tried to decide the vexed question as to whether this consanguinity exercises a good or bad influence on the progress of the race, but it is impossible to say more than that the evidence is inconclusive.

Some European travellers, who, like myself, have resided among the Moï, say that marriages are forbidden between first cousins on the mother's side. They deduce from this fact that the natives consider the part played by the mother in the transmission of hereditary qualities more important than that of the father.

This theory, interesting and valuable as it might be if it applied to a race in a higher stage of development, is probably unsound with regard to the Moï, the phenomenon on which it is based being probably merely the effect of coincidence. There has been an increasing tendency of late years to attribute to half-civilized races scientific knowledge which we have only recently acquired ourselves, and to consider certain customs and beliefs primitive merely because they are ignorant and coarse. Both tendencies are liable to lead to error and require careful watching. In nine cases out of ten such customs are not inspired by any exact knowledge of physiological phenomena at all.

Only a few groups permit exogamy, that is marriages with others than members of the clan, and even where the system persists it does not seem to be due to any defined totemic rule.

Totemism is a semi-magical, semi-religious system which is based on the belief in a bond of relationship between a group of human beings and some species of animal regarded as protector, " totem." It has been noticed that a characteristic feature of totemism is the prohibition of marriages between men and women with the same totem and therefore belonging to the same clan.

The Moï are a strictly monogamous people, for the very natural reason that the males outnumber the females, and this again for the equally natural reason that the men are hardier and more able to

FAMILY LIFE 57

survive the manifold mischances of infancy. Another contributory cause to their moderation in the matter of wives is their financial disability to keep more than one. But it is not a matter of principle, and a man would not hesitate to add to his stock if a sudden windfall made it possible.

A woman's commercial value depends on her age and social condition and varies also in different localities. In most cases she is paid for in instalments to her parents, for the future husband is too poor to give the presents which constitute the purchase price, and his only resource is to sell his labour to pay off the debt. Accordingly there is a stage more or less prolonged during which the young man combines wooing and the duties of maid-of-all-work in the home of his beloved. No arrangement could be happier in this country where labour is scarce. The real object, however, of this cohabitation on trial is to make sure that the characters of the two young people will harmonize and that their affections will survive continuous personal contact. Here, as elsewhere, there are cynics who say that familiarity breeds contempt.

If the engagement is broken off the man must pay an indemnity fixed beforehand. He pays his pig and takes his leave.

This custom is also in vogue among the Annamites, who call it " The Son-in-Law in the making." A similar institution is found even to-day in France, in certain villages of Haute-Savoie. The future son-in-law comes to reside with his future wife's parents. In popular phraseology he "makes the goat's marriage." The allusion becomes clear when we know that in this country it is usual to lead the he-goat to the she-goat, whereas in the case of other animals, such as bulls and horses, the female is always taken to the male.

Returning to the question of a woman's commercial value, I made inquiries in every province we visited, but found it seldom higher than the equivalent of fifty francs.

The final act that seals the marriage compact is a reciprocal scratching. While I was still in ignorance of this custom I received a severe rebuff from a girl to whom I offered some ointment for the scratches that disfigured her face. She refused it with scorn, for the nail-marks with which her lover had adorned her cheeks were, in her eyes, no other than his signature to the marriage-contract.

The rites and customs relative to betrothal and marriage vary greatly in different parts of the country and among different groups. One rule, however, is universal, and that is that the first step must be taken by the man's parents, who approach those of the girl, not without trepidation at the outset, for nothing is more humiliating than to be rejected. Accordingly the first interview is popularly dubbed the "Visit of the little gift of betel to the little garden gate."

If the parents' advances are received with favour

a second visit follows and the presents are more valuable than on the first occasion, generally including chickens, rice, and still more betel. This last substance is considered throughout the Far East as the emblem of fidelity.

The dowry is met with only among the more prosperous groups. Of course it is the future husband who provides it, a far more reasonable arrangement than that with which we are familiar in Europe. In this happy land worldly considerations count for nothing; dressmakers and fashion-plates are unknown. The most expensive jewellery is of copper, the finest coiffures are the superb orchids which abound in the forests. There is no need to save up for the children to come. Books are unknown. The sons will learn to hunt, their sole education, and the girls will be taught to spin and weave. Far from being a burden to her husband a wife is his most valuable assistant, so it is only fair that the husband should make some compensation to her parents for the loss he occasions to them.

The Moï, thanks to the kindly influences of the Laotians, have a much higher idea of the status of womanhood than their neighbours the Annamites. The husband always takes his wife into his confidence and consults her in all the crises of life, and the wives reward their husbands with a very high degree of fidelity. I remember one occasion when I offered a trifling gift to the wife of one of our coolies. She refused it point blank with the one word " bao "

("I am married"). She was not familiar with our gallant European manners, and regarded the acceptance of a present from a man as the first step towards the rupture of the marriage tie.

The penalty of adultery is renowned for its severity. There was a woman in our camp who was feeding her new-born baby. One night I was roused by a succession of screams, and thinking that a fire must have broken out, I called my boy and asked him the cause of the disturbance. He adopted a tone of lofty cynicism and told me that a husband was thrashing his unfaithful wife. Next day the woman was unable to go to work and the child was nowhere to be seen. It seems that her husband had suddenly conceived doubts as to its paternity, and, suspecting his wife of adultery with an Annamite soldier who was in our escort, he had turned himself into an instrument of justice, beaten her without pity and cut the baby's throat. I complained of his conduct to the Pholy (village chief), but far from taking any proceedings he delivered himself in these words: " My only regret is that the betrayed husband did not kill both the adulteress and her paramour." I learnt thereby that the Moï regard an act which may enfeeble the race as a crime against the community and punishable with the utmost severity. The Annamites take a similar view, for their code provides no punishment for a husband who kills an adulterous wife and her paramour if caught in the act. The other alternative is to arraign them before the provincial tribunal, which usually means a sentence of ninety strokes with the lash. In most cases this severe penalty has fatal results, but it may always be compounded at the price of one franc per stroke, the redemption money being paid to the husband as damages.

Divorce is easy and can be demanded at the instance of either party or by mutual consent. The village elders meet to hear the charges and complaints and assess the amount of compensation. If the dissolution of the marital tie is the wish of both, the care of the younger children is confided to the mother, that of the elder to the father. Divorces, however, are uncommon. The husband does not want one, for it will be difficult to replace the partner who represents half his capital and perhaps all his labour. The wife is equally reluctant whatever her sorrows may be, for any change may easily be for the worse. If she marries another she will be little more than his humble slave. All the heavy farm and household work falls on her shoulders, including arduous duties which in civilized countries are assigned exclusively to men. She crushes the rice, shells the corn, attends to the harvest and assists in clearing the brushwood. Pregnancy makes no difference to the burden of her daily tasks except for the entirely inadequate period essential to delivery.

If the husband's means permit she will have no objection to his taking a companion to himself. On the contrary, the newcomer will be an addition to the household staff to whom she will assign the largest burdens. She knows that as first wife her position will never be seriously challenged, and as undisputed mistress of the household she will exercise authority over the other "wives." This unwritten law prevails throughout the Far East. A widow has little difficulty in remarrying, as the area of choice is extensive, owing to the numerical superiority of the men.

I was once honoured with an invitation to a Moï wedding. It was in the village of Lebouy where I resided for some time, and my host was no other than the chief himself, who couched his request in the following terms :

" My elder brother, the great Giver of Tobacco " (this being the name under which I was popularly known), "will, I hope, do me the honour of sharing a buffalo which I propose to offer up at the marriage of my daughter."

It would have been ungracious to decline an invitation expressed in terms of such old-world courtesy. I exhibited my appreciation of the honour by offering him a large glass of Madeira. He hesitated at first, then squatted on the ground as a compliment to the excellence of the liquor, took the glass gingerly in his hand and slowly emptied it. The slaves who formed his bodyguard watched him with evident admiration.

The evening before the wedding the bride-elect went to the banks of the Da-Nhim, a river which flows at a distance of a few hundred yards from the village. All her relations formed themselves into an escort, for it is absolutely imperative that the whole family should be present at the kind of ritual bathe on which she was bent. The entire company plunged into the water, and after a few seconds of merry splashing emerged and dried in the sun.

The opening item of the next day's festivities was the slaughter of the buffalo which is, so to speak, the foundation of the feast. The young warriors of the village armed with lances formed a circle round the victim and hurled their weapons in turn, until at length one struck a vital part and the beast fell over dead. The carcase was dragged to the foot of a pole wreathed round with bamboo-shoots, and the amateur butchers proceeded to cut it up into strips, of which some were reserved to be smoked at a later stage.

The nuptial ceremony proper then began and was marked by an extreme simplicity. The Guru, or Sorcerer, placed the couple and their parents before a row of lofty posts adorned with the horns of recently killed buffaloes. With great solemnity he then drew his knife, seized a white cock and cut off its head, throwing the body over his right shoulder. The headless bird struggled for a moment, flapped its wings in a last spasm, and finally remained motionless on its breast on the ground. The Sorcerer spat into a copper vase, not so much to relieve his feelings as in satisfaction, for the victim's position foretold a numerous posterity to the young couple. He then took a cotton thread and bound the right hand of the man to the left hand of the woman. This act made them man and wife and was of the same force as the exchange of rings in our own country. A rapid invocation to the Spirits of the Hearth followed, and then the feast began.

First I was requested to take my place on a rush mat under a huge shed built for the occasion. A number of women appeared bringing fried locusts, spices, bitter oranges, spirits of rice and meat, almost raw and cut into strips. The newly married couple overwhelmed each other with attentions, filled each other's mouths with rice and accepted in good part the food which all their friends and relations thought it necessary to offer them. Perhaps this rite is a symbol of the principle of mutual help which ought to actuate not merely a family but also tribes and nations.

Meanwhile a woman was conducting an orchestra of four all but naked boys who beat a tattoo on huge gongs. Lest this should become monotonous a musician played a melody in the minor mode and not without a strange haunting charm. The instrument was a large empty gourd on which three bamboo tubes were fastened. The range of this original organ was confined to five notes, but the tones blended pleasantly and in spite of the dragging time the tune was anything but discordant.

We encouraged this artist with an offer of some

A Sorcerer performing the Marriage Ceremony before the Sacrificial Posts.

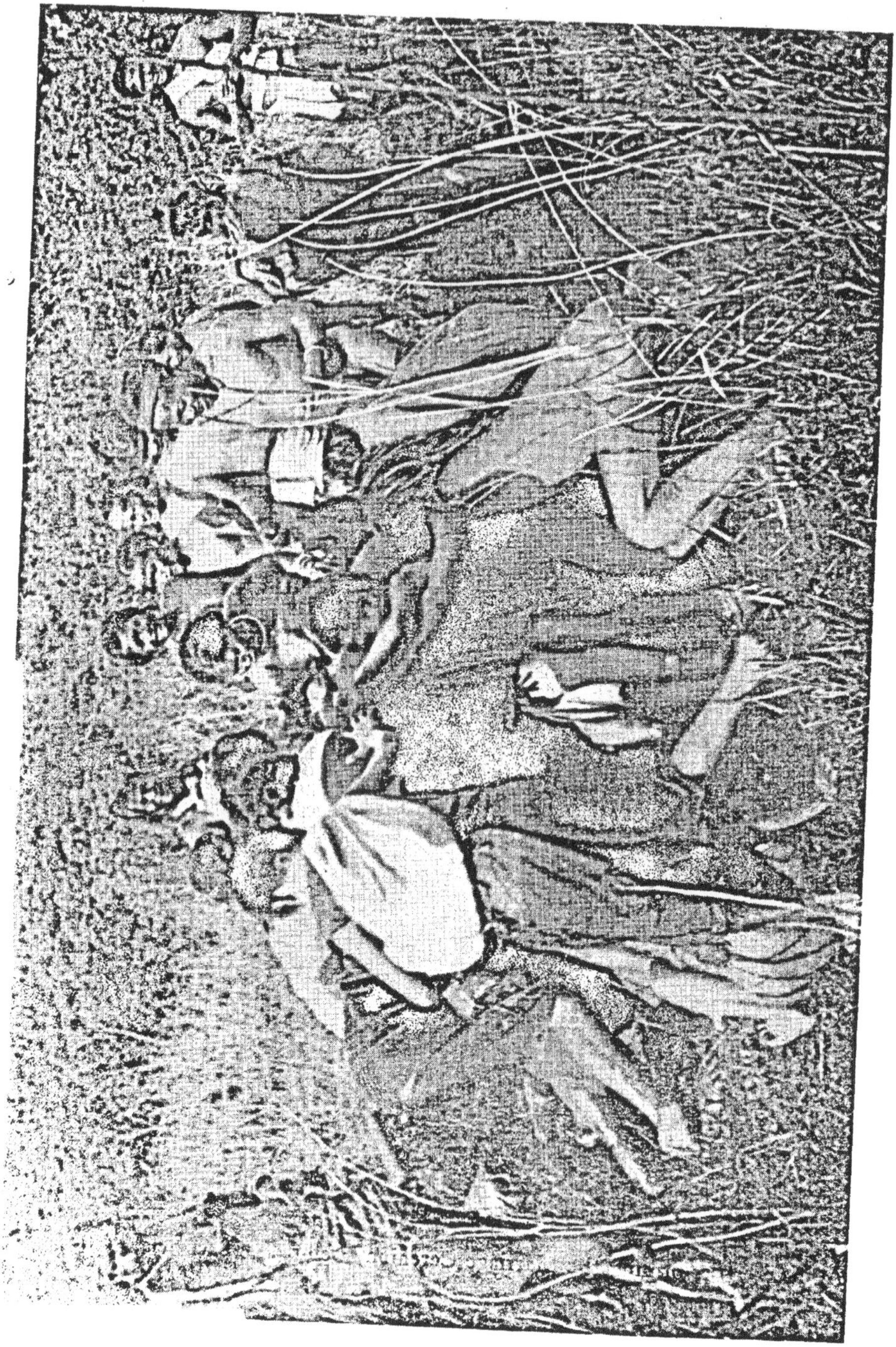

cigarettes, and presently he began to play for a dance, of which the principal movements seemed to be raising the feet in turn, and striking the ground with the heels or a stick. These operations became more rapid and ended with a tremendous contortion of the whole body. It reminded me forcibly of the well-known "bear dance," and is not peculiar to the Moï, being also popular in Thibet.

Both the musician and the dancer were rewarded with the most unstinted applause and invited to take a well-earned rest in view of the orgy which now followed. On such an occasion the Moï regard sobriety as an insult to the host, and indeed the charge could not have been levelled at any of the guests then assembled. The last stage of the proceedings was the distribution of presents, for interest can always seal the bonds of friendship. At a given signal the husband flung lemons, mangoes, areca nuts and other fruits among the crowd, who scrambled for them without the least regard for order or good manners. For some moments a free fight seemed imminent, but good humour finally prevailed and the combatants dispersed chewing the inevitable betel and bidding each other an inebriated farewell.

Among the Moï, as everywhere else, the birth of a child is an occasion for rejoicing both to the family and the village. Such is the fear that malevolent spirits will assail the mother during the critical period that a special hut is made for her accommodation and all strangers are forbidden to enter the village itself. This prohibition, or "taboo," is known as "Dieng" in some regions and as "Calam" in others. The experienced traveller will never dream of attempting to evade it and expose himself to a summary vengeance at the hands of the inhabitants, who are under orders to see it enforced. Foreigners stand in no privileged position and we ourselves had frequent occasion to bewail this absurd regulation. Imagine our rage after a hard day's march under a tropical sun or soaked by torrential rains when we found ourselves condemned to spend the night perched in trees for fear of tigers, with the fires of a tabooed village burning almost under our noses! The punishment of Tantalus was nothing to this, and little consolation is to be derived from inveighing against the ignorance which is the offspring of such blind superstition.

The house in which the mother-to-be is lodged is distinguished from the others by a tuft of pompelmoose and a piece of charcoal suspended from the roof. About the time when the happy event is to take place all the inhabitants forgather in a special place to await the good news.

Even to-day in certain European countries custom forbids the husband and family to be present during labour.

If the group is not altogether destitute, sacrifices must be offered to conciliate the Spirits, especially if it seems likely that complications are threatening. Of course, the villagers offer no more than they can help. The bidding, so to speak, for divine favour generally starts with an egg and rises if the complications continue. The egg will be followed by a chicken, then a goat, then a pig, and finally an ox in cases of extreme necessity.

Only the woman's nearest relations are allowed to be present at the accouchement, for which she assumes a sitting position. As soon as labour begins they rub her stomach from top to bottom with tiger's gut and make her lean against the knees of a female nurse. This is not a universal practice, for in the North, among the Tho, for example, the woman stands supported by two cords passed under her armpits. Immediately after the birth the child is washed and anointed with cocoa-nut oil. The navel-string is then cut with a sharpened bamboo and the severed end tied up with a cotton thread or a blade of long grass. The placenta is buried either in the house itself or in some place adjacent.

It is interesting to compare these rites with those which accompany the same event among certain African races. Among the Bushongo of the Belgian Congo the woman adopts a sitting position and is supported by the knees of a midwife. The placenta is likewise buried and also, at a later stage, the foreskin of the child, if male. In Mandeling (on the western frontier of Sumatra) the child is first washed and then kept in confinement in the house, the natives claiming that this procedure secures the child against evil influences.

After delivery the Moi woman lies on a low bed

and a fire is kept burning at her side day and night, the ashes from which are left smouldering in earthenware vases to keep the room at an even temperature. The smoke is supposed to act as an antiseptic. All the young woman's friends demonstrate their devotion by bringing wood for the fire, taking care to select the dead branches of certain species of trees. Drifting logs from a river must on no account be used. They bring fearful convulsions and certain death to the child.

A potion composed of simples which stimulate the circulation is now administered to the invalid and the effect is augmented by rubbing her all over with ginger. Her first meal consists of ginger, eggs and rice. She is allowed to drink a concoction made from the horns of a young stag. Strange as it may sound, this beverage is a valuable tonic, which we ourselves used at times with great effect.

Ten or fifteen days after the birth the woman resumes her usual arduous occupations. The baby is hung on her back in a little cloth sack, secured over her shoulders to her girdle. His feet dangle on each side of her, and in this position he passes the days cradled by his nurse's movements.

The child is fed at the breast until between two or three years of age, a custom which is a great strain on the mother. To lessen this she gives him manioc and rice, taking care to soften them in her own mouth first. The net result is that the baby's stomach attains an unnatural size and his digestive organs suffer.

The nursling's first meal is the occasion of a special ceremony. The mother is not yet ready to feed him herself, so the duty falls on one of her attendants, who takes her seat on an upturned earthenware jar. The position of this jar is highly significant in the eyes of the Moï. A jar so placed can hold no water. Similarly a child's stomach can hold no food, for it empties itself as fast as it is filled. Dyspepsia, it would appear, is unknown among this fortunate people! After this first meal an attendant goes through the pretence of flattening the child's head against the centre pole of the hut. This is to ensure that the head may not become pointed later on, a physical peculiarity which is regarded as a sign of bad character. Another favourite superstition in these regions is that certain odd numbers are lucky and certain even numbers unlucky. Every mother hopes to give birth to a three or a seven. Her fear is that the birth may occur during the last quarter of the moon. As everyone knows, this belief in the efficacy of certain numbers is almost universal and dates from remote times. The Hebrews and Egyptians furnish many examples, and many more are met with among the peoples of the Far East. Thus the Brahminic Trinity comprises three persons, Brahma, Vishnu and Siva. Angkor was built in seven days, as the Bible tells. The stars which the faithful of Asia worship are seven in number.

The child is not named for the first two years of his life and is doubtless happy enough to be called

"Con-Nie," which to all intents and purposes corresponds to our term "baby." Both the Moï and the Annamites regard the naming of a child as a matter of great moment, for the future depends on a fortunate choice. Nothing can be done before the Sorcerer has been called in to consult the Spirits. This official suggests a name, which is usually whispered into his ear by the mother or the person who presided at the birth. The popular name for a boy is "Squirrel," for a girl "Mouse." A large bowl filled with rice is brought in. The Sorcerer empties it, taking out the grains two at a time. If at the end of this operation only one grain is left at the bottom the proceedings must be repeated until that ill-omened result does not recur. It is not surprising, therefore, that occasionally several days elapse before the ceremony can be continued. The Sorcerer has an interest in the prolongation of these rites, for throughout the whole time he is the guest of the family. If the child dies or is attacked by one of the infantile affections so common in this treacherous climate the mischance is attributed to the choice of an unlucky name. The only hope is to change it at once, which involves a repetition of the ritual rigmarole.

When the child is old enough to bear a light burden he will carry on his back a basket, or even a younger brother, securely rolled up in a kind of sack. Nothing could be more amusing than the solemnity with which the youngster performs his function of dry nurse.

Among certain groups the children's hair is always kept short except for a long wisp at the crown, which gives them a curiously old look.

Clothing is forgotten, as a rule, till the sixth year is past. Sometimes a metal disc is hung from a cord round the waist, and a favourite ornament is an anklet of iron with a small bell attached, which is made and fitted by the village blacksmith. It is a badge of servitude, for henceforth the child is devoted to the service of the Spirits, who, in return, make him an object of their peculiar care.

During their early years the boys are active and intelligent and readily absorb knowledge of all kinds, but as manhood approaches they become apathetic, lazy and incapable of sustained effort. I once undertook the experiment of training a boy to act as my servant. He was about twelve years old, with a remarkably bright face, and very quick and graceful in his movements. In a short time he had learnt to read and count. His eyesight was so good that we always used him when taking sights for our geodetical instruments. He was never happier than when I gave him a rifle to carry during our shooting-parties. After a year, however, his character changed completely. He became intractable and moody, and fiercely resented any criticism. We were a long way from his tribe and he could not return home except through a forest infested with tigers. The prospect of a long and dangerous journey seemed to have no terrors for him. He begged me to let him go, and jumped with joy when I gave my permission. In a twinkling he was out of his European clothes and had donned the old loin-cloth, which he had preserved with the greatest care as a mark of race. He bowed three times, took up his basket and disappeared with every expression of jubilation. His obvious glee was some consolation for the annoyance his departure caused me, for I had set my heart on softening his savage nature and winning his affection. It was with real regret that I confessed myself beaten. On the other side of the account must be placed the feat of Madame Cunhac, the wife of one of our governors, who successfully brought up a Moï girl. The child grew to have an unshaken belief in her mistress and followed her about like a faithful dog, showing her affection and gratitude on every possible occasion, nor could she be induced to return to her village by threats or bribes.

A child receives nothing that can be dignified with the name of education. His incessant occupation consists of playing all day with his little companions. Many of the games played are extremely interesting and we spent many an hour in the evening watching them. Perhaps the favourite is a game they call "The Pig-Snatcher," in which there are three principal *dramatis personæ*, the Snatcher, the Shopkeeper and the Pig. The greatest competition is for the position of the two former, so the candidates are subjected to a preliminary trial. They all take turns at catching a twig on a long pole and balancing it, and the two most expert are rewarded with the rôles of Shopkeeper and Snatcher respectively. The next plays the part of the Pig, which consists of saying nothing, but grunting vigorously at intervals.

The unsuccessful candidates join hands and make a ring round the lucky three.

The Snatcher now approaches with slow steps and interrogates the Shopkeeper as follows·

" Hello, maternal aunt ! Please give me some fire."

" O elderly brother, the fire is under the ashes."

" Well, then, give me a gourd of water."

" The water is at the bottom of the well."

" Then give me a guava."

" The guava is still on the tree."

Feigning dismay at these repeated rebuffs the Snatcher takes a few steps backwards and suddenly stops, for the Pig, in the person of a small urchin of barely five years old, gives forth a timid grunt.

" What is the animal I hear in your stable ? "

" It is a spotted pig."

" What kind of spots has it ? "

" Red on its paws and white on its tail. It has every perfection, and the less I feed it the fatter it gets."

" Really ! Will you take a Mat for it ? " (A Mat is a piece of iron which is used for exchange and worth about a penny.)

" No, it is not for sale."

The dialogue continues, the Snatcher increasing his offer up to a set of gongs, but the Shopkeeper is not to be tempted. At length the Snatcher is weary and pretends to leave the shop. The game seems to be over, but the children enjoy it too much to allow it to be cut short; so there is a general burst of laughter when the Shopkeeper in her most wheedling voice recalls the customer before he has proceeded very far.

"Here, Pig-Snatcher, come in! I have changed my mind and I will sell it to you for a broken cup."

The Snatcher, delighted at this unexpected turn of events, hastens to secure his prize, but is prevented from moving out of the circle formed by the children. He clasps a girl of about twelve who represents one of the doors of the house and shakes her by the shoulders.

"What is this door made of?" he asks.

"It is of ironwood," replies the Shopkeeper. Burglary in that quarter is doomed to failure, he thinks, and finds a younger girl.

"Of what wood is this one?"

"Teak."

"Still too strong. What of this third?"

"It is made of rotten fibres," the Shopkeeper cries.

On that the encircling chain snaps suddenly. The Snatcher, who is no other than the Tiger in human form, darts at the Pig. Despairing squeals. A savage roar. The village dogs appear upon the scene, and amid peals of merry laughter the game comes to an end.

CHAPTER IV

SOCIAL LIFE

Property—Slavery—Utilitarian morals—A bashful race—The Levirate—Law and custom—An amateur arbitrator—Principles and practice of the Ordeal.

THE Moï who inhabit the more northerly portion of this country have largely fallen under the domination of their neighbours the Laotians. In the south, however, in spite of their proximity to the warlike and powerful Annamites, the Moï have, to a large degree, resisted absorption and preserved their independence. Consequently their immemorial institutions have survived the chances and changes of the centuries without appreciable modification.

The unit of administration is the village, which forms a kind of anarchical republic with a nominal chief who is elected. As a general rule these shadow potentates are chosen either for their physical prowess or reputed moral superiority. The Chief's powers are not transferable and lapse on his death.

It sometimes happens that several villages of the same region are united by community of interests or family alliances. The union is then cemented by the formation of a league with a view to defence against common enemies. From such associations for mutual insurance the tribe takes its origin. In many cases one of the first signs that this new organization has become a social or political entity is the appearance of an obligation on its members to intermarry.

It is well known that in the primitive ages of the Aryan races the tribesmen were not only shepherds rather than warriors but also essentially nomadic in habit. It was in the character of owners-in-common that they held the land on which they pastured their flocks. Later, when they began to settle in defined localities to till the soil, the ownership of property ceased to be collective. As population and the area under cultivation increased, private property appeared at first as the right of the family and finally as the right of the individual.

Even to-day, however, we see traces of such primitive collectivism in the "Mir" of Russia, the "Dessa" of Java, and the "Zadruga" of Bulgaria. The peculiarity of the Moï is that they exhibit the three forms of ownership, collective, family, and individual, in conjunction.

Evidence of the communistic basis of their proprietary system is plentiful and cumulative. The whole group takes part in the acquisition and development of a tract of land sufficient to satisfy all their needs. The trophies of war, the spoils of the chase and the harvests are divided equally among those entitled to them. Inequality of distribution is almost unknown. The Chief reserves a portion in addition to his own to offer as a sacrifice to the Spirits or to dispense in hospitality to strangers.

There is equally strong evidence of the system of family ownership of property. Every family has its private residence and household implements. This economic dispensation accounts for differences of wealth and station among members of the same communal group. For example a family in which there are many grown-up girls will become rich on the proceeds of their skill in weaving, pot-making, and other spheres of activity.

The individual ownership of property seems to be confined to jewellery, pipes, weapons, and similar objects which any man can make for himself. Further, any member of the group is entitled to do what he likes with the portion of food distributed to him. In most cases if he does not consume it himself he will lend it to some less thrifty neighbour who finds his store exhausted. If the day for repayment comes round and the liability is not discharged, the borrower, his wife and children, become the absolute property of the lender whose sole obligation is to support them. The debtor thus becomes a slave, or rather, to speak more accurately, a servant for life. It is not at all unusual in times of great scarcity for the Moï to sell both themselves and their families when faced with the prospect of starvation. These facts are well known to our Government, which is powerless to prevent such evils so long as the imperfect means of communication prevent the easy transport of food supplies from a fertile region to a famine-stricken province.

Trading in slaves is prohibited, but there is no doubt that it goes on in secret.

In principle the debtor-slave can procure his own redemption by his own labour. But the value of that labour is calculated by the master and at so ridiculous a figure that in practice hardly any slave earns his freedom before his death. The annual value of the labour of a strong man is reckoned at about five francs more than the cost of his support. Further, if a slave does not satisfy his master he may be resold at a price which represents an increase of twenty-five per cent. on the original debt.

The system may truly be described as in every sense an exploitation of human misery. At the current rate of calculation it may take several generations of sufferers to pay off the first debt.

In theory there is another mode of redemption. On his master's death a slave can recover his liberty by sacrificing a buffalo and placing a small portion of the flesh in the mouth of the deceased. The mere idea of a debtor-slave having the means to buy a buffalo is one to provoke bitter mirth!

Any reform should aim at an equitable calculation of the value of the services rendered and the rate of interest should be drastically revised. This rate, which is extremely exorbitant, soon trebles and

A Little Kha (Slave Girl).

Our Native Prisoners.

The Village Musician serenading a Young Couple about to be married.

even quadruples the amount of the original debt. It is to be noted, however, that a slave shares in the family life, is consulted in any crisis that may arise, and, if a woman, may inherit. Cruelty and ill-usage are rare, and even where they exist there is some safeguard in the slave's right of appeal to the village Elders.

A female slave is protected against any abuse of authority by her master. If he violates her she is freed at once by the act.

In Babylon the law was equally favourable to slaves and even went so far as to permit them to contract independently of their masters under the ingenious system of *peculium*. It was also quite usual for anyone to escape from an embarrassing financial position by entering on a kind of voluntary servitude which could be terminated in time by payment of a sum for redemption out of the earnings of the service. Further, it was enacted by Hammurabi's code, two thousand years before the Christian era, that a creditor, after three years, must set free the wife or daughter of his debtor if he had accepted them as sureties for the debt.

The laws of the Hebrews likewise permitted an insolvent debtor to sell himself and his family into bondage to extinguish a debt. A peculiar feature in this case was the debtor's right to sell his wife or daughters and himself retain his liberty.

The laws of the Annamites forbid this same transaction, but there is no doubt that it frequently takes place. Custom in these matters is of far more force than the law, and the actual nature of the contract is concealed under various disguises.

The Chinese code contains a special provision relating to "The letting on hire of wives or daughters."

Another force working to the same end is the fact that in countries in which individualistic ownership of land prevails, and where labour is scarce the owner stops at nothing to increase the number of hands on his estate. This necessity is the mother of all manner of abuses, to which the weakest naturally fall victims.

The Sorcerers, for example, impose the most exorbitant fines on those who have failed to carry out the least detail of the rites. A penalty thus inflicted constitutes the delinquent to all intents and purposes a slave of the offended Spirit. He has to place himself at the disposal of the Sorcerer, the representative of the deity. Another species of slavery is created by the capture of prisoners of war. There are no provisions in law or custom for their redemption or liberation except by way of exchange. Otherwise the servitude is deemed perpetual.

The independent Moï have recourse to a raid on their neighbours, the Annamites, when their stock of slaves falls low. The prisoner of war is considered as belonging to an inferior order of creation with no status and few rights. A woman may not marry and neither male nor female may inherit; but the law contemplates the case of a free woman marrying a male prisoner of war. The father and the male children become the slaves of the woman. Female children are freed. If the children are all boys or all girls they are divided and one half become the slaves of the other.

In short, although less cruel and inhuman than wholesale slaughter, slavery is one of the most blighting institutions in these barbarous regions. The Moï prefer the milder to the more drastic treatment, not from any motives of altruism but solely from considerations of self-interest. The death of an individual for religious disobedience or even the commission of a crime profits no one, but material benefits accrue both to the private citizen and to the state from the fine imposed or the services exacted as punishment. The most superficial investigation reveals the essential utilitarianism of the conception of justice which obtains among the Moï.

No less utilitarian is their conception of morality. They never ask whether an act is good or bad in itself, for abstract standards of right and wrong are unknown to them. They merely ask whether the act is prejudicial to private or public well-being. It follows from this that crimes against the individual are punished far less severely than crimes against the state, and further that the most serious offences are those which touch material prosperity and enjoyment. A theft of rice from the public granary is punished by enslavement, for rice is the staple food and an indispensable necessity to the whole group. The same theft from a private individual is regarded only as a minor offence punishable summarily by fine. In this case Society does not suffer, or at least only indirectly and to an imperceptible degree.

In the same way a murderer receives no punishment if his act is one of vengeance for a similar crime. He is exacting the price of blood, and the blood-feud is recognized and approved. It is highly meritorious to kill a foreigner or a public enemy, and the slayer becomes *ipso facto* a popular hero.

This conception of morality is the production of tradition and has been influenced in various ways by the jurisdiction of the Sorcerers over a number of offences, especially those relating to sex and ritual.

It has long been popularly supposed that races in a rudimentary stage of civilization enjoy absolute immunity from regulation in the matter of sexual relations. Nothing could be further from the truth, the evidence all pointing the other way. Indeed, paradoxical as it may seem, it is none the less true that sexual relations of primitive peoples are more restricted, more bound round by various interdictions, than those of peoples which have reached a higher stage of development. It is plain that we have often confused complete sexual licence with the exercise of perfectly limited and defined rights which are only permitted during certain public festivals. It is only necessary in this connection to remind ourselves of the Saturnalia in Rome

The same error appears in the popular attitude towards polyandry, which is frequently attributed to the moral abandonment of the women. In reality the system is no less organized and regulated than that of polygamy. Further, all educated travellers who have lived long enough among primitive races to attain some degree of intimacy have expressed surprise at their reticence in speaking of these matters They display the most marked repugnance to give any information about their women, and if pressed to answer questions, take refuge in evasion or refuse to continue the conversation.

It is only after years spent amongst them, and, after winning their confidence, mainly by medical services, that a European can penetrate at all into that region of mystery from which he is jealously excluded.

Some of the following observations are the result of personal investigation. Others are made on the authority of several of my countrymen with the experience of a long residence in the country behind them, while others again are founded on information supplied by the natives which I have myself verified. Some of my remarks apply only to a tribe or a particular region, but in many cases they hold good of the whole group, and even of a wider circle, for it must never be forgotten that resemblances are encountered everywhere between the customs of these folk and those, not only of other peoples of the Far East, but also of the semi-savages of Africa and Polynesia.

I have had occasion to speak before of the custom, practised by several of the Moï tribes, of killing the firstborn if no one comes forward to claim the paternity. Thanks to this convenient institution, it is quite usual for a young girl to become a mother solely to prove her fertility.

We find this same custom among the Bohindu of the Belgian Congo, where the girls indulge in promiscuous prostitution until conception takes place. This event guarantees them a husband, for sterility is a ground for divorce, and the man looks upon fertility as the highest virtue in a woman. Thus, calculated prostitution, if I may use the phrase, is not regarded with disfavour by some primitive peoples. Where the motive is other than the desire for maternity it is regarded merely as mental aberration or weakness of mind. If a woman gives herself without love, she is not a criminal but an idiot. The same attitude is displayed by the Abahua of the Belgian Congo. Each time that we made the acquaintance of a Moï tribe the Chief was careful to demonstrate his hospitality by the offer of some female slaves instructed to put themselves at our disposal. It seems that this act of courtesy is invariably extended to strangers of their own race, and consequently their astonishment was all the greater when we declined the honour.

This magnanimous custom is also found among several of the races which inhabit equatorial Africa, notably the Medgé and the Mangbetù.

Incestuous relationships are by no means uncommon among the Moï. I once spent several months in the village of Lebouy, where the chief was the father of his daughter's children. Nor was any exception taken to his action, which was regarded merely as the exercise of a right which immemorial precedent had sanctioned.

These incestuous connections are by no means confined to the eastern archipelago, but are constantly met with in Africa also. I need only mention the Avura-Gura of the Congo as an example. It is a mere matter of history that incest was practised and recognized by the royal family in ancient Egypt. The most usual instance was a union between sisters and brothers. The object, of course, was to ensure that the royal blood should be transmitted from generation to generation without any admixture of alien strains, and thus preserve its identity with its true and first origin—the union of a god and some creature, such as the hawk or gryphon. The example of the princes soon found imitators among their subjects, and after being confined to the nobility and ruling classes, it spread among all orders of society. We possess an accumulation of proof, which places the matter beyond doubt, in the documents and inscriptions which archæological research has brought to light.

By way of contrast, a custom obtains among certain groups in Indo-China (though almost unknown elsewhere), especially the Man Coc, and Man Pa Tọng, which formally prohibits intercourse between a woman and her father-in-law or uncles, and likewise between a man and his mother-in-law, his aunts, or his sisters-in-law. I shall have occasion further on to investigate this peculiar veto which is enforced by certain African tribes also.

The Levirate (from "Levir," a brother-in-law, in Sanscrit *dêvar*) is also found operating as a stringent injunction.

This, as everyone knows, takes its name from that law of Moses which commanded a brother-in-law to marry his deceased brother's widow (in cases where there had been no issue) in order to provide an heir to the family and to perpetuate his name. It was a species of "adoption beyond the tomb."

In the same way, there are laws among certain of the Moï tribes, such as the Radé, by which a widow is compelled to remarry with some member of her husband's family. Various reasons are assigned for this injunction, but primarily it is dictated by a desire to secure the inheritance to the family of the deceased.

I was told of several cases of bestiality which seemed to me, even if proved, to present no features worthy of comment. Sexual perversions of this character are not confined to any one country nor any one period, and it is sufficient to remark that nearly every race has legends of gods changing themselves into animals with the aim of uniting themselves with mortals. These fables are not mere fictions of a poet's brain but reminiscences of a distant period

SOCIAL LIFE

when Egyptians and Greeks worshipped animal-gods whom superstition had endowed with mortal offspring.

One fact which I was able to prove to my own satisfaction was the dietary regulations to which pregnant women are subjected. Among the prohibited foods at that period figures the flesh of all male animals which have not been castrated. Here, without doubt, is an analogy with the law of the Man-Coc that no sexual intercourse may take place after the third month of pregnancy. In particular, the mother-to-be must abstain from fat and green vegetables. She may undertake no kind of work not even the most trivial of household duties.

Like other races with a low degree of civilization, the Moï attribute to physical excess of all kinds a loss of force which puts an individual at a disadvantage in his contest with the powers of the earth or the air. On this belief are based the rules which prescribe the preparations of one who is about to face some judicial test or ordeal. He must pass the previous night in a state of complete abstinence, so that his moral and physical condition shall be perfect for the trial he is to undergo. The golden rule is summed up in a motto of the Adio of Central Africa· "No man may face the ordeal if not pure in body and mind, sinless and unstained." It seems doubtful whether the origin of this belief is religious or experimental. We know that it flourished among the Egyptians from an early period.

It is impossible to obtain even the most superficial

understanding of many Moï laws and institutions without investigating the peculiar conceptions of morality on which they are based.

A Moï woman appears before the Council of the Ancients with a charge that some man has touched her without her consent. A fine is inflicted on the accused varying in amount with the importance of the part of the body which he touched. If there has been complete seduction and the seducer refuses to marry the complainant the fine is doubled.

Perhaps it is a husband who complains that his wife has committed adultery on three different occasions with three different men. He himself will be punished, and the sentence will be accompanied by some withering reflections on his incompetence and complacence, hardly flattering to his vanity. I ought to add that this curious judicial perversion is met with only on the shores of the great lakes, where morals are less rigid than in other parts of Indo-China.

I was told that among a few groups adultery is not considered criminal if the woman's accomplice is a relation of her husband. The Batua of the Congo also seem to regard this as an extenuating circumstance, but their neighbours, the Medgé and the Mangbetù, take a precisely opposite view and rigorously forbid brothers to seduce each other's wives. All the Moï consider it a gross aggravation of the offence if the seducer takes advantage of the husband's absence in war or the hunting-field.

I have already recorded that I was frequently prevailed on by the Moï to act as arbitrator in their disputes. I have the gravest misgivings that my judgments did more credit to my kindly intentions than to my legal knowledge.

I always made a point of using all my resources to impress the litigants with a due sense of the importance of the occasion and the dignity of the tribunal.

A scarlet cloth is thrown over my folding table. Next the huge blue-cotton umbrella, whose humble function is to protect our theodolite from the sun's rays, is commandeered to shelter the miserable packing-case which serves me for my curule chair. I don a wide-brimmed Boer hat and my revolver-case is reverentially attached to my belt by my boy, who is crier, clerk, and usher all in one.

To-day the case in the list is ·

"Annamite *v.* Moï."

It would be altogether a miracle if the plaintiff did not herald his appearance with a present of some kind, in this case chickens, eggs and bananas. He is convulsed with astonishment when, incorruptible, I reject his bribes. His ordinary judges, the Mandarins, have other and better manners. They have not prepared him for such a rebuff.

The Moï, on the other hand, has brought nothing with which to seek my favour. Perhaps he is too poor or perhaps he has already sufficient faith in my impartiality.

The case opens with a recital of the facts in issue.

The Annamite tells his story first.

He bows three times, kisses the ground and remains on his knees throughout the hearing in accordance with the procedure prescribed for the plaintiff.

"I am a dealer in pigs," he tells me, "and I was bringing four of them to market in the hills.

"While passing through this Moï village the heat and my weariness compelled me to break my journey; so I sought out the Pholy with a request for hospitality and the shelter of my pigs in his sty. You may imagine my amazement when, on resuming my journey, I discovered that my fine animals, all more than two years old, were nowhere to be seen and had been replaced by four miserable creatures which are hardly six weeks old.

"I demand therefore that the great soldier Mandarin shall restore to me what is my own."

Questioned in turn, the defendant swears by the Spirit of the Hearth that the plaintiff's story is a mere tissue of lies. His version is that the Annamite took advantage of the previous night to steal some of his young pigs which had got loose in the neighbourhood, and that, failing to procure sufficient food for them, he had attempted to exchange them legally for animals of greater value.

Under these perplexing circumstances I find Solomon's mantle weighing heavily upon me,

Suddenly an inspiration comes to me, doubtless a gift from the Spirit of the Hearth.

If the animals have really been stolen from the village they will surely be able to return to their homes by themselves. They have fasted since the morning and it will be strange if their empty stomachs cannot spur their memories to something more than normal activity.

Accordingly with the becoming solemnity of a just and wise judge, I order the plaintiff to drive the four animals in dispute before him through every street in the village. The procession forms up, the Tribunal, strangely nervous as to the result of its experiment, bringing up the rear.

The Annamite assumes a swaggering air and brandishes his whip like a man sure of his facts, but a significant contraction of his eyebrows gives me the impression that he is not wholeheartedly in agreement with my plan. Sure enough, before the troupe has progressed more than a few hundred yards, one of the pigs hesitates, sniffs suspiciously, and wags its tail, then, uttering a vigorous grunt, dashes into a stable with a certitude that leaves no doubt of its familiarity.

A few steps farther on a second animal repeats the comedy, with the same features of hesitation, recognition, and precipitation. The Annamite thrashes the air with his whip and swears by Buddha that he is the victim of a pernicious conspiracy. All in vain. Soon all the pigs have recovered their native haunts and there is nothing left for him to drive. The Ministry of Justice has an easy task in constructing a case against him and the impudent rascal is unanimously convicted of theft, aggravated by abuse of hospitality. He thinks himself lucky to escape with the loss of one of his gold rings as a fine and compensation to the Head of the village.

I wonder if I was right?

Happily for my reputation as judge, this *cause célèbre* was positively my last appearance in the rôle. A few days afterwards I was a spectator, by official invitation and on the principle of reciprocity, at one of the native trials.

No luxurious court-house, no gilt and trappings here! The Pholy, following the example of St. Louis, administers justice beneath a sacred fig-tree— the most majestic object conceivable—beneath whose all-embracing branches a concourse, vaster than any that throngs our courts at a sensational trial, could find shelter. The chiefs surround their President and form a truly imposing tribunal. The Sorcerer, too, is there, and he will play the chief part to-day.

Some cattle have been stolen a week or so ago and every man suspects his neighbour of the crime. The real malefactor, however, is known only to the Spirits, and they alone can expose him. As their cares and interests are too multifarious to permit them to appear in person on the earth, our Sorcerer declares that they have assigned to him their powers and functions for the occasion. To-day he will be their mouthpiece. He takes an egg lightly between his thumb and first finger, pressing the ends with two other fingers. At his request a young assistant proclaims in a wailing voice the names of all the neighbouring lands. He cannot believe, he tells us, that a fellow countryman should be guilty of so dastardly an outrage. But the recital is over and the egg has not trembled. There is nothing left but to call out the name of his own village. Alas! No sooner are the words uttered than an ominous crack is heard and a sticky yellow fluid issues from the shell, now broken in two. Recourse must now be had to the evidence. The circle of inquiry is narrowed and it only remains to discover the guilty individual.

The first experiment has proved far too successful to be discarded in favour of any innovation. An egg, balanced in the same way as before, will be the sole cost of the continued investigation. The same unsophisticated youth now proceeds to recite the names of all the inhabitants of the village. In most cases he designates them by their nicknames. The " Squirrel," the " Pagoda Cock " and the " Marabout " are at present white as snow. They all appear to heave an immense sigh of relief as their names are called out without any sign of expostulation from the egg. It is plain that their belief in the justice of the Spirits is far from profound. They lose no time in vanishing from the scene.

Suddenly, just as the youthful voice proclaims " The Scorpion," the egg unmistakably collapses.

The malefactor thus indicated is a broken-down old man, an object more of sympathy than of suspicion. His rickety frame is supported with considerable difficulty by his legs, which are swollen to an unnatural degree by gout. But the eye of the Spirits is piercing, their justice unfailing. No escape for the guilty is possible. However, as the accused protests his innocence with all the emphásis at his command, the Pholy condescends to allow him to prove it by submitting to the ordeal prescribed by the Gods. Two alternatives are offered to him, the ordeal by water and that by boiling resin, in which an innocent man may plunge his hand and withdraw it unharmed.

" The Scorpion " is not slow to choose the former. The divine instrument of trial is near at hand in the shape of a river which flows within a short distance of the sacred judgment tree. While the preparations for the ordeal are going forward, the accused asks for permission to make a preliminary statement. If he can associate an accomplice with him in the crime it will doubtless mitigate his punishment. Accordingly he formally names another villager as his partner in transgression. The alleged partner's vigorous denials are followed by immediate arrest. The question now is as to the respective degrees of guilt, a point which the river will ultimately settle. Two stakes are driven into the middle of the stream at a point where the depth is about ten feet. The unfortunate victims are conveyed by canoe to the spot and left clinging desperately to the stakes while trying to keep their heads under water as long as possible. The test is quite simple. The one who loses his breath and comes up to the surface first stands convicted of being the principal in the theft, while his larger-lunged rival is cleared of everything save the charge of complicity.

In a few seconds the performance is over, for the unhappy " Scorpion," already paralysed by fear of the immersion, cannot hold his breath at all, and bobs up to the surface immediately, half asphyxiated. The Sorcerer, delighted at the result of his experiment, expresses his appreciation in a series of approving gestures.

The principle of the ordeal rests on the belief, prevalent among the great majority of half-civilized races, that the tutelary deity of any individual withdraws his protection and assistance if his " ward " has violated any of the fundamental principles of morality, or neglected the rites and ceremonies enjoined by his religion.

This notion of loss of protection of a higher power may possibly be associated with the vague idea of a conscience. It is certainly one of the most curious conceptions which research into the science of divination has brought to our notice. The submission of a suspected criminal to trial by ordeal is an invitation to the Spirits to give a manifestation of their desires.

There are many forms of this species of divine

interrogatory, varying in number and character in different parts of the world. Fifty varieties at least are met with in Africa. It is not to be believed, however, that every ordeal is dangerous or even necessarily harmful. Many forms are known far less cruel than those which arrest the imagination of the traveller by virtue of their more inhuman incidents, such as the ordeal by boiling water, molten lead, or poison dropped into the eyes.

Thus, among the Moï, a favourite ordeal is to compel the accused to drink an excessive quantity of water or alcohol resulting in temporary discomfort without danger or permanent injury.

In Africa cases are known where an ordeal is carried through without the suspected criminal knowing of it. For example, it has been considered sufficient to observe the direction in which the smoke of a chimney is blown, or to set a trap in some place known to be frequented by rats. The innocence or guilt of the accused will be determined according to whether a rat is caught or not.

To judge by the enormous quantity of spirits consumed by the Moï I should have said that this form of ordeal was the most frequent incident of daily life. My flask of ammonia was in perpetual requisition after I had, in an evil moment, revealed to them the peculiar property of ammonia gas, which dissipates the fumes of alcohol.

Perhaps I am doing my friends an injustice. Perhaps there was a more edifying explanation of the run on my flask. May it not be that it furnished a magic potion to some lover of the " bottle " with which to renew his stock of dreams ?

A psychologist friend of mine once said that man cannot do without his " dream-world."

The Moï is no exception. He, too, needs an artificial paradise and finds it in the bottle. He drinks to see life rosy !

CHAPTER V

RELIGIOUS BELIEFS AND RITES

Similarity between the philosophical conceptions of uncivilized races— Most of the ritual derived from magic—Dualism—Private and public talismans—The Pi—The Legend of the Dog-King—Totemism— Sorcery—Rebel Moï.

A STUDY of the general history of mankind reveals many striking resemblances between the crude ideas which pass for philosophical conceptions among nations in their infancy.

Whether the Moï is considered as an undeveloped or a degenerate being (and the consideration will be determined by the school of thought to which the inquirer adheres) it is beyond dispute that he must be classed among the half-civilized portion of mankind, if only because his ideas of the supernatural are those which the brain of the savage has evolved at all times and in all places. Unlike the civilized races, he has never been able to distinguish the natural from the supernatural. He still believes that the world is controlled by invisible forces set in motion by Spirits constituted like himself, susceptible to emotions and passions like his own, and

RELIGIOUS BELIEFS AND RITES

ready to shape their actions at the dictates of humour or caprice.

This belief is the foundation of the multifarious rites which accompany the most trivial daily act of the group which we are now studying.

Since the invisible Beings who thus direct and sway the fortunes of men are susceptible of love, pity, and even, it seems, of fear, it is both possible and advisable to appeal to these emotions to secure their assistance, or, at least, their neutrality.

It will readily be accepted that experience of life does little or nothing to shake this belief in the perpetual intervention of the supernatural, for naturally it is seldom that the desired event does not follow, sooner or later, the particular ceremony in which that desire finds expression.

For example, a great sacrifice is celebrated to secure a cessation of drought. Even if there is no rain for several weeks afterwards, it will still be regarded as an answer to supplication.

The Moï is still in utter ignorance of the connection between cause and effect, largely because he has only the most elementary notions of time and space.

It is an almost universal rule that from the earliest times religion grew out of a belief in magic. Indeed it is worthy of remark at this point that most of the customs and traditions found among civilized races are in essence forms of ancient magical rites which have been adapted to changing conditions.

The most recent investigations by the most

eminent ethnologists confirm the view that a great number of ritualistic ceremonies are founded on the principles of imitative or sympathetic magic. This fact must be kept in mind

Imitative magic is based on a belief which obtains general currency that the effect resembles the cause which produces it. The rudimentary intelligence of the savage infers from this that it is possible to bring about the commission of some act merely by imitating it.

Suppose a Moï desires success in the chase. Before starting on his expedition he will prick himself with one of his arrows, or else he will go through a series of contortions resembling the struggles of an animal caught in his net. He never doubts for a moment that by imitating his action, his prey will become an easy victim to his toils.

"Sympathetic" magic is based on another equally prevalent belief that objects which have once been in contact will continue to influence each other after the contact has ceased and that such continuance of influence remains unaffected either by time or distance.

It follows as a logical conclusion from this belief that all that is necessary to obtain or maintain influence over any person or object is to get possession of some part of that person or object. Accordingly the Sorcerer's first task is to secure some portion of his intended victim, a few hairs, perhaps, or some blood, or a piece of nail. By tormenting the image he will inflict the same sufferings on the original.

"*Les Tribes Moi*"] [*By Henri Maitre.*
A Hut of **Propitiation** containing **Offerings** to the Gods.

rom "*Les Tribes Moi*"] [*By Henri Maitre.*
Tombs fenced with Bamboo and decorated with Elephants' Tusks.
[*To face p.* 100.

Photo by] [*A. Cabaton.*

Woven Bamboo Baskets used to carry Offerings to the Priests.

RELIGIOUS BELIEFS AND RITES

In the same way a rejected lover will dress a burnt-clay figure in a fragment of the robe of his mistress and by supplications addressed to her representative seek to turn her hard heart towards himself.

Thanks to the new light thrown on these fundamental principles by the untiring efforts of Frazer, van Gennep and other eminent ethnologists, analysis of the better known beliefs of the Moï has become both practicable and intelligible. We can at any rate distinguish their salient characteristics.

As the Spirits are susceptible to human passions their natural inclination is to be malevolent towards man, for passions excite to ill-will and ill-doing rather than to benevolence. To counteract this baneful tendency it is highly desirable to incite the supernatural powers to turn their anger upon one another, and this is the more easy of accomplishment because they are numerous, jealous, and have each their particular domain.

To this origin must we assign the idea of provoking a supernatural conflict—dualism—which inspires the accomplishment of certain rites.

Further, it is impossible to secure either the assistance or even the neutrality of the superior powers without a talisman. The Sorcerer supplies these indispensable instruments, of which he enjoys the monopoly. Their nature and appearance vary with the object which their wearer has in view. If a native fears the attack of some particular animal his talisman will be some part of the object of his fears. The teeth of wild animals, the claws of tigers, the tongues of serpents, figure frequently among the talismans of those who fear an encounter with these formidable enemies. As a rule they are enclosed in a small wallet and suspended round the neck.

In a sense this is as natural an instinct as that which prompts savages of all races to make a protective amulet of the object of their fears, for, by an analogous association of ideas, they have frequently found the remedy in the apprehended evil itself. Anyone who has lived in the bush knows that immunity from the ill effects of a scorpion's bite can be obtained by injecting under the skin a paste made from the tails of those venomous creatures.

Some of these talismans are valueless to all save their original owner, and sometimes even to him only so long as he remains attached to his tribe and village. They are, so to speak, personal and not transferable.

On the other hand there are what I may call "collective" talismans endowed with powers to protect a family, a community, or even a whole tribe. They are displayed in some prominent position, hung on the doorpost, a sacred tree, the mast of a canoe, or the palisade of a village.

Others are endowed with medicinal properties and are alleged to cure fevers and dysentery. Our portable chemist's shop was regarded as a very sacred grove of the Spirits of Healing. These august deities consented to appear in the form of a white powder

RELIGIOUS BELIEFS AND RITES 103

(quinine) or of fire-water (tincture of iodine) to allay human ills. A bottle of chlorodyne which I used frequently in the many cases of dysentery and cholera was elevated to the rank of a deity.

I must confess also that there were many occasions on which I took advantage of their credulity in these matters. There were times when my request for food and lodging for our party met with hesitation and even point-blank refusal. In such circumstances a simple threat to grind them all to powder produced a prompt compliance with our wishes.

The Moï apply the generic term of " Pi " to all the occult powers whose intervention in human affairs is a matter of daily terror. The word " Pi " roughly denotes the idea of supernatural action. It corresponds to the " Orenda " of the Iroquois and the " Mana " of the savage tribes of Polynesia.

The Spirits who claim sway over the region of the forest-clad mountains are both numerous and quarrelsome. Those whose intentions towards men are known to be beneficent are neglected while worship and sacrifice are concentrated on the propitiation of the malevolent ones.

The " Chicken-Devil " is an object of the greatest terror to women. Legend relates that once upon a time he was imprisoned within the body of an ogress by whose murder he was restored to liberty.

The malevolent disposition of this Spirit is displayed by his habit of poisoning the breath of all the women who cross his path. A woman thus contaminated poisons every particle of food with which she comes in contact.

No less dangerous are the Spirits which have been liberated from bondage by the violent death or suicide of their masters. Woe betide the traveller who encounters them on his journey. If his escort be not large and his weapons of the latest pattern he will go to swell the already lengthy list of victims of the powers of evil.

Farther on lurks a fresh horror.

The road is long, the sun overpowering, the earth a burning carpet. Suddenly a tree offers welcome rest and shelter to the weary traveller. He loses no time in seeking its grateful shade and, selecting a suitable branch for a fly-swish, prepares to cut it with his knife.

Heaven help him if he carries out his intention. The tree is haunted by the spirit of a chief slain in war. It will snatch up the sacrilegious criminal and bear him to the great Beyond.

It is a horrible catastrophe to meet with certain Ghouls, whose method of progression is a rolling motion like that of a barrel, and who devour all the refuse of the roads. If a woman is with you their vengeance will fall upon her. She will become barren and gradually rot away.

On moonlight nights young warriors often meet with ravishing nymphs who beckon them to follow into the depths of the forest. The loveliness and wiles of these mystic temptresses soon overpower

RELIGIOUS BELIEFS AND RITES 105

the strongest will and the young men yield to the spell and disappear in the darkness. Soon the vision vanishes. The victims, terror-stricken, walk round in fruitless circles until dawn. Their tormentors are malignant spirits who assume the form of lovely nymphs solely to gratify their cunning spite by hindering and terrorizing their victims.

Among the numerous uncivilized groups of Indo-China it is curious that only one offers the peculiar characteristic of possessing a totem. The "Man" or "Yaos" believe that their first ancestor was a dog. Accordingly, their veneration for that animal is profound, and it is strictly forbidden to use its flesh for food.

If we are to believe one legend which at least has the sanction of general acceptance, about 525 B.C. Pen Hung, who was at that time ruler of the Chinese province of Su, promised his daughter's hand and the half of his kingdom to the hero who should rid him of the conquering marauder Cu-Hung, who was menacing his security. The invader's reputation for valour had preceded him and was such that no man dared cross swords with him. When all seemed lost a dog named Phan-Hu undertook the task of destroying the enemy, and, having succeeded in slaying Cu-Hung in mortal combat, he returned to claim from the King the fulfilment of his promise.

The King gave his daughter to the victor, but in order to keep to himself the more fertile portion of his kingdom, he assigned only the uncultivated mountain-tops as the dog's share. This unfairness was resented by the Dog-King, and to remedy it special concessions were granted to his descendants.

The copy of a charter in which these privileges are set forth is still preserved among what we may call the archives of the "Man." This apocryphal document has been translated by Colonel Bonifacy of the Colonial Infantry, who was the first to call the attention of Europeans to its existence. On the other hand, if we are to believe the twelfth-century historian Fan-Chi-Hu, the dog Phan-Hu was no other than a savage who took that name and did in fact marry a princess as the prize for a very remarkable triumph in a personal combat.

However that may be, it is incontestable that individuals are found in every country whose excessive hairiness suggests a striking resemblance to the dog, especially as regards the face. The Toda of India and the Birmans have recently furnished several striking examples of the freak which is popularly known as the " dog-faced man." But to return to the legend, we may at least conclude that the marriage took place at a much earlier period than that suggested.

The " Man," the issue of this union, have shown a marked tendency to expand. From the mountain-tops which formed their original kingdom they have penetrated into Tonkin, Annam and the region of the lakes. They seem to have made ample use of a provision in their ancient Charter which entitled them to set fire to any forest which impeded their progress. They claim that this authority is still valid and subsisting, and we had the greatest difficulty in enforcing obedience to our forest regulations. The most interesting feature of this ethnical group is that it shows undoubted traces of the existence of an alliance formed in immemorial times with some species of animal. Now the underlying idea of totemism is that of a compact between an aggregation (family, or group) of human beings and some animal species from which has sprung a relationship at once physical and social.

The recent controversy over the definition of totemism seems to make it both redundant and impertinent for me to enlarge on a subject which is still fresh in the memory of all. Nor is the matter of great moment, for I am convinced that, with few exceptions, if the peoples whom I am studying have any connection with these quite special phenomena, that connection is too remote to be regarded as a basis for any satisfactory deductions.

Besides, it is well known that competent observers have frequently confused totemic practices with certain customs whose origin is rather to be looked for in zoolatry or theriolatry (*thēr*, a wild beast).

Theriolatry embraces such curiosities as tiger and crocodile-worship, while zoolatry signifies the worship of the domestic animals. It must be admitted that when the totem of a group is a wild beast the totemism is probably theriolatric, but it is impossible to dispute van Gennep's statement that all theriolatry is not necessarily totemic.

Organization in groups or totemic clans is only found among races that are just emerging from barbarism, and proof is not lacking that several peoples in classical antiquity had passed through that stage of progress before the period of recorded history begins.

Sorcerers, among the Moï, fall into two categories, those who are gifted with the faculty of divination whereby the guilty can be detected, and those whose exorcisms are confined and directed to the healing of disease.

As a rule the Spirit himself selects the individual whom he proposes to endow with these divine functions.

The first intimation to the happy mortal on whom the choice of Heaven has thus fallen is a feeling of violent colic or sickness of a peculiar kind which leaves no doubt as to its message or mission. The sufferer suffers gladly.

It is by no means the rule that initiation is followed by an immediate assumption of the divine functions. In most cases a prolonged interval elapses, for a candidate who feels unequal to the rôle thus suddenly thrust upon him will prefer exile rather than a return to the ranks of common mortals, a set-back which would make him a public laughing-stock.

Among the Djarai, one of the most important of the Indo-Chinese groups, there are two sorcerers of the greatest renown, known as the " King of Fire " and the " King of Water."

It is probable that these mythological names

originally personified the incarnation of Agni, God of Fire, and Varouna, God of Water, and are themselves traces of Brahminism which at one time exercised immense influence over the southern Indo-Chinese peoples and which cannot be said to be entirely defunct to-day

The Hindu god Agni is always represented as armed with a lance. The " King of Fire " carries, not a lance, but a sword, to which an extraordinary magical power is attributed. If its guardian were to draw it merely an inch or two from its scabbard the sun would cease to illumine the earth. If he drew it out altogether a paralysing lethargy would settle upon his subjects.

Hardly less astonishing are the powers ascribed to the two fetishes which are in the official keeping of the " King of Water." One is the fruit of a creeper which shows not the slightest trace of decay though it was plucked at the time of the Deluge. The other is a sacred rattan which, though of immemorial antiquity, looks as fresh as on its first day of existence. The owner of these talismans has only to utter a word and the universe will disappear beneath the celestial cataracts.

The Cambodians and the Cham assert that these talismans formerly belonged to their kings and were stolen from them by treachery. More than once they have organized expeditions to recover their treasure, but the Spirits have willed otherwise, and the Djarai have never had any difficulty in repelling the invaders.

The predecessors of Norodom, as long as they held sway and directed the destinies of Cambodia, brought presents each year to their cousins, the Kings of the Savage Lands. These gifts took the form of an elephant gorgeously caparisoned, a quantity of brass and some superb pieces of silk destined for the sheath of the sacred sword. As a fitting reply to this act of homage, the King of Fire condescended to leave the imprint of his august finger on a cake of wax, which was then sent to Pnom-Penh, and on two gourds filled with rice.

India, as well as Cambodia, is familiar with the custom of preserving the print of the foot or hand of anyone who has become an object of veneration. Oil of sesame figures frequently in ritual sacrifices, especially when offered by those guilty of intemperance. It is said to purify the worshipper and be grateful to the outraged Spirit.

Wax and corn are alleged to have a remarkably soothing effect on Spirits with a tendency to active malevolence.

But to return to the two Potentates, it must be admitted that they have no effective political authority, though their influence in the sphere of religion is unchallenged.

Their residences lie at a distance of several miles from each other on opposite sides of the watershed between the rivers of Annam and the lakes.

Their offices are hereditary and, if we are to believe the current legend, the family are always present

RELIGIOUS BELIEFS AND RITES 111

at the death of a pontiff to assist his passage to the next world. This is not from any urgent desire to succeed him but to accomplish a traditional rite The next step in the proceedings is remarkable. The individual on whom the mantle of the deceased has fallen by hereditary right takes refuge in flight. He is pursued and caught, and in spite of his repeated refusals is compelled to continue the dynasty.

This solemn mockery, parading as a custom, is by no means confined to the group of which I am speaking. In all lands and all periods men are to be found who meet their appointment to places of high honour with sincere or insincere refusals. For one case of genuine apprehension of unfitness there are ten of mock-modesty.

In many cases, it must be admitted, the office of Chief is both onerous and precarious. Sometimes the Chief is only the titular head of the tribe, bound hand and foot by custom and tradition and held responsible for all the misfortunes that overtake his country during his reign. In these circumstances it is hardly to be wondered at that there is some misgiving among those elected to the burdensome office. The Princes of Loango, the Sheik of Gardaia, and the King of the Hobbé in Central Nigeria all take to ignominious flight when their turn comes to assume the reins of government.

In most cases, however, the refusal has become a tradition, whether spontaneous in its origin or not. The Moslem is doing no more than to imitate

Mahomet's modest denials when the angel Gabriel came to announce his selection as the prophet of Allah. Even in our days, how many times have we not seen the good citizen professing his unworthiness of a proffered honour and accepting under the pretence of compulsion that on which his heart has long been set!

We have an interesting account of a visit to the " King of Fire " from the lips of Commandant Cupet of the Pavie mission. The Potentate put every conceivable obstacle in the way of the expedition and spared no pains to make their residence in the country as uncomfortable as possible. Having surmounted these obstacles, however, the explorers were faced with a flat refusal to allow them to depart. The situation was becoming extremely strained when a happy accident relieved it. The Pontiff chanced to see a compass, and was so impressed by the movements of the magnetic needle, which he attributed to some magic power, that he withdrew his opposition and allowed the expedition to proceed unmolested.

Tragically otherwise was the experience of my friend Prosper Odend' Hal, Director of the Indo-Chinese Civil Service, during the archæological and ethnographical mission of 1904.

Some days before the departure of his expedition under the auspices of the French School in the Far East, he came to ask me if I would lend him my Moï vocabularies, which he wished to complete during the journey. In the course of our conversation he

RELIGIOUS BELIEFS AND RITES 113

told me of his intention to dispense with an escort other than an interpreter and a few boys, with a view to facilitating movement and saving time. I had already had sufficient experience of the insecurity of the regions he proposed to explore to know the danger of such a course, and I exhausted every argument to turn him from his purpose. The country was far from pacified and the guerilla warfare which detached bodies of the Moï carried on against us seemed likely at any moment to break out in open conflict. Nothing appeared to me more foolhardy than to go among them defenceless at a time when force was the only argument they could appreciate. Unhappily Odend' Hal remained firm in his conviction that a mark of confidence would fire their imaginations and touch their hearts. He professed a high regard for these unregenerate savages and endowed them, quite gratuitously, with all manner of virtues

This blind confidence was the cause of his undoing. He started from Phan-Rang at the end of March, crossed the Annamite range, the mountains of Langbian and the plateau of the Darlac, then penetrated into the interior of Phuyen (Annam), the land of the " King of Fire."

It seems that from the first he had made up his mind to see the renowned sacred sword. After much negotiation, its royal owner had intimated his pleasure to gratify the desire and invited the explorer to a great banquet to be given in his house.

On the seventh of April Odend' Hal attended, accompanied only by his interpreter and unarmed, to demonstrate his confidence in the loyalty of his host. Some hours later his servants were aroused by a report of fire. In an isolated hut, already wrapped in flames, they found the bodies of the two victims pierced through and through with spears.

Odend' Hal was a senior officer of the same standing as myself. He had taken part in our earliest expeditions at the time of the conquest, and lived more than twenty years in the country, where his kindness and outstanding ability had won universal respect

More than one punitive expedition had to be sent out after this outrage, and some of them met with open and unremitting hostility from detached bodies of the Moï. I have mentioned before that even during the mission on which I was engaged MM. Canivey and Barbu, who were in command of the Militia, had to organize a flying column to operate to the north of Langbian, where we were then engaged on a topographical survey. These two officers themselves commanded the force, which was composed of fifty militiamen and the same number of coolies.

They left Dalat, where we had made our headquarters, and marched in the direction of the Darlac. Within a few days they were in touch with the rebels, who pursued the policy of retiring before their advance, abandoning their villages and attempting to draw the column into the forest-clad mountains, where numerous defiles offered special advantages for guerilla warfare. Captain Canivey was not to be deceived by such tactics, and advisedly gave the order for retreat, leaving the subjugation of the rebels to a later occasion.

When the first stage of the return journey was almost completed the advance-guard reported towards evening that their progress was impeded by small bamboo stakes fixed into the ground. Rifle in hand Canivey at once went forward, suspecting an ambush. Behind the palisade of thorny bamboo he thought he detected several dark dots moving hither and thither. Suddenly two arrows, then a third, struck him, and a fourth followed. Captain Barbu, who rushed to the rescue, was received by a shower of missiles.

The Linhs, or native soldiers, threw themselves flat on the ground and fired volley after volley in the direction of the attack. The Moï replied with an avalanche of arrows and javelins, but the rapidity of our fire soon proved too much for them and, after their ranks had been seriously depleted, they gave way and fled, leaving all but a few of their wounded. We made prisoners of all the rebels thus left to their fate and buried the corpses in an effective, if summary, manner.

It was long before MM. Canivey and Barbu recovered from their wounds, but after many anxious moments their natural vitality triumphed, and within a short time a new expedition was organized which proved a complete success.

CHAPTER VI

RITES AND SUPERSTITIONS (*continued*)

Tribal and proprietary signs—Tattooing and mutilation—Principles and practice of the taboo—Its survival in modern Europe—The incarnation of Spirits in stones, trees, and animals—Belief in the magic powers of the tiger—Animal-poison—Bones as a charm—A protecting ear—Ex-votos offered to the Spirit of the tiger—Superstitions about monkeys—Hunting rites.

MOST of the barbarous races of all countries seek to preserve their identity and distinguish themselves from their neighbours by some marked peculiarity either of dress, jewels and ornaments, or even by some particular mutilation of the body.

Africa shows a wonderful variety of tribal symbols. Among the most general of these are the elliptical or concentric marks of a red-hot iron on the face and breast which are considered such an embellishment by the Bangendi of the Belgian Congo. Another common form is the artificial elongation of the breasts caused by cords or the weight of heavy ropes of pearls. This fashion is in vogue mainly among the Isambo of the same region. Then again it is quite usual for certain classes to dye their hair red, shave off their eyebrows and tear out their eyelashes and moustaches. The most widely practised form of mutilation, however, is that of the jaw. The Bushongo, also of the Belgian Congo, extract the two incisors of the upper jaw, and some of the women have the lower incisors cut in such a way as to form a hollow in the centre.

Some of these practices are found among the Moï and more particularly the elongation of the ears and breasts and the extraction or pointing of the teeth. This last mutilation takes place at the age of puberty, a fact which suggests that it forms part of the complex of rites which mark the passing of the young from one state to another, or which celebrate their initiation into the full status of membership of the group. If so, it merely follows a custom which is encountered in all latitudes.

Among the Moï the operation of filing lasts from ten to fifteen days. The instrument employed is a hard stone, which is found in the bed of certain rivers, notably the river of Phanrang. It is the subject of a flourishing export trade to the tribes of the interior. The incisors of the lower jaw are filed to resemble a triangle, or perhaps the teeth of a cat, those of the upper jaw are cut in the form of a semicircle or filed down to the level of the gums. Although this mutilation is extremely painful, so great is the influence of tradition that no man would dream of dispensing with it. For as the piercing of the lobe of the ear devotes a woman to perpetual spinsterhood, so the neglect to be filed deprives a man of the right to found a family.

In Australia the young men submit to the extraction of several of their teeth at the moment of initiation. Sometimes the teeth thus removed are hidden under the bark of a tree unknown to their late owner. If he dies the tree is dried by fire and becomes a monument to perpetuate the memory of the deceased. This is a striking example of sympathetic magic, of which I have spoken before.

In Africa the village blacksmith is the appointed minister to perform the rite of dressing the teeth. He places a small iron ring against the tooth and strikes it with a light hammer. It would be natural to suppose that this process would be even more painful than the filing. What matter! In the eyes of the savage the suffering involved is the most meritorious part of the operation. Our coolies could hardly contain their indignation at the suggestion that an anæsthetic should first be administered. Painless filing would be a stigma to man, an outrage to Heaven!

In Africa the practice is extended to women as well as men in several groups, though only after marriage, but in Indo-China I never met any women who had undergone the treatment.

It is well known that mutilations of this kind are not the only badge of race which distinguishes one group from another, for it seems plain that tattooing also originated in a desire to serve the same purpose.

The islanders of Timor employ hereditary marks tattooed on the cheeks, the chin, or the breasts of

RITES AND SUPERSTITIONS

the women, to distinguish the different families. The same custom is followed in New Guinea. Most of these symbols are compounded of an ideograph and a letter of the alphabet. Their use is extended to distinguish owners of such things as shields and weapons. Here they form a kind of trade-mark of which the owner alone knows the meaning, and which all others are prohibited from infringing. (If I had known of this peculiarity during my travels among the Moï, I should have been more careful in noting the tattoo marks which are to be met with among the dwellers by the lakes and also the signs which are engraved on various objects. As it was I merely observed the blue markings which adorned the legs of the men and the curious red hieroglyphics inscribed in rectangles on their arms and backs. It is very likely that these were also the symbols of relationship or ownership.)

It is well to remind ourselves that the custom exists even in Europe to-day. Some of the Catholic women of Bosnia still practise the tattooing of the forearm or chest with the form of a Latin cross. The practice seems to date from the twelfth century and to be inspired by a desire for a visible sign of their religious isolation, for they live among a Mohammedan population which has never been distinguished for its tolerance.

In whatever manner the custom came into being there is little variety in the substance used in the process. The skin is firmly stretched and the figure lightly sketched upon it. Then a number of punctures very close together are made with a needle dipped in the staining matter and wrapped in cotton almost up to the point. The part is then bandaged until the lapse of a fixed period, after which all covering is taken off and the indelible traces, changed in colour to a Prussian blue, remain on the skin.

Of course the operation is attended with all manner of prayers and ceremonial. It may not take place on certain days which are regarded as unfavourable, and never without the approval and assistance of the Sorcerer. This again recalls the custom of the Catholics of Bosnia, who invariably select Sunday or some other holy day for the ceremony of engraving the sacred sign.

Like the Moï, the youths of the lower Congo reside in a specially reserved dwelling when the time has come for them to undergo the rites associated with initiation into full citizenship. In Africa, however, this residence is always outside the village and the profane are prohibited from entering under pain of death. Further, its principal function is to accommodate those who intend to enter the sect of the "Nkimba" (meaning "initiation"), members of which take the name of "Nkissi" ("enchanted"). Sometimes this voluntary retirement lasts as long as a year.

A widespread, but unfounded, belief prevails that races in a rudimentary state of civilization enjoy greater licence than those which have advanced further along the path of progress. On the contrary, the savage

RITES AND SUPERSTITIONS

is subject to all manner of restrictions which make freedom of will almost a mockery. Not alone his acts but even his feelings and desires are hedged about with repressive regulations. The simple explanation is that he sees the supernatural in a very different light from us and brings it into the smallest action of his daily life. Once granted that he is not a free agent, and that unseen powers have to be consulted at every end and turn, it follows logically that a number of prohibitions arise which it is convenient to refer to in this book as " Taboos," a generic term which has been used by the Polynesians and now adopted almost universally by ethnologists.

Taboos are of every conceivable kind, royal, sacerdotal, sexual, proprietary, and they all spring from the fundamental notion that it is necessary to regulate every action in accordance with the probability of arousing or conciliating divine displeasure. Some of them follow as a corollary to the belief in the effect of magic by imitation or contact.

Thus, since in time of drought rain can be caused by spilling water on the ground, it is taboo to perform that operation at a period when a cessation from rain is required.

Other taboos are prophylactic. Thus certain persons, contact with whom is considered to be prejudicial to morals, are isolated to preserve the virtue of the others.

I have already recounted the prohibitions of every kind which regulate the behaviour of a woman during pregnancy. Here again the motive is the same. The rules as to isolation and the restriction of diet have no other object than to preserve her from dangers which are ever hovering around.

Other taboos are directed towards the preservation of health and physical strength, and apply largely to kings, chiefs and officials. Thus in Japan princes were never permitted to put their feet on the ground. The Mikado was compelled to spend several hours motionless on the throne. He violated the injunction if he even turned his head. The sun must never shine on his face, and on no account must he cut his nails, hair, or beard. Even to-day the King of Cambodia is not allowed to be in a house of more than one story lest some human being should pass over his head. Accordingly the ceilings of his palace are made of glass so that no one shall commit such an act of treason unobserved.

These curious regulations become more intelligible when we remember that the chief of a savage tribe is regarded as the depository of the health and strength of the whole group, which is thus directly interested in the preservation of its ruler from every form of malady and mischance. It is possible that this very ancient idea is the origin of many of the rules of etiquette which are so punctiliously observed by the Courts of certain States.

An explanation of many of these taboos may also be sought in an examination of the religious systems on which they are based. For example, in totemic

RITES AND SUPERSTITIONS

groups unions between persons who have entered into a compact with the same totem are invariably prohibited. Accordingly we should expect to find, and do in fact find, that exogamy is the rule among members of the same clan.

The most superficial observation of the religious systems of all nations reveals the existence of taboos in some form or another. They appear in Christianity as in Buddhism, Brahminism, and others which dispute among themselves the title of the true faith.

Even outside the sphere of religious observance we know that certain acts, insignificant in themselves, are habitually avoided. This can only be attributed to a traditional prohibition dating from ancient times. I myself know many devout Christians who would gaze at me in astonishment if I told them that many of their most cherished beliefs can trace their descent from the precepts of pagans. But I spare them any such inward perplexity and merely smile to myself when I see them hasten to put out one of three lights burning in a room, or ostentatiously separate two forks which some clumsy servant has put crosswise on the table.

But besides all these taboos which apply without distinction to all the members of a group, there are others which concern one or other of the sexes, such as the regulation which appoints certain occupations and pursuits as proper for women only, and vice versâ.

Thus, among the Moï the women do all the work about the farms and in the fields, though this would seem to be the natural province of the men. It is easy to suggest laziness as the reason for this reversal of the natural order, but probably the origin is to be sought in some ancestral tradition long since forgotten. More noble occupations, such as war and the chase, are reserved to the men, and their wives, proud of their husbands' glorious duties, are quite content to play the part of beast of burden. The difference is illustrated in many humble actions. A woman must carry a burden on her head or her back. A man submits to no such indignity. He divides the load into two parts, hangs one on each end of a bamboo pole and balances them across his shoulder. It is again necessary to recall that Europe shows traces of this conception which have hitherto remained unexplained. Why is it natural for a woman in Austria to act as a mason's labourer, while in France it would be deemed an outrage to impose such laborious duties? Why is the office of lemonade-seller confined to men in France, while in Austria that rôle is invariably played by women? The list of these anomalies is lengthy and would furnish evidence for a plausible argument that the feminist movement is no more than the belated revenge of a sex whose activities have been too long checked by the arbitrary prohibitions of man.

We have now seen that certain persons, natural and supernatural, certain objects, and even actions, are deemed harmful and to be avoided at all costs. It is therefore not altogether surprising that the ruly righteous avoid even referring to those persons, objects, or actions.

The Moï, for example, will never utter the word "Tiger," an animal he regards with a kind of holy awe, and which has been raised to the rank of a deity. If he must refer to the creature he calls it "The Master" or "The Lofty One," or else uses some obvious paraphrase the sense of which escapes no one.

Hunting one day in the forest, I happened to meet a little girl who was gathering bamboo shoots for the family meal. I chanced to ask her whether peacocks and heathcocks were to be found in those regions.

"Oh, yes," she replied, "there were several here just now, but they have gone. . . . There is no peace among us," and a few moments after, "We fear."

I had little difficulty in guessing the object of her terror though she dared not put it into words, but to convince myself, and partly, I fear, from an unmannerly enjoyment of her confusion, I feigned ignorance and asked again:

"But what do you fear?"

She hesitated a moment, half paralysed with fear at the thought of uttering the dread name, then recovered her composure and with sly malice replied:

"We fear Heaven."

Heaven, that was the Tiger without doubt! The following week I learnt with tragic force how natural were her fears, for she fell a victim, by no means the first, to the terrible enemy.

The incident remains engraved on my memory both for the melancholy interest attaching to it, and also because it was the first time I had come into actual contact with the taboo which forbids certain names to be uttered or requires the employment of a special language when prohibited subjects are to be referred to.

Explanations have often been attempted of the belief commonly held by savages in the incarnation of Spirits in forms other than that of a human being. The most natural theory is probably the most obvious. Since the world began all peoples have noticed that man is one of the most perishable of the objects about them. Is it likely, they ask, that the Spirits would choose so destructible a home for their earthly habitation? Surely they would select a place with greater chances of permanence, a stone, for example, or a tree? Hence the worship of these objects, not for any intrinsic value, but because they are housing Spirits.

Among the Bahnar, a Moï group, certain flints of immense age are objects of the greatest veneration. Frequently one of these stones is raised on high on a pedestal of bamboos and the more curious they are in appearance, the more reverence is bestowed upon them. The conception of the incarnation of a deity in an animal must be traced back to the same idea. Primitive man naturally attributed to animals, which sometimes preyed upon him, powers superior to his own. He was far from thinking himself the lord

RITES AND SUPERSTITIONS

of creation and ascribed that superiority to the presence of a Spirit incarnated in the animal and directing its actions. The Egyptians worshipped the crocodile under various names, such as " Lord of the Waters," and " The Devourer." If such a belief prevailed among an advanced people such as these, it is hardly surprising that the barbarous races of Indo-China should fall into the same error.

We find, in fact, among these races clear traces of litholatry (from the Greek *lithos*, a stone), dendrolatry (*dendron*, a tree), and theriolatry (*thēr*, a wild beast).

It is quite usual to find some hoary guardian, such as a fig-tree or ebony tree, stationed at the entrance of a village. It shelters with its spreading foliage a minute house raised on piles and dedicated to the Genius of the Soil or the Master of the Earth. Within this pagoda is a brazier from which the fumes of incense are always rising. The offerings which are brought will call down the blessing of Heaven on the harvest, and in particular will inspire the Genius to wreak vengeance on thieves who attempt to rob the public granary. A few canes hung on the walls of this little building serve to put a holy fear in the less imaginative visitors. They are the symbol of the punishment which will be meted out to robbers.

Unfortunately, the harvest has to encounter not merely the depredations of the evilly-disposed, but also the attacks of animal enemies such as the boar and the deer. To ward off this class of mischance a stretched bow is hung on the roof, threatening with its arrow any animal bold enough to approach. I may add that the farmers frequently use this hut as a lair from which to shoot the marauders. By thus doing the work of the Genius they augment his reputation and benefit themselves, a very satisfactory arrangement.

Similar rites are to be found in every part of the world from the earliest times. In ancient Egypt the festival of Sokari (the hawk-headed Osiris) at Memphis always concluded with the erection of a pillar called "Tat" or "Ded" in the form of a tree without foliage. The same custom obtains among the Siamese, the Cambodians, and the Laotians, where the "Tat" is often to be seen. Its origin is plainly ritual. In the region of the lakes the "Tats" are to be found placed so close together as to look like a nursery garden. As a rule these monuments are made of simple hewn masonry and vary greatly in size. The same variety is to be observed in their form and design, which seems to be determined by the individual caprice of the architect rather than by any conformity to established custom. They generally resemble a pyramid in shape, the base being either circular or square, the apex assuming the form sometimes of a Byzantine roof or that of a spire. Their erection is usually the fulfilment of a vow or the commemoration of some fortunate occurrence in the family. Among the Laotians the number of "Tats" which a man raises is considered the measure of his piety.

In Europe the same conception appears in the familiar festivities of the maypole.

It sometimes happened in the course of our geodetical survey that we were compelled to cut down a tree which interrupted the field of view of our instruments. A most interesting scene preceded the act of destruction. The "foreman" of our Moï coolies approached the condemned tree and addressed it much as follows:

"Spirit who hast made thy home in this tree, we worship thee and are come to claim thy mercy. The white mandarin, our relentless master, whose commands we cannot but obey, has bidden us to cut down thy habitation, a task which fills us with sadness and which we only carry out with regret. I adjure thee to depart at once from the place and seek a new dwelling-place elsewhere, and I pray thee to forget the wrong we do thee, for we are not our own masters."

This harangue, accompanied by spitting and an immense obeisance, being concluded, the foreman addressed another in very similar terms to the Lord Tiger, which in its character of undisputed King of the Forest has jurisdiction over every tree within it.

The tiger, indeed, thanks to its fearful ravages in this land of hilly jungle, is easily first among the animals which popular superstition has endowed with supernatural powers. Nor is this to be wondered at, for Europeans who live in the country are frequently obliged to confess themselves thwarted and even driven away by the depredations of this ferocious beast. I have already mentioned an occasion on which, after fourteen nights of inactivity, I was compelled to withdraw and abandon the place to a tiger which had carried off one of my natives before my very eyes. It was during this same fruitless attempt to get rid of the pest that I learnt from my escort the popular superstitions concerning the powers of this formidable foe.

In the first place their beliefs are determined by terror. Everything concerning the creature is fantastic, mysterious, marvellous.

A fearsome natural power resides in its whiskers, which produce the awful thing known as animal-poison. The right and ability to invoke this phenomenon pertain to the Sorcerer who proceeds in this wise. As soon as a tiger has been killed or captured he pulls out its whiskers and encloses them with the utmost care in a hollow bamboo stick. A hundred watches later a snake emerges from this prison and takes refuge in the garden. The Sorcerer seeks out the place where it lies hidden and once a year on the fifteenth day of the seventh moon he takes it a few grains of maize, which constitute its sole nourishment. The creature rises from its hole, rears itself aloft, swallows the gift, and if it finds it to its taste leaves a few drops of poison on the ground as a sign of gratitude. The Sorcerer collects these carefully in a saucer. According to the rites he must use this poison before the year is over under penalty

Memorial Stone erected to a Tiger.

A Hunting Party.

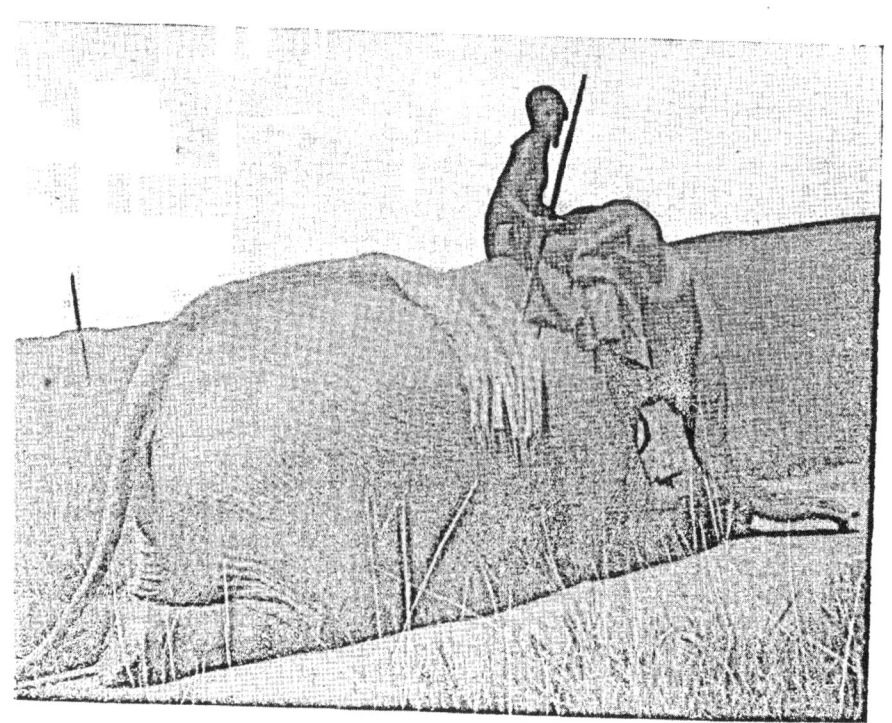

An Elephant and his Driver.

[*To face p.* 131.

of himself becoming impotent. His duty is to mingle it with the food of certain persons whom the Spirits will designate.

After a short time disturbing symptoms make their appearance. The patient is seized with a trembling fit which agitates his whole frame. Convulsions follow, or else he loses his sight, or hearing, or sense of smell, while his stomach swells in a manner alarming to behold. The disease soon defies all treatment and the wretched victim expires amidst the most atrocious sufferings.

It is easy to scoff, but every traveller in these regions has known cases of sudden attacks of a particularly virulent form of fever which manifests itself in most alarming forms, such as suicidal mania, epilepsy, pronounced deafness, or swelling of the abdomen.

I myself had an unpleasant practical illustration of the unshakable belief in animal-poisons and their baneful effect. There was a native member of the mission who believed himself bewitched in this manner. Although he was in a high fever, he stolidly refused all medical assistance and immediately coughed up the mixture which I attempted to force down his throat. Within four days he was dead, a victim to his own superstitious ignorance. The most unfortunate effect of the tragedy, however, was that it only served to confirm his companions in their belief.

It must not be believed that everything pertaining to the tiger is necessarily harmful. On the contrary certain parts of its body are credited with some remarkably beneficial properties. Thus some small bones of the shoulder are frequently carried about as a charm against the attacks of the animal itself, and also to give their owner physical superiority over his foes and preserve him against an unfavourable result of the ordeal, should he be called on to face that trial. It is therefore little surprising that competition for this talisman is often bitter and bloody and that its market value sometimes exceeds that of a buffalo.

Another widespread superstition is that a tiger which, in springing upon its prey, is clumsy enough to damage the ear, will abandon its victim immediately and never return to devour it. Curiously enough we received from the mouths of two members of the mission, M. Millet and Sergeant Valutioni, proof that this belief is not altogether devoid of foundation. The former once spent four days watching over the corpse of a buffalo with a torn ear which had been killed by a tiger. The animal never returned to carry away its prey. Now we know that the habit of this carnivorous beast is to return nightly to devour its victims when their weight is too great to permit of their being carried off immediately to its lair. So was it simple caprice which prompted this strange behaviour or had the tiger perhaps been wounded in the encounter? It is impossible to bring the question out of the realm of surmise.

The Sergeant's experience was somewhat similar. He was riding at nightfall when his horse suddenly swerved and nearly threw him out of the saddle. Picking himself up, he saw a huge tiger leap upon his horse, only to abandon it immediately and disappear into the jungle. He examined his mount for injuries and discovered that the only damage was that a piece of its ear had been torn off. The natives who had witnessed the attack manifested no sign of astonishment and recounted the numerous occasions on which they had observed a similar occurrence.

Whatever the truth may be, it is in virtue of incidents such as these that the Moï attribute to the tiger the faculty of reasoning out all its acts. It is considered the most vindictive of creatures, and rather than expose themselves to its vengeance they will let all its misdeeds go unpunished, contenting themselves with a philosophical resignation to fate. Sometimes the inroads of tigers cause the abandonment of an entire village, the natives preferring exile to gradual decimation. Sometimes, however, they resort to charms to ward off the dread plague. For instance, they will place a box, on one side of which the figure of a tiger is rudely carved, in front of the principal house. This is a favourite device of the Annamites, among whom these ex-votos distinguish a region infested by the pest. Every time a stranger passes the spot it is his duty to leave a stone or a twig in honour of " Duc-Thay " the Noble Master, the Spirit which has jurisdiction over the tigers, perhaps the tiger itself.

A supernatural character is also attributed to the

monkey, largely on account of its agility, its imitative ability, and its cunning in escaping from its pursuers. The creature is held in high esteem by many peoples, and it will be remembered that the Hindoos regard it as an incarnation of Vishnu. The white gibbon with black whiskers is regarded with great veneration. One of my colleagues once tamed one of this species and taught it to perform various domestic duties. The creature made his bed, washed up and waited at table. But it was extremely jealous and went into transports of anger if any stranger seemed to monopolize its master. Of course, the natives attributed these accomplishments to the presence of a Spirit, so my colleague was baulked of the credit due to his patience. Among the Phuyen, an orang-outang of about human proportions enjoyed a most unenviable reputation. It was supposed to snatch the unwary traveller in its huge, hairy arms and shake the breath out of him while uttering screams of fiendish glee. To escape such an embarrassing encounter the natives who inhabit the forests in which the creature lives always carry an armful of long bamboo shoots. If they are attacked the shoots prevent the orang-outang from getting a proper grip of its victim, who thus escapes without difficulty.

A widely prevalent superstition in Langbian is that certain monkeys of the species known as *semnopithecus* never put foot to ground. They are supposed to progress by hanging on to each other and thus forming a living chain, one end of which

RITES AND SUPERSTITIONS

is attached to a tree overhanging a stream. I can myself bear witness to having frequently seen them bridge the space between two trees in this manner and accomplishing the most astonishing acrobatic feats on a trapeze consisting of their companions.

Hunting rites are numerous and for the most part rest on the same conception which we have noticed before in relation to other rites, namely the belief in the power of imitative or sympathetic magic.

Thus a hunter never eats the flesh of the hare or deer for fear of becoming as timorous as these creatures. This species of food is only permitted to old men, women and children. If a wild-boar hunt is in prospect the hunters taking part must abstain from fat and oil. Without this precaution the animal would undoubtedly slip through the meshes of their nets and escape its pursuers. When the Laotians slaughter elephants for the sake of their ivory the women are absolutely forbidden to cut their hair or nails, otherwise the monsters would infallibly break the stakes of the palisade in which they are entrapped. So long as an elephant-hunt lasts the hunters may only communicate in a special language which has conventional terms for objects of common use. (We shall see later that a special language is also employed by the Cham on their annual expeditions in search of eagle-wood.)

Another regulation concerns the chief of the hunting-party, who may not set foot to ground. If the necessity arises that he must leave his elephant a carpet of leaves is spread beneath his feet.

Whenever we killed an elephant the natives flung themselves upon the victim. The first-comer drank its blood with relish and the others had to rest content with the great drops which reached the ground. The next step was to cut off the little triangle in which the trunk terminates. This object is a much prized amulet. Next the genital organs are severed for the evening meal, and finally, as something is due to us for presenting such booty, they offer us hairs from the animal's tail for toothpicks. To be offered these hairs is the equivalent of being presented with the brush in Europe.

Another widespread superstition among the Moï is that the urine of savage dogs is able to blind the prey that they pursue. M. Millet tells us that in the province of Tay-Nhinh he saw wild dogs tear out the eyes of a boar, pin it against a tree and rip it in pieces. One of them seemed to be told off to distract the victim during these operations, the distraction consisting of biting the creature's head to prevent it from turning round and goring its foes with its tusks. The combination of ferocity and system displayed by these wild dogs has always greatly impressed the Moï, who believe that it is quite impossible to kill or capture them. We must admit that, though during our operations we killed almost every kind of wild animal, we never did anything to shake that belief. A wild dog was never in the day's bag.

CHAPTER VII

RITES AND SUPERSTITIONS *(continued)*

Agrarian rites—How Me-Sao, King of the Moï, opens the jar—Rites of initiation and " coming of age."

THE Moï being essentially an agricultural people it is not difficult to believe that a large number of agrarian rites enliven the monotony of their daily life. We must also remind ourselves that these rites are generally based on a belief in imitative or sympathetic magic. They are seldom propitiatory in character.

Thus before each harvest the Mnong plant bulbous or fibrous-rooted plants in the corners of their rice or maize fields and water them with spirits. At sowing time they cast some of the leaves of these plants among the seed in the hope of thus attracting the Spirit of the grain. The ceremony is completed by sacrificing a pig or chicken, and the proceedings terminate with a great feast. This method of celebrating sowing-time with a feast was famous in antiquity. The sower assumes that by filling his own body with food he can stimulate the fertility of the grain. The place and time selected is the largest plantation the sower can find and the season of the new moon, as if to invite the harvest to coincide with the last quarter. If the sower is a woman she will let her hair hang loose, in order that the stalk of the cereal may, by imitation, be as long as possible. At harvest time she will clothe herself very lightly, and the ball of rice, in imitation of her slender form, will be small, and accordingly of better quality.

Reasoning along these lines the savage often believes that the sexual act during seed-time will have a great influence on the harvest to come. Sometimes this influence is considered beneficent, and accordingly the work of sowing is accompanied by the most licentious orgies. Sometimes, on the contrary, this influence is regarded as baneful, and chastity is recommended, or even ordered. The famous ethnologist Frazer considers that to this order of ideas must be traced the rigid abstinence observed by Catholics during Lent.

Even to-day the Karens believe that illicit love affairs bring a bad harvest to the guilty parties.

In this connection it is only necessary to observe that ancient history has much to tell us of lascivious festivals in which the laws of morality and decency were relaxed almost to the point of extinction during the sowing-time. The Saturnalia of ancient Rome, taking their name from Saturn, the god of agriculture, are an example which occurs readily to the mind, and modern equivalents are to be found in certain half-pagan, half-religious ceremonies of eastern Europe.

It is also not without a certain significance that all these agrarian rites, no matter the group which practise them, are celebrated in the open air and not in a temple, and that their observance is not the function of a professional priestly class, but the duty of all, from the highest magnate to the humblest slave.

The Moï preface every religious ceremony with the opening of a jar of spirits of rice. To omit this prelude would be to invite disaster. In the dead of night the discordant voice of the tom-tom suddenly breaks upon the stillness, and, as often as not, its message is one of invitation to the opening of a jar. We obeyed the summons at first mainly out of curiosity, but finding the proceedings monotonously similar, we soon came to take no further interest. One of the best-known chiefs, Me-Sao, who enjoyed the title of " King of the Moï," had a grandiloquent manner on these occasions which is worthy of record.

His house, or rather conglomeration of huts, was certainly not less than a hundred yards in length. The stage was thus fully worthy of the scene to be presented. As the guests arrive, the host invites them to be seated on a row of stools, very large but so low as to give the impression of sitting on the ground. A number of attendants immediately take off the visitors' shoes, anoint their feet with various oils, after which the guests rest their legs on a low, iron railing fixed in the ground and worked into a rude pattern. In front of the audience is a post to which is fixed an enormous jar containing perhaps twenty-five to thirty litres of spirits of rice. A Moï seated before the post recites our praises in a drawling voice. Our skill in the hunting-field, our physical strength, the efficacy of our medicines form a theme on which the bard lets his fancy play freely. When he has recounted our individual virtues, another warrior imprisons our right wrists in a thick copper bracelet, an act which signifies the conclusion of a compact and an oath of blood-brotherhood. The great jar is then solemnly decanted after an invocation to the spirits. The King of the Moï introduces a long hollow straw into the liquid, draws up a mouthful, and graciously offers the other end to those whom he deigns to honour with his friendship. It would be the height of ill-breeding to decline this mark of friendship, and there is no alternative but submission. One by one we take a sip from the stalk, which is kept filled from a small drinking-horn with a hole in the middle to regulate the flow of the liquid. Those who drink first are the most to be pitied, for the jar is corked with a mixture of glazed earth and bran, and in spite of the cup-bearer's skill some of the solid matter always gets into the tube. By a happy convention there is nothing to prevent the guest from spitting out his dose, in fact the action is regarded as a high compliment to the character of the vintage. This ceremony frequently lasts all night to the accompaniment of selections by the band of native musicians on enormous gongs. When the distinguished strangers have been thus honoured the tribesmen, in order of rank, take the tube in turn, and after them the women also, by which time the liquid has become perfectly innocuous, thanks to its successive dilutions.

The offer of a jar to a guest of rank is a mark of respect and allegiance in all these parts. Wherever we went we were always received by the chiefs with a preliminary greeting of this kind.

Spirits of rice consist of a mixture of paddy and water which is allowed to ferment for not less than ten days and not more than three moons. Another favourite offering was that of a white cock flanked by an odd number of eggs and served on a kind of cane tray, of which the bottom was sprinkled with a layer of snow-white rice. In exchange for these courtesies we returned presents of brass needles, and, if our reception had been particularly cordial, mirrors, which the women almost tore from our hands. This exchange of presents was the sign of an alliance and was seldom followed by any act of treachery. We soon came to realize that we had little to fear from groups who gave and received these hostages.

Superficial observers often attribute to superstitions certain modern customs of which the origin is to be sought in moral or legal decrees. Many of these customs which seem without significance become quite intelligible when viewed in the light of recent research into the institutions and ways of life of societies which have long since disappeared. In the same way our opinion will be sensibly modified by a close examination of the customs of primitive peoples whose rites and ceremonies we are apt to attribute too readily to abstract symbolism.

For example, research into the origin of the practice of circumcision has brought some authorities to the view that this custom has at some time been substituted for that of human sacrifice when the victor offered the body of the vanquished as a gift to the gods. When David came to Saul to demand the hand of his daughter, the King replied that the only dowry he required was a hundred foreskins of the Philistines. In other words, Saul's conditions were the sacrifice of a hundred of his enemies, and do not seem to be unreasonable under the circumstances. Again the Dyaks of Borneo are not allowed to take a wife until they have at least one scalp of their foes to their credit. Later, by a prolonged process of substitution, circumcision of the boys and excision of the girls have taken their place as rites which mark the admission of the young people into the full privileges and fellowship of the community and signify the passing of childhood.

Most of the groups which practise these rites set apart a special hut for the accommodation of the boys and girls during the celebration. No one is allowed to enter, and the novices are subject to a multitude of disciplinary regulations which are designed to promote physical courage and endurance, obedience to superiors, and respect for established tradition. Certain kinds of food are rigorously prohibited during this period of seclusion, which lasts until the wounds made by the operation are healed, an event celebrated with great pomp.

These ceremonies are only consistent with the theory that among certain races circumcision is not a piece of pure symbolism but an act of physical and social initiation. The candidate for admission to the full rights of citizenship must be instructed in the duties and responsibilities of his new status. He must be initiated into the traditions of his clan. In nearly every case some distinctive feature of dress or hair, or some tribal mark, such as tattooing, deformation, or mutilation indicates the critical period. In Rome the young man put on the toga to indicate his assumption of the rights of manhood.

It must not be imagined that the attainment of puberty in a physiological sense coincides with admission into full membership of the tribe. It is possible for these events to be separated by a long period, though many observers have fallen into error in ignorance of the fact.

The Catholics regard the first communion as the point at which the innocence of childhood passes, and manhood, with its burden of temptation, begins. Accordingly the communicant-to-be is prepared for this ceremony by a period of initiation, during which he makes a reverent study of the traditions of his faith and the articles of his creed.

The Moï, too, celebrate the attainment of puberty by a series of rites and festivals. The period of seclusion in a special house which no one may enter points clearly to a belief in the necessity of a period of initiation, during which the candidate prepares himself for the new life.

The Moï also exhibit traces of usages regulating the sexual relation which are of very ancient origin. We have already noticed the innumerable prohibitions obligatory during pregnancy. The rites to be observed during the menstrual period, and particularly at the time of the first menstruation, are no less rigorous and complicated. A woman must not touch meat at that period, and must be particularly careful to avoid contact with either of her parents. The girls of the Lolo, a people on the Chinese frontier, as soon as they have reached a marriageable age, are subjected to a vegetarian diet and have their food, from which every particle of meat and fat is carefully excluded, cooked in special pots.

On the other hand the Moï seem to have no special rites to mark the menopause.

Similar customs are to be found among most of the races in the Far East. The Blimyar, a Dravidian people from southern Mirzapore, reserve a certain part of their houses, under the outer verandah, for the women during the menstrual period. The Parsees forbid their women to look on flame. Europe itself is familiar with regulations of the same type. In the country districts of France the peasants think that the presence of a woman in the condition in question is enough to turn the beer, convert the wine into vinegar or even ruin a whipped cream or mayonnaise! The belief seems to spring, like so many others, from the long accepted convention that contact with blood is a cause of impurity.

Another very curious rite is that which ethnologists have agreed to call " avoidance," which means the prohibition imposed on both parties to a marriage to touch, in the case of the husband, his mother-in-law, and, in the case of the wife, her father-in-law. Colonel Diguet of the Colonial Infantry deposes that this taboo is found also among the Man-Coc and the Man-Pa-Teng, tribes of mountaineers near Tonkin, whose customs bear strong resemblances to those of the Moï. Speaking for myself, I can advance the case no further, for to all my questions on the subject the natives answered with that obvious reticence which is the sign of their dislike to be catechized on sexual matters.

Africa and Australia furnish many examples of " avoidance." The Bovandik of South Australia even have a special language for conversation between a husband and his wife's mother, or a wife and her husband's father. In Uganda a son-in-law may not look at his mother-in-law and not even speak to her except through a partition or carefully closed door. Madagascar provides examples of the separation of the sexes. The Mahafaly and the Sakalava build their houses with two doors, one facing north for the husband and another facing west for the wife. The woman may eat hot foods but the man may not. On the other hand, the wife may not sit on the same mat with her husband during his meals. This practice of eating apart is common throughout the East. The Moï are no exception, and even carry it to the length of taking their meals in groups, each group consisting of members of the same clan or village. We had the most bitter experience of this custom and its resulting inconvenience during the expedition. It was our practice as a rule to have the midday meal in the open at any place where we happened to be at the moment, and the time was naturally short. But however short the interval, the coolies never failed to waste the larger part of it in sorting themselves out into clans.

Primitive peoples regard the fertility of their women as a national asset, and all kinds of rites are celebrated to avert the crowning disaster of sterility, which is neither more nor less than a public calamity. The Laotians, who cannot truly be described as primitive, make family pilgrimages to a temple in which there is a famous statue, probably of the goddess Kâli. The figure is of a woman of a black race standing with a linga in her hand. Each day she receives a large number of visitors, who show their devotion by sprinkling her lips with cocoanut oil in the hope of gaining her favour, and thereby assuring to themselves a numerous posterity. The walls of the temple are hung with votive offerings, the nature of which leaves no doubt as to the character of the requests made to the divinity. In this connection it may be mentioned that a similar practice obtains in certain villages of the Italian Tyrol, Bavaria, and Rhenish Prussia, where the traveller will find the votive offerings, consisting of a spiked ball, a symbol of the matrix, directed to the same end.

In lands less enlightened, where sculpture is but in its infancy, this act of devotion is replaced by a ceremony enacted by the Sorcerer. The Tho, for example, make a small model bridge of bamboo and place it near the house of the childless family. The bridge is a standing invitation to the Spirit of Fertility to enter the house and accept the hospitality of the inmates, rewarding them by granting their request.

Among other tribes the Sorcerer makes a small figure of the barren woman and adjures it to submit to the yoke of maternity. It will be remembered that the rite of *envoûtement* (casting a spell on a person by transfixing an image of him) is based on sympathetic magic, so that it is essential that the operator should possess some portion of the person on whose behalf the ceremony is performed. A piece of hair, some nail-parings, or, best of all, some of the menstrual blood, are most commonly used on these occasions. This rite is practised by almost all savage tribes, but generally with a view to accomplishing the destruction of the original of the model rather than obtaining favours for him.

Among the Moï certain plants which they call "Begand" are endowed with magical properties, malevolent or otherwise. All these roots belong to the family of the *Zingiberacae*. Sometimes all that is required of the sick man is to rub himself with the herb. The spirit which has caused his illness will then acknowledge the efficacy of the treatment and withdraw. Sometimes, on the contrary, a single leaf mixed with food is quite sufficient to cause a mortal disease. When mixed with tobacco the "Begand" acts either as a love philter or as a means of procuring an abortion. Among other tribes the species is known as "Magan," and the Sorcerer alone is allowed to cultivate it, since it forms one of the principal ingredients in the small figures of friends or enemies which play so large a part in magical ceremonies. This rhizome is also reputed to have a powerful effect upon animals, and a few leaves are invariably placed in traps and nets to ensure a successful catch.

The missionary Father Durand, who laboured for years among the Moï, says that the Magan is worshipped as if it were a god, and confirms the view that it possesses valuable therapeutic properties.

While on this subject it is interesting to recall that all the research of modern travellers has so far failed to discover the plant which furnished "Soma" to the Vedic tribes and "Hom" to the Iranians. If this discovery is ever made it will set at rest any doubts which may exist as to the original seat of the most ancient religion of the Indo-Iranian race. The only Soma of which we know anything is that of the Brahmins, and this, indeed, differs in vital respects from the sacred beverage celebrated in the Hymns, for, instead of producing inebriation, it seems to have acted as an emetic. The "Hom" of the Kirman Parsees, or rather the "Nireng," which is a mixture of "Hom" and cows' urine, likewise possesses the properties of an emetic. This is perhaps merely a coincidence of the kind which is frequently observed among different groups among whom religion is little more than sorcery.

It has always been my regret that I never had an opportunity of witnessing the ceremony of *envoûtement*. M. Millet, however, of the Woods and Forests Department of Indo-China, saw it more than once and gave me the following graphic account.

A Moï who has some cause of complaint against one of his fellow tribesmen observes his tracks and follows him until he reaches the spot where his enemy has relieved himself. He marks the place with a short bamboo inserted in the ground. A short time after, perhaps, his enemy falls ill, and then he visits the place at frequent intervals and either thrusts the bamboo deeper into the ground or else draws it out, according to his desire to aggravate or diminish the malady.

It may be, of course, a pure coincidence that the illness follows the ceremony I have related, but it is at least open to conjecture that the victim hears of what has been done and fear of coming vengeance unnerves him and produces the evil physical effects he expects. Everyone knows how human beings, especially highly strung and nervous human beings, can make themselves ill by anticipating an evil which they dread.

M. Millet was also responsible for the following account of an hallucination of which he was the victim, and as he is a gentleman of unimpeachable veracity, and neither weak nor superstitious, I see no reason to hesitate in accepting his statements.

"I was stationed at Djiring in Annam and the night in question was dark and rainy. I was sleeping in a hut of straw which, by exception in these tiger-stricken regions, was not raised on piles. About midnight I was awakened by the sound of a prowling tiger, a sound which left no doubt of its origin. It is quite impossible to mistake the short 'cop-cop,' the tiger's hunting signal, as recognizable as that of a motor-horn. I got up, seized my rifle and prepared for the intruder. The walls of the hut were made of a network of palm leaves and so flimsy that the beast could have burst through at a bound. I waited in silence and in a few seconds heard a noise as of a heavy body falling, followed by the piercing cry of the victim, a young fawn, I surmised. The tiger growled and then gave vent to its feelings cf satisfaction in a series of curious mewings. I went out, and though it was too dark to see more than a yard ahead of me I made for the spot from which the sound proceeded and fired point blank. There was an unmistakable sound of a huge creature springing up and bounding away,' then silence.

"At daybreak I searched the neighbourhood for footprints and traces of the struggle. The ground was of clay and had been soaked by the rain. It was bound to reveal marks of the presence of any animal, however light. To my amazement the only footprints visible were those I had made myself! I repeat that I could not possibly have mistaken the sounds I had heard, for I had distinguished even the noise made by a large animal passing through the bushes.

" The explanation of my Moï attendants to whom I related this adventure was very simple and plausible. The Spirits were responsible for the trick played on me!"

Colonel Diguet relates a case of indirect *envoûtement* which he observed among the Man.

If a native has a serious complaint against another he commits the cause of action to paper, or rather the native equivalent of paper, along with the name of the accused and his village. He then rolls this up into a ball and thrusts it down the mouth of a goat, which he afterwards suspends by bands from the branches of a tree. He then beats the unfortunate creature with a cane, not without many apologies for the evil treatment which circumstances compel him to mete out. One by one he recites to the animal the matters of which he complains and begs it to plead his cause with the Spirits. To ensure a proper zeal on the part of the advocate he enumerates a series of torments which await it in the next world should it fail in its mission. He then departs in the sure and certain hope that his prayers, and especially his threats, will have the desired effect. The unhappy goat is then left to die of starvation.

It will be remembered that from the most ancient times the ceremony which has for its object the expulsion of a disease from an individual, or the transference of that disease from his body to that of another, is effected by means of an intermediary, generally a goat, which has come to be known as the " scapegoat " by reason of the part it plays on these occasions. He who performs the ceremony is supposed to have lodged in the body of the animal the evil thing which he wishes to expel or transfer. The comparison of this practice which, as I have said, dates from a remote antiquity, with the curious proceedings among the Man of which Colonel Diguet speaks is thus very striking.

The practice of direct *envoûtement* is also met with among the Man. It takes the form of making an image in rice-paper of your enemy and piercing it with arrows or spears.

Something very similar was practised in the Middle Ages, for there is hardly a museum of archæology or ethnography which has no show-case of small figures transfixed with nails, especially in the region of the heart.

RITES AND SUPERSTITIONS 153

The museum of Tervueren in Belgium is peculiarly rich in specimens of this kind, most of which were collected by the ethnographical expedition sent out from England to the Congo in 1907, under the direction of Mr. E. Torday, of the Anthropological Institute of Great Britain and Ireland. The method of investigation followed by the explorers is worthy of note, for the leader, thanks to his unrivalled knowledge of the dialects, was enabled to dispense with the services of an interpreter. The information which the natives willingly supplied as to their rites and superstitions has thus come to us unadulterated by translation, since it was immediately transmitted to Mr. T. A. Joyce, the Honorary Secretary of the Institute in England, who forwarded a series of supplementary questions to Mr. Torday when a point seemed to require further elucidation. Mr. M. W. Hilton Simpson, and the artist, Norman H. Hardy, were also members of this mission, of which the results were such as to deserve special mention.

The expulsion or transference of evil spirits is not always effected by indirect means such as that of the scapegoat. In the majority of cases the method followed is the direct one of exorcism. The rites of exorcism vary greatly according to the beliefs and traditions of the different tribes. It is generally accompanied by flagellation, which has for its object to purify the voluntary victim from the stain of sin. The Spirit which torments him, finding that the repeated blows make his habitation untenantable, resolves to evacuate the place. It is plain that this is the true and original purpose of this chastisement and that the idea of purification by pain only crept in later.

Like all peoples in an early stage of civilization the Moï attribute disease and even death not to any natural cause but to the presence of malevolent spirits, the "Pi." All efforts must then be concentrated on persuading the harmful intruder to depart, if not by bribes then by threats. If the illness seems likely to terminate fatally, the Sorceress is called on to expel the evil spirit by incantations and sacrifices. This ceremony has many features of note, and I witnessed it on several occasions in spite of the inveterate reluctance of the Moï to allow us to take any part in their public life.

The Sorceress is a priestess who enters the house of the dying person clad only in a full, white loincloth. A rough plank serves for an altar and on it she places a bowl of rice and six small candles, which she lights. Then to the accompaniment of a series of peculiar writhing movements she chants a litany, which gets quicker and quicker as the candles get smaller. Her contortions also become more rapid and violent and in the end she is seized with a fit of hysterics, which signifies the frantic struggles of the "Pi" before they yield to the power of the incantation. All at once her movements cease and she commences to indicate the hour in which the cure will take place. This is done after consultation

RITES AND SUPERSTITIONS 155

with the Spirits, during which she takes the rice out of the bowl at the rate of three grains at a time. Then she takes a mouthful of water, which she returns over the patient's body in driblets while she presses his stomach as if she were attempting to squeeze the life out of something. Just as the last of the candles is on the point of going out she utters a cry of triumph and holds up a stone of about the size of a nut before the eyes of her astonished and admiring audience.

The cause of the malady has gone! The "Pi" have departed, leaving this trophy of victory to the conqueror who seems so exhausted by her efforts that several gourds of spirits of rice are necessary to restore her strength.

It sometimes happens that the patient takes a good turn after this ceremony, either as a reward for faith or else by pure coincidence. But if the reverse occurs and the patient dies shortly after the exorcism, the unfortunate result is attributed solely to the parsimony and ingratitude of the deceased, whose offerings were not deemed sufficient by the Spirits.

As I have said, the method of exorcism varies with different groups. For instance, it takes the following form among the Tho of Tonkin. The priest addresses himself to the Chicken Devil who is in possession of the patient, first inviting him to take the food which has been prepared for him and extending the invitation to all the Chicken Devils of the five cardinal points. (Throughout the Far East the centre of the earth is regarded as a fifth cardinal point.) He then throws two coins into a cup of rice and calls on the Male Element and the Female Element to make the first come up heads and the second tails. Whether the operation succeeds or not the Sorcerer then lights several sticks of eaglewood, pours some spirits of rice into a cup, and addresses all the Chicken Devils in the following words

" I beg to inform you that the patient I am about to cure has been brought to his present condition by the malevolent intervention of one of your number. I adjure you to command your brother to leave the place and torment my patient no longer. Let each of you return to the cardinal point from which he came; otherwise you shall not partake of the feast which we have spread for you. . . ."

The Chicken Demons, however, are slow to take the hint, for the patient's condition shows no sign of improvement. The spokesman betrays no sign of annoyance at this obstinacy, but his tone changes from one of studious moderation and politeness to one of command.

He continues

" I am an intimate friend of the Emperor of Jade and on the best of terms with Lao-Quan. It is they who speak by my mouth, and at your peril you refuse to obey the behests of these holy and powerful persons."

His speech now becomes more rapid and his gestures more agitated.

"I hear the approach of the four sacred animals, the Dragon, the Unicorn, the Phœnix, and the Tortoise. . . . I hear the voices of the fearful Spirits they are bringing to fight you, I see the armed warriors that escort them. . . . Fly ! . . . Fly quickly, lest they slay you for your obstinacy ! . . ."

By this time the speechmaker is quite out of breath and can do no more than ring his bells, while his companions rouse the whole neighbourhood with their gongs and tom-toms. This ear-shattering symphony is intended to imitate the titanic contest which now takes place between the Chicken Devils and the sacred animals, who finally rout their enemies and drive them away in confusion.

In Babylon also, exorcism was practised in cases of illness, which was invariably attributed to the flight of the soul and the possession of the body by a demon. The first step was to interrogate the patient so that the priest should know for what reason his soul had abandoned him. The patient related all his acts and the priest enumerated all the sins he might have committed. The list of sins is interesting to anyone familiar with ancient civilizations.

There were the usual transgressions against oneself and one's neighbour, adultery, murder, theft, injustice, but there were also sins against the code of commercial morality. To judge by the number of these last, offences against good faith such as the use of fraudulent balances and false money were extremely common.

Analogous lists of forbidden sins have been found in some of the Egyptian tombs.

It is to be noticed that the divinities of primitive groups are thought to punish only those crimes which touch their own dignity and worship. They take no account of offences which cause no loss to themselves. When the group advances along the path of progress we find that their gods are supposed to be angry at any act which may be prejudicial to the interests of the whole community. We also find that their vengeance consists of withdrawing their magic protection from the delinquent. It seems plain, therefore, that in the earlier period religion is considered as a thing apart from morals, while in the later the two conceptions blend and intermingle. This would certainly support the theory that law has grown up from ancient prohibitions which in origin were no more than ritual.

The apparatus of the Moï sorcerers and sorceresses is simple and scanty. No special clothing is worn, consisting as it does of bands of coarse cloth, perhaps two inches wide, which they strap over their shoulders and about their loins much like rustic braces. The mountaineers of Tonkin, whose rites are more complicated, have more elaborate ceremonies. .

Among the Man-Tien, for example, the sorcerer-priests wear a most remarkable costume when they perform their sacerdotal functions. It consists of an apron of unbleached cloth, a kind of embroidered bandolier, and a head-dress resembling the helmet of a French cuirassier and made of a framework of bamboo covered with a piece of cloth dyed indigo blue.

The accessories to ritual ceremonies are generally the following ·

A short cane of wood with a veneer of red lacquer and prismatic in shape.

A sword made of coins threaded together in such a way as to cause a jangle whenever it is moved.

Some seals to resemble those which are found on the books of magic to demonstrate their authenticity in the next world.

A number of images on cloth or paper with which the Sorcerer adorns the house of the person who has invited his assistance.

In every place and among all tribes no ceremony takes place without the harsh discord of incidental music made by gongs, tom-toms and cymbals.

It would not be fair to leave this topic without paying my tribute to the extreme fervour and conviction which are displayed by all who take part in these ceremonies. On the various occasions on which I was a witness I was always impressed with the fact that a belief based on faith only is entitled to respect; and I hesitate to regard as mere superstition anything which seems incomprehensible to me. Even in Brittany there are many sanctuaries where rites are practised which have in view the expulsion of evil, and Doctor Hébert has made a detailed report of an occurrence, one of thousands, which took place at the celebrated sanctuary of Saint Goulien at the Point du Raz. Here believers resort in immense numbers in the belief that they can obtain a cure for neuralgia by having the little bell (which was used by the saint to summon the catechumens) placed on their heads by the sacristan, who then rings it furiously. The sound of this bell is supposed to drive away the malady and restore the patient to health. If the desired effect is not produced, the failure is attributed to the pilgrim's want of faith or else to the sins which still hamper his soul. He must therefore purify himself and entrust his recovery to one of the innumerable saints whose sanctuaries are scattered throughout this region. At the worst he has had a pleasant tour in one of the most curious and interesting parts of France, an event which contains in itself some elements of a cure.

The Festival of the Dead: Carrying Home the Sacrificial Buffalo.

The Festival of the Dead : Poles erected for the Celebration.

[*To face p.* 161

CHAPTER VIII

BELIEFS AND RITES (*continued*)

The origin and observance of funeral rites—The ceremony of the Commemoration of the Dead—Burial rites and various methods.

ALL students of primitive man have observed that egoism is one of his most prominent characteristics. Hence it is not difficult to believe that the extravagant attention he pays to the dead is due not so much to any sentiment of reverence as to the necessity of looking after his own interests.

Among primitive races the general idea is that after death man has exactly the same feelings and necessities as during life. Accordingly, his spirit will have to seek food for itself if the living fail to provide it, and this will always be the case where the deceased has been buried without the proper funeral rites. The dead man must then take by force what has been denied him. In this way many common thefts are accounted for. The loss to the owner is a vivid reminder that he has been neglecting his duties and a warning that further disaster will overtake him unless he mends his ways for the future. The fact is that the spirit has not yet been received into the society of the dead because the deceased has not yet been officially buried, and, on the other hand, he has ceased to belong to the company of the living. In this painful and anomalous position he conceives a great hatred of those who are responsible for it and wages war on them.

The folklore of all countries shows traces of this belief. In every country the most fearsome ghosts are the spirits of those who have died a violent death, for example by fire or drowning.

At a later stage, fear of the vengeance of the dead is a less powerful motive to the living than the hope of obtaining favours from those who regard their late companions with a feeling of gratitude, a feeling which the departed spirit manifests by granting his protection to the living and interceding for them with the gods.

In Egypt the development of this last idea coincides with the inception of the practice of building the immense tombs in which we find innumerable inscriptions detailing the end in view.

"He who guards and cherishes my double shall find favour in the sight of the Great God, and shall become a liegeman. He shall not die save in the plenitude of years." (Dehasheh, Fifth Dynasty.)

From that time forward the living believed that material prosperity on earth was a reward for their devotion to the departed, and they spared no pains to make them as comfortable as possible in the life beyond. We have abundant proof of this in the

BELIEFS AND RITES 163

objects found in the tombs. Nothing that could conduce to the well-being of the deceased has been omitted. He was supplied not only with all the luxuries to which he was accustomed in life, but also with companions of both sexes, attendants, slaves, and even women of the harem. As these persons were unable to enter the abode of the Spirits, they were ruthlessly sacrificed in order that their double might rejoin their master and be at his service in the new existence. This idea of the necessity of a change of state before entering the spirit world was so fundamental that even the domestic utensils destined to the service of the deceased were broken to signify a symbolic death.

In Egypt also, as in many other countries at a similar stage of development, we find the practice of offering up sacrifices of animals and fruits which were intended as nourishment for the dead. By degrees the sacrifice is replaced by a symbol, and finally gives way to the mere recital of a set formula, which is considered to have as much validity as the original ceremony. This seems obvious from the fact that at this later period a word or a look was reputed to have special magic powers. Thus eyes are painted on the sides of the coffins to ward off malevolent spirits, and even to-day no Chinese junk that sails the seas is without an enormous eye painted on each side of the prow to protect it from the attack of the Dragon.

There are some names which no man may utter,

such is the magical power attributed to them. In Egypt, for example, even the gods themselves refrained from pronouncing the dread words " Ra " or " Osiris "

Our knowledge of ancestor-worship in Egypt is singularly full, thanks to a century of archæological research, and we should be fortunate if even half the efforts had been expended on investigating the same phenomenon in the Far East. In the circumstances it is impossible to advance any conclusions as final, though it is certain that ancestor-worship throughout the Far East plays a part, the importance of which it is difficult to overestimate. Indeed, it is not too much to say that in all probability it has been the basis of most of the religions to be met with in this region. At the moment ethnologists are in doubt as to the exact nature and extent of the native belief in the physical needs of the dead. They have not even settled on the precise location of the spirit world, nor on the amount of influence exercised by the dead over the acts of the living. It has been established beyond dispute, however, that certain funeral rites in the Far East are based upon the same conceptions as those we have seen obtaining in the West.

Thus, for example, we find food and domestic utensils left in the tombs for the use of the deceased, and the same fear of being deprived of proper burial. What further proof could be required that man is regarded as possessing a double personality and that

BELIEFS AND RITES

the soul is not deprived of physical needs by its separation from the body?

Even in the details of the burial ceremonies in Indo-China we find striking resemblances to those with which we are familiar in civilizations now vanished. The sacrifice made in honour of the deceased, and obviously with the end of furnishing him with the means of existence in his new life, is still observed by the Moï in a manner almost identical with that which prevailed in the land of the Pharaohs.

The Egyptian sacrifice was attended by the following circumstances.

The animal was first caught with the lasso, a method which does not imply that it was wild, for at that period the herds were allowed to roam at large, and even domestic animals had to be taken in this fashion. The victim was secured by an approved method and its carotid artery severed, invariably in the same manner and with the same instrument. The blood which flowed from the wound was carefully collected in a jar which an assistant then handed to the " Sounou " (doctor) with these words :

" Taste this blood."

The Sounou wetted his lips with it and answered ·

" It is pure."

This tasting of the blood was necessary to demonstrate that the beast had been well chosen. Finally the animal was cut in pieces, beginning at the thigh, which was considered the choicest part, and to crown the occasion its lungs and intestines were removed.

I myself can bear witness, after seeing many similar ceremonies observed by the Moï during their festival of the Commemoration of the Dead, that the proceedings show no substantial variation from those I have just recounted. The fifty centuries which have intervened might as well be fifty days, so perfect is the resemblance.

All religions afford many illustrations of the ability of certain rites to defy the hand of time. Among the ethnographical collections in the British Museum are a large number of instruments of stone used for the purpose of sacrifice by peoples who had long since abandoned stone as a material for all other weapons.

The great festival of the Commemoration of the Dead is celebrated by the Moï in June of every year, in a manner which varies little in the different tribes. I was always invited on these occasions and never failed to attend, for the occasion is one of the highest interest.

The previous eight days are spent by the women and children in collecting bamboos on which to hang garlands of leaves and flowers. At intervals tall poles are erected from which various trophies are suspended, and the whole village exchanges its usual dirt and squalor for an appearance of irresponsible gaiety. The thatched roofs of the huts are the only sombre note in the variegated colour-

BELIEFS AND RITES 167

scheme. The small canals which intersect the plain seem to be engaged in a perpetual chase and in the distance the lofty Annamite chain rears its proud head as if to shut off this smiling land from the rest of the world.

As soon as the day breaks every family rises and proceeds in Indian file along the high banks guarding the ricefields to the family tomb, where the loved dead are resting. The sepulchre is a small building not unlike a hut from a distance, but distinguished from it by the line of the roof, which is curved instead of straight, a peculiarity which produces the form of a pagoda. The relatives renew the thatch of the tomb where necessary, sweep the floor with the most elaborate care and replenish the store of victuals with fresh supplies. A few prayers are uttered and then they continue in silence to the place of sacrifice. This is a vast clearing on which several lofty poles have been erected. Securely tied to the foot of each pole is a young buffalo, selected by the warriors from the tribal herd. The number of victims to be sacrificed is determined by the number of males who have died in the previous year, the loss of females being reckoned, with true oriental gallantry, as a matter of no moment.

The moment the sun appears from behind the curtain of mountains four assistants drag one of the clumsy beasts to the ground in such a way as to expose its throat to the priestly executioner, a man of great size, who promptly thrusts in a long, shining blade. The blood spurts into a wide-necked copper jar, produced for the occasion. The sword flashes once more and a groan escapes from the victim in its death agony. The great body oscillates and falls to the ground with a thud. The ceremony is consummated. One of the assistants now dips a small broom in the jar and takes up some of the blood, and the members of the family gather round the carcase. The women crouch on the ground with their hands before their faces and utter hollow groans. The dead beast is now covered with the clothing of the deceased, consisting of the cloak, the skirt, a pipe, or some other object he has cherished in life. The Sorcerer in the rôle of High Priest advances and commences to recite the virtues of the dead hero in a hollow voice.

"He was strong."

"Strong," repeat the company in chorus.

"His arrow was both swift and sure."

"Swift and sure," comes the echo.

Each time the Sorcerer's words are repeated a terrific bang on a gong makes the distant mountains ring. The litany proceeds until the catalogue of the great departed's deeds is complete.

This ceremony recurs without variation until all the victims have perished.

The first time I witnessed such a scene no less than nine animals were sacrificed, though the village boasted of only twenty-five families.

When the last rite has been accomplished the

BELIEFS AND RITES 169

assistants drag away the carcases and proceed to the distribution of the haunches and intestines, after which the remains are hoisted to poles adorned with garlands. The horns are severed from the base of the skull and suspended from the sacrificial post until the same ceremony in the next year.

The only variation I have ever been able to discover on these occasions is the following. Among certain groups the buffalo is stricken down by the warriors who stand round it in a ring and hurl their javelins in turn. Once down, however, the death-blow is administered exactly as I have described above, and the blood allowed to flow to the last drop. This last incident is of the utmost importance in all ritual sacrifices, for all primitive races agree in regarding blood as the most acceptable offering to the gods.

Ceremonies of a ritualistic character also take place when a death occurs. The corpse is immediately propped up against one wall of the hut, a little rice is thrust into its mouth, and each member of the family bawls into its ears in turn. One of the women goes out to the nearest stream with a jar and brings back some holy water. The body is then laid out in a somewhat summary manner and sewn up in a sack of coarse cloth which serves for shroud, after which a few branches are strewn over it. The children begin a melancholy chant accompanying themselves on gongs and wailing women take up the refrain. The house is lit day and night by torches which emit a strong resinous odour. If the dead man is a person of importance the inhabitants of the neighbouring villages are invited and the funeral ceremonies may last several days A huge metal pot is then placed under the open piles on which the hut stands. Its purpose is to catch the liquids which may exude from the putrefying corpse, for the belief is general that malevolent Spirits are particularly fond of this form of nourishment.

When all the mourners are assembled the interment proper begins. With the first signs of day the bearers take up the body, convey it rapidly through every room of the house, and after wrapping it in large palm leaves secure it to a stout bamboo pole. The next matter is to get it out of the house in such a way that it will never know the point of exit. Otherwise the Spirit will surely find its way back and continue to haunt the living. Accordingly, an opening is very carefully made in the thatched walls or roof, so that the breach will close of itself when the corpse has passed through. The next stage is the procession to the burial ground. The mourners and relatives form up in Indian file and the whole party proceeds in a direct line westwards. After marching a few miles the bearers stop short in the depths of the forest. They proclaim that the corpse has suddenly become heavier by way of asserting its predilection for that particular spot. In truth and fact this piece of pantomime is merely set form, for in nearly every case the presence of several newly-made graves indicates that the family burial-place has been reached.

BELIEFS AND RITES

The bearers now choose a tree, which they proceed to cut down, hollow out, and transform into a rude coffin. At the same time others of the party dig the grave itself, which is only deep and wide enough to accommodate the bier. The body is always placed in such a way that the head points westwards.

The women gather round the corpse, crouching on the ground, wailing and tearing their hair. The men stand about, affecting an air of utter indifference. The deceased is now placed in one half of the hollowed trunk, into which the relatives throw amulets, domestic utensils (carefully broken first), rice, maize and various kinds of fruit. Sometimes a hollow cane is passed through the lid of the coffin and the earth above, ending in a small funnel through which liquids can be poured.

As soon as the earth has been returned the bearers stamp it down with their feet and cover the spot with brambles to keep off marauding beasts. A kind of roof of palm leaves is erected over the tomb and on this are placed the broken pieces of the deceased's cooking-pot and cup and a further supply of provisions which are renewed at each new moon during the first year but less frequently afterwards. The mourners now leave and strive to forget their grief in a feast which varies in magnificence with the influence and social position of the departed brother.

Apart from the renewal of the provisions and the annual commemorative festival, I noticed no other particular mortuary observances among the Moï.

The individual gravestone which is met with everywhere in China and Annam seems to be unknown among the uncivilized groups of Indo-China.

The chief sign of mourning is to keep the hair cropped quite close for a period varying from one to five years. The return to ordinary life is marked by a ceremony, in the course of which some animal is sacrificed. The liberated mourner boils its head and carries it to lay on the tomb of the deceased, after which all are at liberty to make short work of the rest of the animal.

It is hardly surprising that mourning is not expressed by any change of dress, for the scanty supply of flimsy wrappings does not permit of much variation.

This is perhaps a convenient moment to mention certain burial rites, which seem peculiar to the savage tribes of Tong-King, where the influence of Chinese customs and manners is easily traceable.

When a Tho dies the family strew the floor of the house with a vast number of minute pieces of gold and silver paper. These baubles attract the Spirits, which can then be easily captured. A cloth mask is placed over the dead man's face and goose feathers are fastened into his clothing to enable him to soar over the rivers which might otherwise impede his progress in the world beyond. A complete set of writing materials is put in the coffin so that he may have no difficulty in communicating his ideas and experiences to the living. The Sorcerer furnishes the deceased with a passport and complete directions

BELIEFS AND RITES

as to his behaviour in the new existence. The grave is not dug until the Geomancer has determined the exact spot by means of two sticks and a piece of cord. An immense catafalque painted in five colours is raised over the corpse, and under this imposing arch the dead man's sons pass in procession, leaning on their " Weeping Sticks " and preceded by an attendant who throws handfuls of maize into the air to distract the attention of evil Spirits.

When the interment is over the Sorcerer proceeds to burn the catafalque, which, being no more than a slender framework of bamboo covered with sheets of paper or flimsy material, offers no resistance.

A few days after this ceremony those of the dead man's sons who have founded a household of their own raise a small hut near their own establishment to accommodate the personal belongings of the deceased.

Lest the soul should grow weary in its new abode pipes of opium are constantly prepared for it and placed in this hut. Further, occasional diversion is provided by organizing a ritual dance, in which many persons take part. To complete the entertainment of the Spirit, the dancers wear quite special costume, consisting of a mask representing the marabout stork. From this mask falls a long veil which completely conceals the dancer's body and produces a resemblance lively enough to give to this ceremony e name of " The Dance of the Marabouts."

The burning of the catafalque by the Tho calls

to mind a curious burial rite observed in some places in France. When a Savoyard dies his relations put on gloves, fasten an armlet on their sleeves, and themselves carry the coffin to the cemetery. Before the earth is returned to the grave they throw these gloves and armlets into the bier and take back the pall to the curé, who burns it. If this custom is originally due to the fear of contagion from anything which has come into contact with the coffin it can hardly be disputed that we are face to face with a true prophylactic rite.

Among the Meo, when a man dies the relatives tie a lacquer dog to the end of a string, which is put in his hand. The reason for this is the belief that the animal will lead its master through the tangled by-paths of his new domain. The corpse is taken to the tomb seated in a chair. A plank is laid at the bottom of the grave and the body lowered on to it.

A similar custom is found among the Indians of British Columbia, who believe that the dead warrior must never be put in his coffin in the house, lest the relatives should lose their souls which would be attracted by the bier and try to get into it. They also follow the practice I have described above of taking the corpse out through the roof or a hole made in the walls.

Another custom popular in Tong-King is for the mourners, as soon as the funeral rites are accomplished, to walk through a narrow passage made between trees or bushes set very close together. By rubbing

Funeral Rites: The Body in a Coffin made from the Hollowed Trunk of a Tree.

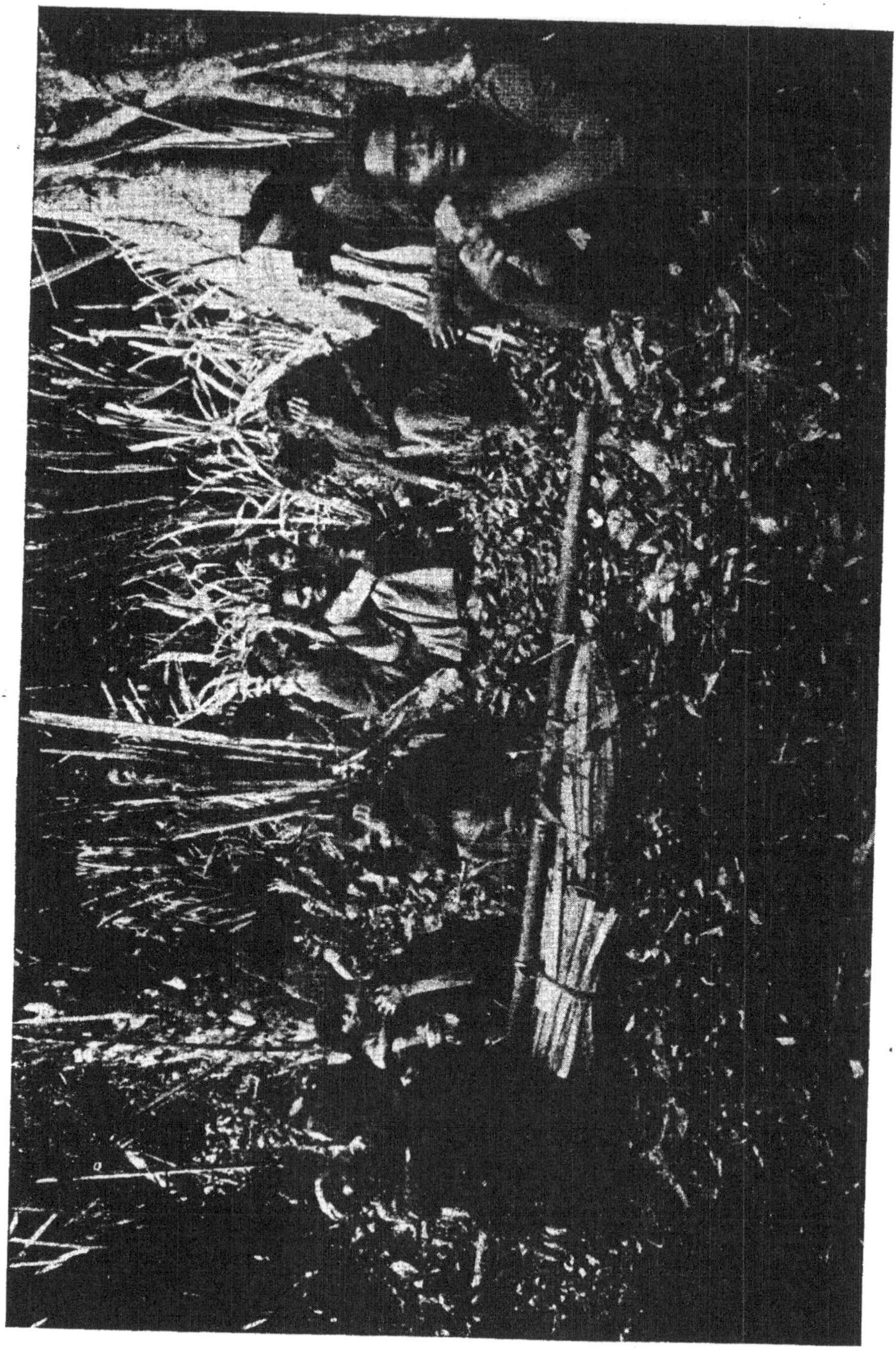

themselves against these obstacles they shake off any Spirit which might have attached itself to them during the interment.

The direction in which the corpse faces is everywhere considered a matter of the utmost importance. Certain races of the Congo, for example the Bongo, have one rule for the men and another for the women, the former facing north, the latter south.

The Moï cemeteries vary greatly in different regions. Some tribes favour a kind of family burial hut, on the floor of which the coffins are laid in rows. The interstices of the coffin are then carefully filled up with cement made of clay and pulped leaves. This mausoleum is always in the middle of a rice or maize field at a convenient distance from the village. As a rule the edifice has no distinct decorative features, but is usually surrounded by a wooden palisade carved with rough figures. A circular ditch, a yard wide and two yards deep, is dug round the cemetery. The earth thus removed is accumulated on one spot and gradually forms a conical mound. I have occasionally seen such a mound surrounded by a palisade of which each post had received individual artistic treatment.

A common feature of all cemeteries is a wooden shanty looking like a European pigeon-house, in which are stored the bones of the victims offered up in sacrifice for the dead. These charnel houses are often painted with the blood of slaughtered animals.

A funeral pyre is reserved only for the Kings

of Fire and Water. Burial in the earth is the rule among all branches of this group. Among a few tribes the coffins are hoisted to the branches of trees and secured with rattan threads. Pieces of coarse cloth wrapped round the corpse are considered sufficient to protect it from the weather. These aerial cemeteries are also found in Borneo.

In all parts of the country the natives displayed the greatest anxiety that we should not disturb their tombs. We paid due regard to their susceptibilities, carrying our respect for their customs even to the length of abandoning a valley which seemed an ideal site for the track of the Trans-Indo-Chinese railway, but which was honeycombed with graves.

CHAPTER IX

ART AND CULTURE

The relation between the evolution of artistic expression and social development as illustrated by the Moï and the Laotians—The intimate connection between Music, Dance and Stage—A Moï orchestra and war dance—Deficiencies in the sense of sound due to lack of artistic education—The effect of a gramophone—Predominance of the analytical over the synthetical faculty—Exaggerated respect for form—Impression produced by the stereoscope—Decorative arts—Sports, fêtes, and public amusements—Extensive use of marks for ritual and other purposes.

IT has often been said that the craving for æsthetic expression, inherent in human nature, lies dormant until men have taken their first steps in the path of civilization, but that after that stage has been passed its own growth is commensurate with the advance that is made.

Whatever may be the truth of this, it is undoubtedly illustrated by a comparison between the artistic intelligence of the uncivilized Moï of Annam and that of his immediate neighbour, the Laotian.

The former, living among a society which exhibits few traces of organization or corporate existence, seems totally innocent of any desire to exploit his æsthetic emotions for the benefit of others. If he sings, it is for the good of his own soul, not for the entertainment of his neighbours. His song consists of a rhythmic cadence produced either by a series of inarticulate sounds or by a meaningless repetition of an interjection, a syllable, or a word. He is not sociable, much less altruistic. Why, then, should he give himself the trouble of manœuvring his feet or acting a scene for the sole benefit of the spectators? Accordingly these two artistic manifestations, dancing and music, are almost unknown among the Moï.

The Laotian, on the other hand, is a gregarious animal and likes nothing better than to express his sociable instincts in public rejoicings of all kinds. He is not satisfied with song by itself but accompanies his outbursts with pantomime of various kinds, and also dances which are intended to recall the past or provoke desire. The favourite scenes which are represented are an elephant hunt or a combat, if the feelings to be relieved are particularly warlike. If, however, the singer-dancer-actor is in peaceful mood the scenes enacted will be those of ploughing, sowing and harvest. These mock plays vary greatly with the degree of civilization to which each group has arrived.

It has been said that music usually excites the listener to movement or action. This is probably because, originally, music was always associated with miming and dance, and the effect is still felt after the cause has disappeared. However that may be, music has always inspired to high deeds, whether by acting as an intellectual stimulant to the listener whose brain dwarfs his muscles, or as a physical stimulant to the listener in whom matter dominates mind. Music inspired Dante to some of his greatest poems and John Stuart Mill to some of his profoundest and most original philosophical speculations.

One explanation of the fact that song is the first artistic manifestation of primitive man is the probability that his first articulate utterances were either cries or actually sung. Even to-day a child which is completely isolated from birth will be able to sing but will never learn to talk. All mothers know that a child's first cries are attempts to sing. Only after the lapse of a year does it accustom itself to employ the speaking voice. It does not seem altogether presumptuous, therefore, to believe that in the infancy of man Music was the æsthetic imitation of his first vocal utterances.

Later, man realized that it was possible to add volume and variation by accompanying the sounds with rhythmical beats produced by some object within reach. Of such objects are the familiar stick, with which the aborigines of Australia mark time, and the heel of the Moï dancer which sets the measure for a warlike march with its regular taps on the ground.

Soon other embellishments follow. The gourd finds itself the rustic tom-tom, a popular instrument among the Moï as among the native races of Africa. The hollow bamboo stalk appears in all the glory of a flute. Finally, the orchestra makes its bow with the invention of stringed instruments and gradually supersedes the human voice, which it was originally only designed to accompany.

The evolution I have outlined was brilliantly illustrated in Greece, where we can easily follow the successive stages by which Music liberated itself from the trammels of Dance and Pantomime and emerged as a self-contained art of its own.

There is little to be said about the Moï dancing, which shows lack of imagination and invention. The funeral and war-dances are characterized by conventional steps with few features of distinction, a fact which corroborates the view expressed above that artistic development follows in the path of civilization.

The orchestra comprises various instruments which can be used both for purposes of solo and accompaniment. The lower parts are entrusted to a wooden box measuring a yard across, with a series of holes over which a buffalo skin is tightly stretched. The volume of sound is augmented by metal buttons secured to nails distributed over the surface of the instrument, as also by bells of different sizes. This discordant and formidable sound-box is vigorously thumped with a mallet and accompanied by brass or copper gongs, which are frequently hung from the roof and played like bells. The "Rade" and "Djarai" groups also use wooden or metal discs joined in pairs, which are clashed together after the manner of cymbals.

The instruments to accompany the voice are various species of fifes and flutes, of which the most popular consists of five or six bamboo tubes of different lengths soldered with clay to a large gourd.

Each district has its favourite tunes which gradually become recognizable to the European ear and, though at first they seem devoid of all musical qualities, it is surprising how soon a particular rhythm or melody fixes itself on the mind and tickles the fancy.

Singing seems to be a form of diversion confined to the women. On the other hand, a woman in an orchestra is an exceptional phenomenon, and it is only on rare occasions that she is allowed to take part even in a dance. The song seems to be nothing more than an emission of sounds having no musical relation to each other whatever. It is a monotonous recitative, broken only by more or less passionate interjectional explosions. The series of notes is dependent solely on the singer's sweet will. She seems to have no idea of what she is singing, for frequently when a particular phrase caught our fancy and we asked for it again she confessed her utter inability to repeat it. The sounds are harsh and piercing, and usually recall the cries of wild beasts.

Strange though it may sound, it is nevertheless true that the hearing of the Moï is extremely quick and well trained. He can recognize the ticking of a watch ten yards away and the sound of a rifle at a distance of four miles. Of course there is all the difference between having quick hearing and a good ear for music. The latter quality depends, not on the physical construction of the organ, but on artistic education, in which the Moï have always remained lacking.

It is an old saying that the savage always prefers something which appeals to him by its violence. The more harsh and strident are the sounds the more they will appeal to his musical taste. To put this theory to the proof we frequently tested the native preferences with our gramophone.

No one could imagine the curiosity aroused in the village the first time we gave a concert on this instrument. Our geodetical operations were in full swing and, apart from the interest created by these, we had gathered huge audiences of women and children by filling up the intervals of our work with impromptu performances for their benefit. Our main "turns," which never varied, but of which they never seemed to grow weary, were as follows. We used to light a cigarette from a distance by means of a magnifying glass, or show them a compass of which the needle seemed to move exactly where and when we pleased. Other objects of immense popular interest were our watches with their mysterious ticking, the cork-screw of a wonderful eight-bladed knife, and, marvel of marvels, the astronomical telescope which made it possible to recognize a friend at a distance of more than three hundred yards and which compelled him to walk on his head!

In view of these wonders our fame spread abroad, and when our concert was announced each man told his neighbour that a trick yet more marvellous than any yet seen was about to be performed by the bearded strangers with pockets bulging with tobacco !

In a very short time the huts were empty though the heat was appalling. Even the village sluggards left their perpetual siesta, and in many cases women and children brought their menfolk by main force. No one was allowed to remain behind on so important an occasion. Soon the audience was gathered round us, the children in front, the mothers squatting in groups, the warriors standing about with an affected air of lofty indifference. A lively dispute as to the choice of records roused public interest to fever heat, and as no two of us thought alike, each holding out for his favourite piece, we settled the vexed question by drawing lots. The choice fell on the " Spring Song," which, however, met with little favour. The audience evidently had no opinion of Mendelssohn. The small children made for their mother's arms in terror and were only consoled with difficulty. The general feeling was one of astonishment passing to displeasure. We hastily took off that record and replaced it by a hunting-chorus well sprinkled with the blare of horns. This met with a most enthusiastic reception.

The standard and canons of musical taste among he Moï were thus brutally revealed to us. We took the hint at once. The beautiful collections of chamber-music which had so often charmed our ill-temper with its memories of far-away France were hastily dismissed to the bottom of the box. We put on all the loudest band records we had and then raided our stock for selections on all the noisiest instruments. The neighbouring forest was soon echoing the strident notes of xylophone, banjo, ocarina and trombone. We went to the music-halls and called on the singers and whistlers, and when the interval was announced after " Fou Rire," the entire audience went off almost convulsed with attempts to imitate it.

Quite recently we prevailed on the Chief of a neighbouring tribe to allow us to make a record of his speeches at a wedding-feast to which we had been invited. Without giving any warning we then turned on the disc. The audience pricked up its ears and seemed intensely interested to hear the well-known voice under such novel circumstances. Suddenly, before the record was half-way through, a slave seized hold of a jar of spirits and tried to empty its contents down the trumpet of the instrument. It took all my strength and eloquence to dissuade him from this fell purpose. The audience, however, seemed to take his intervention as a matter of course. The explanation of this unforeseen attack was simple. The gramophone, faithfully recording the utterances of the chief, had demanded, on its own behalf, something to drink!

After this, of course, we had to go through our repertoire, at the end of which an escort appeared to take the marvellous apparatus home. The grateful audience surpassed by smothering it with wrappings of all kinds. They would rather have died than allow such angelic voices to run the risk of catching cold.

Another explanation of their tastes in music is the love of exaggeration in any and every form which seems to sway the savage. The sound that pleases him must be explosive. A colour must be brilliant, an outline striking or grotesque. The more we examined examples of their decorative art, a branch of activity for which the Moï display real aptitude, the more we realized their over-emphasis of the dominant lines. Another characteristic, common among all races with a low standard of culture, is their repugnance to leave bare places in a scheme of decoration. There are no such things as contrast, foil, or background. Each part of the design has as much importance as any other. If they decorate a room, for example, they do not leave the smallest space without treatment of some kind. It follows from this that the Moï, as critic, is concerned solely with details and has no thought of the inward meaning or larger significance of a composition.

I frequently demonstrated the truth of this observation by the following experiment. When I visited a new group I used to make a bid for popular favour by a generous distribution of tobacco to the few children who overcame their alarm at my beard and strange costume. Thus encouraged, they soon flocked round when I drew out my pocket stereoscope and a box of slides consisting of photographs of children of the neighbouring tribes, taken at a moment when these restless rascals were still. The astonished exclamations of my juvenile audience soon brought their mothers, grandfathers, and even some of the less shy sisters on the scene. The men, of course, were either out hunting or busy with a siesta which must on no account be interrupted. A circle was formed round me and every one had a look in turn.

"What a big nose!" said number one. "There's the red mark of betel on his mouth," he continued. "Look at the lovely white ring in his ear! Why, it's a whole head! I believe it's 'Little Buffalo' who came here with his father for the last harvest!"

He was right. It was indeed "Little Buffalo," whose resemblance was thus not established before our savage had examined every detail of his face.

Shouts of laughter greeted the discovery and it was plain that they all really thought "Little Buffalo" was there in the flesh. They all put out their hands to feel him, and great was the amazement when they only touched the back of the card. My box of slides soon acquired a baneful reputation as the abode of Spirits.

One day a woman came to see me to announce that her baby had died a few days after I had taken

A Medical Examination.

Looking through the Stereoscope.

[*To face p.*

Three Boys of our Native Guard.

[*To face p.* 187.

ART AND CULTURE 187

its photograph. I was hardly surprised, for the child was very ill at the time.

"Great Master," she said, "my baby is in your box. Please give me another at once, but this time it must be one already brought up."

She was astounded when, to grant her request, I sent her off to her husband!

Doctor O. Munsterberg, in an interesting study, has advanced the view that in its origin art is nothing but realism. It is undoubtedly true that the savage mind seems entirely preoccupied with the concrete, and entirely incapable of comprehending abstract ideas. It is equally true that we have changed our methods of teaching the natives in the light of this discovery and that the results obtained illustrate the inevitable failure of our old system. No one doubts that a child learns to reproduce a drawing of some familiar object far more easily than a symbol, such as a letter of the alphabet, which is not identified with anything having a concrete existence.

The art of the Moï is nothing if not realistic. It is also solely and totally utilitarian, since it is confined to industrial use. The figures employed for ornamentation are invariably taken from the animal or vegetable world with which they are familiar. For instance, popular subjects for reproduction (not without remarkable transformations) are the tracks of a hen in the dust, the marks on the skin left by the bristles of a boar, the teeth of a saw, the scales of a turtle, or the crested ridge of a fish's back. It will be recalled in this connection that many of these signs are adopted as tribal or proprietary symbols.

The favourite objects for decoration are pipes, quivers and drinking horns. When the artist has finished his design he smears blood over the subject, both to throw up the outlines of the figure and also to add a touch of violent colour.

Sculpture is still in its infancy. In many of the cemeteries the traveller will find figures of seated women, their hair lank and dirty, supporting their elbows on their knees and covering their faces with their hands. These are the widows, who, in a truly life-like attitude of desolation, weep for the departed. The impression of reality is heightened by covering their heads with human hair and their bodies with ragged clothing.

There is a close kinship between the art of the Moï and that of the uncivilized peoples of the Malay Peninsula, another proof that all these races are branches of the same stock. Their art exhibits the same sense of proportion, the same boldness of design, the same horror of empty spaces which is revealed by the overloading of ornament and exaggeration of form.

The Moï by nature is easy-going and idle and displays such energy as he has in devising fresh amusements. The prime distraction for him, however, remains the opening of a jar of spirits of rice.

Certain games of skill are in vogue, of which

the most interesting is a form of fencing in which skill seems to blend with a good deal of flourish. The two combatants are armed with wooden sabres, smeared on the sharper edge with buffalo's blood so as to leave a mark wherever it touches. The point is blunted and cannot be used by the laws of the game. Unlike the European rules, it is not prohibited to strike the lower half of the adversary's body. Accordingly, the fencers do not maintain any fixed stance, but revolve about a central point and use their legs to ward off hostile passes. It is quite usual to see all four limbs requisitioned in an emergency. A high standard of acrobatic agility and sureness of eye and hand is attained.

A few of the Moï who have lived among the Laotians have brought back to their countrymen various borrowed amusements and, among them, primitive stage-plays. Of the plots of these, which are destitute of imagination or construction, the following is typical.

A few girls walk about under the watchful eyes of their parents. A stranger appears and tries to carry off an unsuspecting damsel. A free fight ensues, in the course of which the ravisher is vanquished and pretends to fly, but as soon as the pursuit slackens he returns, waits for a favourable moment, and catches his prey round the waist.

Shrieks for help! The lady faints!

The evil deed seems about to be crowned with success when a Spirit appears, strikes the bold wrongdoer to the ground, and leaves him lifeless at his intended victim's feet.

The women's parts are taken by boys in accordance with the unwavering rule throughout the Far East that females may not appear in any dramatic representation.

The Moï celebrate New Year's Day with a festival that lasts at least seven days. During this period etiquette requires that seven buffaloes, seven pigs, seven goats and seven white cocks should be consumed and this formidable fare is washed down, in accordance with the rites, with the contents of seven jars.

All the neighbours of the Laotians follow that race in the details of their observance of these ceremonies, which are called by their Laotian name of "the Festival of the Dead Year." The participants are formed up in a long procession. The girls sprinkle perfumed water on the boys they like and throw mud at those they dislike. Both the favoured and the despised recipients of these attentions take them with good humour as being part of the day's work. Actors then appear dressed to represent our First Parents. According to legend these two worthies, in the beginning of the world, were covered with thick hair like the beasts. Accordingly, the performers wear a covering made of innumerable strips of bamboo.

The actors who play Adam, Eve, and the Dragon, cover their heads with black wooden masks representing grinning devils with horrible fangs, enormous ears and a tangled mane reaching the ground. So far from exciting fear or even curiosity, however, these blood-curdling apparitions are greeted with a universal shout of merriment. A curious pantomime follows. The three performers fall on their knees, raise their right arms, and manipulate the movable lower jaw of their masks while delivering in concert a wonderful harangue, in the course of which they extol the virtues and voice the most intimate desires of each member of the audience. The last words are a wish for a Happy New Year to the village and every living creature within it.

Amid the riotous plaudits of the crowd the actors then retire with a profusion of bows and capers.

All savage races are familiar with the use of horrifying masks to heighten the effects of religious rites. The fetish worshippers of Africa regard them as an indispensable accessory to the due performance of the ceremonies, and every traveller has seen the performers in ritual dances adorned with their grotesque headgear.

Sometimes the masks have special characteristics to connote the racial peculiarities of those who wear them. The Moï masks, for example, are remarkable for their long flowing hair and it may well be because this people believe that their ancestors were a hairy race.

It is quite usual for the masks to commemorate

some ethnical peculiarity which distinguishes the group.

In Egypt the King usually adorned himself with a mask of the animal-god from whom he claimed descent.

The visitor to the Trocadero in Paris will see statues of the Kings of Dahomey represented as sharks, their bodies covered with scales. The British Museum contains a number of bronze reliefs whereon the King of Benin appears as half shark and half man.

In short, in countries savage or civilized, masked dances are nothing but crude attempts to dramatize popular myths, and accordingly the actors play the rôles either of animals or the legendary heroes with whom they battled.

CHAPTER X

INTELLECTUAL LIFE

The relations between the development of language and social evolution—An enigmatic system of writing—Knotted cords, knotches in sticks, and their accessories—The evolution of literature among primitive races—Length of memory among races that have no written records—Historical value of legends transmitted by oral tradition—Nature of the more usual alterations to be met with in documentary folklore—The most general legends, fables and proverbs of the Moï.

THE main fact which differentiates primitive groups among themselves is diversity of language. To this rule the Moï present no exception, for they offer the choice of a considerable number of dialects. There are very nearly as many dialects as tribes, and, what at first seems even more extraordinary, the dialect of one village is usually unintelligible to the inhabitants of any other. But this singularity vanishes when we investigate more closely, and for these reasons.

The development of a language is intimately connected with the simultaneous intellectual and social evolution of the race which employs it. Now the civilization of the Moï has been stationary, if not actually retrogressive, for a prolonged period, and accordingly it is to be expected that their language, far from consolidating itself, should be subject to all the influences which flow from contact with neighbouring populations.

The learned philologist Cabaton has classified the Moï dialects into three broad divisions, according to the degree in which they have been modified by the tongues spoken by neighbouring peoples who have advanced to a higher stage of civilization. These three divisions comprise :

(*a*) Dialects of Malayo-Polynesian origin.

(*b*) Dialects of Kmer origin.

(*c*) Dialects of Thibeto-Birman, Tai or Chinese origin.

This diversity of dialects is responsible for the fact that the word " Moï " has no ethnical sense at all and that it is a mere generic term which, as I have explained before, can conveniently be used to describe the whole complex of barbarous groups which dwell in the mountain uplands of Indo-China. The word does not signify an autonomous entity with clearly defined characteristics, but merely a medley of various elements, of which many have lost all trace of common origin.

It is even more difficult to catalogue the different races which go to make up the inhabitants of Indo-China than to catalogue the dialects. At first sight some of them seem to be pure, but closer inquiry soon dispels the illusion. There are many reasons to account for this, among which may be cited the

INTELLECTUAL LIFE

prevalence of polygamy, and the perpetual intertribal conflictsin the course of which the vanquished, after a short period, are absorbed by the victors, to the evident advantage of the latter.

If the dialects are innumerable, there is virtually only one method, employed by all the groups, of communicating ideas or transmitting thought. It consists of the use of certain conventional signs. The more common of these are triangular or hexagonal figures of bamboo or rattan, measuring one foot eight inches in their greater dimension and hung in some conspicuous place. These geometrical forms warn the traveller of impending danger or notify a prohibition to cross the boundary of a " taboo " village.

Another method of communication is by means of a string with a series of knots. This practice recalls the *quipos* which were in use among the Peruvians and Mexicans to record important events and as a medium for the transmission of thought.

Suppose two friends want to arrange an appointment to meet in several days' time. They present each other with threads which have the same number of knots and as many knots as there are days to elapse before the meeting. Every day at sunrise each of them unties one of the knots. When at length there are no knots left they know that the appointed day has arrived.

It is very curious that the Moï, whose recollection of facts is almost infallible, are unable to recall either figures or dates without the assistance of mechanical aids to memory.

Doctor Noël Bernard, of the Colonial Forces, tells a very interesting story in his exhaustive monograph on the Kha.

"In a village situated in the plateau of Boloven I found the inhabitants stricken with terror. They informed me that a malevolent Genius had been enraged with them for more than a year and was decimating the population. To remedy their ill-fortune they rebuilt the village in a new place, and the death-rate decreased. I happened to ask them the number of the victims in that fatal year. They could not tell me. I renewed the question and the village chief gave me the figures in a highly novel manner. As he called out each victim by name he laid a small stick down at his feet. When the counting was completed the old man summed up as follows: 'Two died during seed time, three during harvest, four at the beginning of the rains,' and so on, concluding with a tragic, 'What a number!' But not a single native present could calculate that number, though there were only thirteen sticks at the feet of the incompetent arithmeticians!"

M. A. Gaultier de Claubry, when he was Director of Public Instruction in Indo-China, had opportunities of making observations which throw light on the incident just related. He used to teach French to twenty-two natives between the ages of twelve and twenty and wished to follow the ordinary rational method of explaining the meaning of a lesson first and asking his pupils to learn it by heart only after that meaning had become clear in their minds.

After a period devoted to repeated attempts along these lines he had to confess himself beaten and that the method was impracticable so far as these particular scholars were concerned, for the more clearly they grasped the meaning of the words the greater was their difficulty in committing them to memory.

Contrary to all the recognized precepts of sound teaching, the Professor resolved to reverse the process, make his pupils first learn the lesson by heart and only proceed to its translation and explanation when they could recite the words without a slip. The results were even more unexpected, for the more quick and certain their memories became the greater was their difficulty in understanding the meaning of the words.

The Professor repeated this experiment from time to time and the same phenomena always recurred.

It seems, therefore, clearly arguable that in certain individual cases connection between the thinking and memorizing faculties is either missing or only imperfectly established. They seem unable to perform their functions simultaneously. The memory cannot work properly unless all other mental processes are suspended.

But to return to arithmetic, the custom of employing pieces of wood to assist calculation is to be found everywhere in the savage world. Our coolies were collected from many different quarters, but they all carried a bamboo in which each evening they cut a notch to reckon up the number of days of service. On pay days they lined up solemnly side by side and each produced his stick from his loin-cloth and presented it for inspection. It was very rarely that our accountants found any error in the number of the notches.

As will have been gathered from the answers of the Moï chief to Doctor Bernard, the estimation of time by years of twelve months is unknown in these regions. Savages date all the events of their lives by their relation to the occurrences which affect them most, that is to say, the variations of the monsoon and the forward or backward condition of the crops.

No one knows his age, for no practical benefit accrues from the attainment of that piece of knowledge.

The use of sticks is not limited to the purpose I have mentioned but extends to the transmission of orders or information. In the last case notches are cut on both sides of the stick and of various forms and depths. Also they will be separated by spaces of varying lengths. Each of these details has thus a special significance.

This is the method employed by one village to convey a declaration of war to another. Its general terms will be much as follows ·

" Twelve days hence we shall seize any man who crosses our boundary. We will not release him except or ransom, four strong oxen which have already worked in the ricefields, or, failing them, two sets of gongs at least ten years in the making. Our tribe counts more than thirty young warriors trained to the bow, and a great number of old men, women and children."

Before being entrusted to the messenger charged with delivering it to the foe this ultimatum-stick is decorated, according to immemorial usage, with some egret's feathers, a burnt bamboo, and red pimento.

The symbolical significance of these accessories is as follows:

"Messenger! Thou must be as swift as the bird whose feather you bear. Thou shalt not stop by day or night, and this bamboo will point thy pathway in the hours of darkness. Thou shalt not fear if thou neglectest not to eat some pimento such as this."

I have often met women or old men with these notched laths hung round their necks. On inquiry they informed me that each notch represented a goat or chicken promised to the Pi of the forest in return for protection from the Tiger. As their slender means did not unable them to make a sacrifice in advance they were postponing the redemption of the promise until the next harvest.

I was indiscreet enough to inquire what would become of them if by any chance the vow was never fulfilled, but they looked at me in blank astonishment and indignantly denied that there could be any compromise with conscience. One of them, however, took me into his confidence. " I was unable to fulfil a certain vow during the last harvest, which was a particularly bad one, so instead of the five chickens which I first promised the Pi I now owe them one goat. If the next harvest is not better than the last, the goat will have to be replaced by a pig."

It sometimes happened that when we had broken up our encampment and were advancing to a new site some particularly well-inclined Chief dispatched a warrior-herald before us to announce our arrival by means of a notched stick. The contents of the message were such that before we had appeared the rice necessary for our escort and the paddy for our horses had all been prepared.

I must add that I speak of exceptional occurrences. The rule was that no herald preceded us, or if he did his message was of very different tenor. In such cases, the great majority, we could do nothing but seize by force of arms what ought to have been conceded with good grace.

The Moï regarded our written characters as a species of magical invention. Accordingly the powers thus attributed to the letters themselves were speedily extended to the paper on which they were written. They began to furnish themselves with a " Sra," or sheet of paper, whenever they set out on a journey, in the belief that it would guarantee them against delay or mishap *en route*. A courier would always carry an envelope, generally empty and unaddressed. Armed with this talisman he was secured against the attacks of tigers and evil spirits and freed from all anxiety as regards what La Fontaine has described as " bon souper, bon gite, et . . . le reste."

This use of notches as written symbols is also found among certain peoples of southern China. Father Crabouillet tells us something of this in his writings. In the course of his missionary work he discovered that the natives are able to represent by these means not only concrete objects but also abstract ideas. They were familiar with the ideographic characters of the Chinese, yet they preferred to use their own enigmatic system for the transaction of business.

We can only conclude that their object is to keep their affairs private from their neighbours the Celestials, whom they have particular reason to distrust.

The literary evolution of primitive peoples follows soon after their musical evolution, to which I have already referred. In the first stages, poetry, song and dance are inextricably associated. The spoken word plays a quite subordinate part in this æsthetic trinity. It serves to explain the meaning of the rhythmical movements but cannot be dissociated from them. The form of this rudimentary poetry is frequently a simple exclamation, a cry or imitative call. The interjectional refrains which we find to-day among savage tribes are only the relics of those wordless romances which preceded spoken verse in the first stage.

Metre is none other than the outcome of man's natural leaning to measured sounds. The verse of primitive folk is accordingly distinguished by the shortness of its lines. There is no rhyme except that which results from the combination of assonances. The length of a line may be used as a test of the standard of civilization to which a people has attained, for it only reaches appreciable dimensions when rules of metre and prosody have been formulated and enforced.

In China there is a mass of documentary evidence which throws light on this process of evolution. The line in that country was originally of four feet only, and did not attain to seven feet for a very considerable period. In India the Sanscrit line is very short in the Rig-Veda and gradually lengthens in the Epics, concluding with the dimensions of fifteen syllables divided by a hemistich, the relic of an earlier period in which the line was very short.

At the peril of seeming paradoxical I have lingered over the sense of rhythm among primitive peoples because so many travellers have expressed surprise at the immense impression which can be produced on a savage by uttering a poetic phrase or merely inserting a line of verse in ordinary conversation.

One of our party, a poet in his own way, frequently took advantage of the impression thus produced. He always addressed our coolies in verse, and though his knowledge of the language was only elementary, he was better understood and more speedily obeyed than others of us who spoke the dialects fluently. He united with this gift of rhyme a facility of metaphor which was remarkable. His conversation was sown thick with images, many of them quite ridiculous, but yet not so absurd as to prevent even our appreciation of them.

I have already remarked that in the infancy of society æsthetic manifestations were confined to choral dances representing simple subjects of an impersonal character, and no more than the reflection of the current life and thought of the group. But in course of time that way of life and thought became profoundly modified by new influences and movements, resulting from conflicts between rich and poor, master and slave. A new literature arose which expressed other feelings and aspirations, a literature which found voice in the popular artists who invented a new profession in all countries. The rhapsodists of Greece, the scalds of Scandinavia, and the Celtic bards, furnish familiar examples.

Everywhere these wandering minstrels presented the vague popular traditions in set forms. Their works reflect quite faithfully the movements and aspirations of their own day, and being transmitted by oral tradition, they form to-day a body of material which is virtually our only source of information as to the folklore of primitive races.

Accordingly, no study of a group can be complete which takes no account of its legends, myths and fables; if a group has no written records they form our only historical evidence. It has often been remarked that the non-existence of such records has served the purpose of improving the memories of those who have only oral tradition to rely on.

Recent research among primitive peoples in this very subject has demonstrated that the average duration of the recollection of an event is six generations, or about one hundred and fifty years. During that period, if the event is one of importance but yet in the natural order of things such as an earthquake or a flood, or even a political occurrence, such as a change of dynasty or a revolution, its memories will remain practically unmodified. Of course this applies only to groups among which the use of writing is unknown. Otherwise, the absence of any necessity for oral tradition greatly diminishes the length of its life. During our expedition we had many occasions to observe the ease with which the Moï Chiefs recollected events long since past and generally forgotten. Father Durand made the same discovery during his long residence in Annam. He told me of historical events in the eighteenth century of which the Moï had spoken to him with the most circumstantial detail. For example, they remembered the revolt of Thang Khoi in 1834 as if it had been an occurrence of only yesterday, and recounted an exploit, long since forgotten, of two Cochin-Chinese adventurers.

These pirates, some years before the capture of Saigon, managed to force the barrier and enter the

[A. Cabaton.

Photo by]

A Court of Trial on an Annamese Stage.

To face p. 204.

By the courtesy of] [*Mme. Vassalle.*

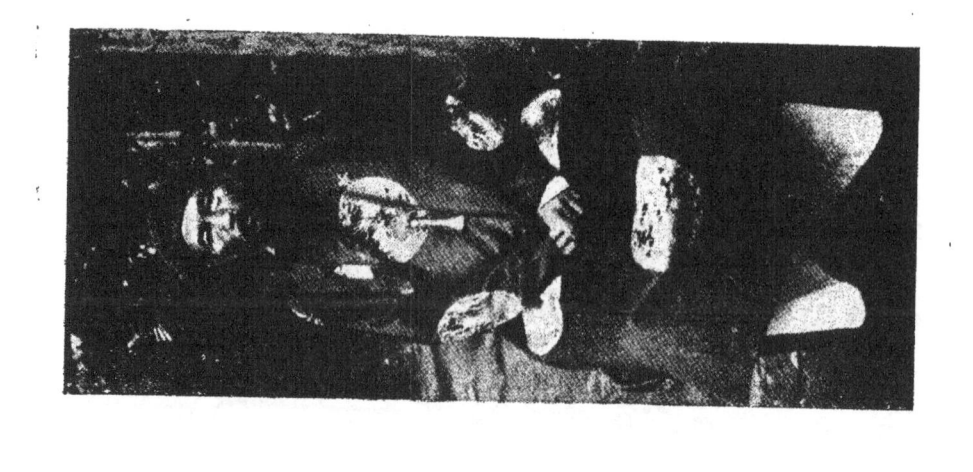

A Group of

Imperial palace under fire from the guns of the citadel of Hué, while the Emperor Tu Duc fled in terror.

The Annamites have a great regard for this retentiveness of memory and their consistent hostility towards all their neighbours robs that regard of all taint of partiality. However, once the fact is established, it follows that many legends founded on actual occurrences but transmitted orally from generation to generation in default of any written record may have as much authority for ethnography as if their authenticity had been established by documentary proof. But it cannot be denied that the imagination of the Moï has equally played a part in the composition of some of the current stories which were originally true statements of fact. Like all other peoples they have been subject to those influences which silently introduce elements of the apocryphal into the well of truth. Their folklore exhibits the same phenomena which can be studied at all times in similar groups. For example, they transform the hero of some particular locality into a hero of the whole group, or, in other words, make a national property of what is strictly a local possession. To the same end they substitute the name of their country for the name of the place where great events have taken place. In these ways all get credit for what only the few deserve, and in the end they have a fine collection of heroes and adventures filched from every source. But in spite of these alterations, the motive of which seems to be the ambition to have more great men and stirring deeds than their neighbours, it is patent that these legends faithfully reflect the principal conceptions of these primitive folk.

As the prevalent superstitions vary in different localities it would be absurd to suppose that all the legends, myths and fables which I am about to speak of enjoy universal currency. On the contrary, some circulate in one part of the country, others elsewhere. But I have attempted in making a selection to confine myself to those which are most widely known. Some of them originated among the Laotians or Annamites. Very few are of native origin, for the imagination of this group has always been undeveloped.

The biblical account of the early history of the world has been curiously adapted and transformed. The great deluge, for example, appears under the following guise.

In the beginning a Genius incarnated in a kite disputed with one of his colleagues incarnated in a crab, and a lively quarrel ensued, in the course of which the latter had his shell broken by the beak of the bird, an insult of which he bears the mark to-day. Casting about for some means of revenge, the Crab-Genius conceived the idea of raising the waters of the sea until they covered the high mountain on which the Kite-Genius was perched. Every human being perished with the exception of a young couple, brother and sister, who saved their lives by taking refuge in a huge pumpkin. This original boat deposited them safe and sound on the top of the highest mountain. The rescued couple at once sought far and wide for any other survivors of the human race, but all in vain. Their fellow beings had all perished. A tortoise which they met with advised them to marry to ensure the continuance of the race. The young man, horrified at the suggestion, cut the creature in pieces as a punishment, but the pieces quickly reunited, a marvel of which the tortoise has ever since borne the traces. The couple then renewed their wanderings and soon met a bamboo which offered the same advice, and was treated in the same way. Again the pieces reunited, and from that day to this the bamboo has always had knots. Finally, a Spirit descended to earth to terminate so embarrassing a situation. He offered the girl eight beans, promising her that if she ate one each year she would conceive on each occasion. In delight at the gift and the prospective fulfilment of all her hopes, she hastened to put the beans in her mouth, and, forgetting her instructions, swallowed them all at once! What the Spirit foretold then came to pass. She produced eight children at a birth and these founded the principal human families.

The tradition of the dispersion of the human race is also perpetuated. The Djarai Moï, for example, give the following description of the event.

" Our own land was the centre of the earth where the peoples of mankind, having outgrown their resources, built the Tower of Separation before scattering over the surface of the globe. The tower was so lofty that the topmost story could only be secured by bands of strong fibre which the workmen fastened by clinging to them with all their weight. Perched on the very top was one who thus surveyed the whole expanse of earth spread out before him. His duty was to indicate to those below the paths which led to the most fertile portions. After a short survey he called out to the workmen who were holding the ropes: 'To the Eastward I see a wondrous plain washed by the ocean, to the Westward a rich valley watered by a great river.' Before he could continue, however, an ominous rumbling was heard, the tower trembled for the space of a moment, and then fell to the earth with a crash, burying him under its ruins. The Annamites and Laotians were the unkind workmen who had all let go in their frantic haste to find the prosperous regions so eloquently described! As for the Moï, they were far too lazy to enter into an exhausting competition, so they remained on the forest-clad mountains which no one envied them."

The story of Joshua stopping the sun is replaced by that of a Spirit exhibiting the same powers.

"In the beginning there dwelt in the land o the Moï-Bahnar a valiant chieftain named Diong, whom the gods themselves were unable to subdue So great was the fame of his exploits that women frequently deserted their husbands in order to follow him. One of these offenders was the wife of the chief of the Moï-Djarai, who resolved to punish the author of his wrong, and declared war on him. The two tribes composed of equal numbers of skilled warriors fought with the utmost desperation, but fortune finally favoured Diong, who ended the day by slaying the injured husband with his own hand. Firmly convinced that his triumph was only due to celestial intervention, the victor begged the Spirits to put back the course of the sun in order to allow him time to annihilate his foes. His prayer was answered, for the gods drew back the sun and started it again at midday."

Most of these legends have been collected by the Catholic missionaries, whose work among the people of Bahnar has met with a large measure of success. It is possible that the higher standard of education to which the people of this region have attained has made possible the investigation of these biblical stories. Other groups, when questioned on the subject, can give no account of their legends whatever. I ought to say, however, that the story of the pumpkin saving the human race at the time of the deluge is well known among all the semi-savage peoples of Indo-China.

Sometimes the individual characteristics of a group are illuminated by a legend or fable which explains their origin. For example, the origin of the Moï practice of filing the teeth may be sought in a Cambodian fable.

When Buddha dwelt among men he was fed by each of his faithful disciples in turn. He visited the Moï and after them the Cambodians and asserted that the meats offered him by the former were much inferior to those of the latter. The reason for the difference was then made clear to him. The Moï were too lazy to pound the rice and contented themselves with grinding it in their teeth. The Master was greatly incensed at this lack of respect towards himself and condemned them to file their teeth in such a way that a repetition of the offence would be impossible. Further they were compelled to wear in their hair the small sticks which served for cooking utensils and, to add to their shame, he pierced their ears and forbade them to wear anything but the plainest clothing. The Moï found these restrictions more than they could bear and they fled to the mountains, leaving the plains to the Cambodians who dwell there to this day.

The extraordinary configuration of the regions inhabited by the Moï was bound to give birth to many legends which would furnish them with some satisfactory explanation of the phenomenon. The chief characteristics of these stories will be illustrated by the following examples, which I have selected at random.

The highest point of the great Annamite chain is a lofty mountain with a curious needle-shaped peak. The summit is inaccessible, and our surveyors had to be content with establishing their geodetical station at its foot. The peak is a well-known landmark and, according to the Moï, none other than the wife of a Spirit, who turned her into stone. In the beginning of creation a company of demigods dwelt on this spot. One day the husband went to get food, leaving his wife at home. She took advantage of his absence to deceive him, and in the fulness of time became pregnant. On his return the Spirit learned of the injury he had suffered and turned on the accomplice who took to flight. The husband gave chase, came up with his rival as he was on the point of casting himself into a river, seized him, cut off his head and turned his corpse into a stone.

Unsatisfied with this act of vengeance the murderer retraced his steps and likewise turned into stone everyone who had assisted the flight of his rival. On entering his palace he observed a crowd gathering round his wife who, in the throes of childbirth, had summoned a midwife and all her friends. The sight maddened him, and with a wave of his hand he transformed every living creature within reach into a mountain. Even the elephants, which in this country serve as transport animals, did not escape his vengeance. That is why this massive group of peaks is known as " The Mother and Child," a name preserved even by our cartographers.

Even more general than legends are ballads, fables and popular songs. Some of the chants which approximate to liturgical psalms are only known to a few select spirits who sing them together on special occasions.

Henri Maitre, the commissioner, has translated one of these rhapsodies which he discovered in the course of his ethnographical researches. A few extracts will illustrate the halting simplicity which characterizes these compositions.

" The Gods created the Earth and the trees. That is why men know how to make gongs and tom-toms with which they accompany their sacrifices to the Spirits. . . .

" Men create jars for spirits and the hollow bamboo tubes through which they suck up the liquid.

" Parents bring children into the world and feed them until they are able to look after themselves. . . .

" Thanks to the protecting care of the Spirits, the children grow up hardy and splendid like a tall tree or a great river. . . .

" Later, they too will marry." . . .

By the side of such outpourings with their sprinkling of archaic words and their more or less religious flavour there are also numbers of jovial popular songs which the young men hum at work or sing to the girls who catch their fancy. If the lady deigns to reply these songs develop into a kind of choral repartee. This practice is confined to the Laotians and their immediate neighbours.

The Laotians also still preserve the Court of Love, which has many features in common with the celebrated European institution of the Middle Ages.

At the period of the year when the rice harvest has been gathered in and work in the fields is temporarily suspended the chief occupation of the young men is to court the girls. Stages are erected on which the Laotian ladies in search of a husband assemble. At their feet burn lamps, by the light of which every detail of form or costume is discreetly brought to the notice of the swains. A plate of betel and a bamboo spittoon pass from hand to hand. Squatting in a row before their lady-loves the young men compose verses in their honour, and the ladies reply according to the burden of their hearts. Each couple keeps up the interchange of vocal repartee before a public only too ready to record its approval when one party or the other scores a point. The couples are not allowed to touch each other. If the burden of a song requires the performance of this act the singer symbolically touches himself. Both the singing and acting are accompanied by measured music, which adds to their charm.

The Malays also frequently improvise rhapsodical poems called "Pantouns," in which two persons converse together. The Malayan literary tournaments have acquired a widespread reputation.

The following is an excellent example of a love-poem sung by a Moï man and girl:

"Hallo, pretty girl. You smell sweeter than an orchid! .

" Your legs and bosom are like ivory!

" Your body is so white that it might have been shaved! .

" Your figure is as sinuous as that of a serpent! . . .

"If you walked in the forest to gather moss and batatas, I should wish to meet you alone to offer you some betel! (That being the emblem of accepted love.)

"If you will marry me I can give you a large rice-bowl, a warm coverlet for the cold nights, and an ox from my stables! . . .

"At night we will lie on the same mat as close together as the legs of a shackled elephant!" . . .

The girl's answer is cruel:

"If you could give me ten silver necklaces and five ropes of white pearls I would have none of you or your offerings, but tell your brother, the swift hunter, that he can have me for a green banana!" . . .

I have already dwelt on some of the superstitions which have gathered round certain animals, and it only remains to say that there is hardly a creature which is not the subject of a legend, a fable, or, at least, a popular saying. From a comparison of the relative importance of these legends or fables, it is plain that the Moï believe in a regular hierarchy in which each species has its place. This belief is shared by the Annamites, and its existence was clearly demonstrated by the following tragic incident.

One morning one of our engineers, a man named Petaud, was found crushed to death by elephants while engaged in tachymetrical operations. He was quite unrecognizable and it was plain that one of the infuriated monsters had flung him to the ground and the whole herd had then stamped his body into dust. We were quite unable to assign a cause for this terrible catastrophe. The only plausible explanation was that the unfortunate victim had been so preoccupied with his observations that he had stumbled into the midst of a sleeping herd and had taken them for rocks. The part of the forest in which he was found was, in fact, studded with huge granite boulders, many of which resembled elephants in colour and form. Without loss of time we set to work to clear the neighbourhood of the dangerous foe. Many of the monsters fell beneath our bullets and it occurred to us to send the feet to one of our countrymen on the coast, with a request to send them by an Annamite junk to Saigon. We knew of a naturalist in that town who makes elephants' feet into stands for flower-pots. Our discomfiture was complete when we were informed that no one would undertake the carriage of the booty to the coast at any figure we named. The following reason was advanced for this refusal.

" The elephant is the highest of the animals which reign on earth, but his powers can only be exercised on land. At sea the whale is mistress and she is very jealous of any encroachment on her prerogative. Accordingly, if we took any part of an elephant into her domain she would manifest her displeasure by capsizing our vessel."

Our prospective flower-pot stands had to wait for the arrival of a European ship!

Wild beasts and, in fact, all animals which may be

harmful to man are given high-sounding titles by the Moï in the hope of tickling their vanity and thus earning their gratitude. On the other hand, harmless creatures, especially those which cannot be used for food and are therefore useless to mankind, are given names of derision or contempt. Further, certain species whose wiles defy all attempts at capture are considered as being emanations of the spirits themselves. Suppose a rat has the impertinence not merely to avoid all the traps, but also to defy the Chief of the tribe and watch from a beam while a jar is being opened. Its ordinary name is immediately transformed. Henceforth, everyone refers to it as "the gentleman with magic powers." The same title is extended to the termite ants who succeed in making a home in cooking utensils in spite of all efforts to keep them out.

Other insects, such as the spider, are considered by their presence to incite married persons to infidelity. Accordingly a wife never goes to bed without making a thorough search for the malignant creature. If a spider fell from the ceiling between husband and wife the lady would know for a certainty that her spouse had torn up the marriage contract.

Popular fancy has also fastened on certain products of the vegetable kingdom. When the millet or rice is in flower no one is allowed to pass by who carries a truss of hay, for these plants are very sensitive and would invariably follow the example of the hay, which bears no grain.

If a pregnant woman were stupid enough to eat a double banana she would infallibly give birth to twins whose fingers would be knotted together.

There are numbers of nursery tales for children, many of which bear strong traces of Hindu influence. The following are good specimens:

THE RABBIT, THE TIGER AND THE ELEPHANT

One day the Rabbit met the Elephant, who looked very distressed. The small quadruped asked the big one the cause of his trouble.

The Elephant, grateful for the sympathetic inquiry, made reply:

"I have wagered my life with the Tiger and lost the wager. To-morrow I must put myself at his disposal and he will eat me, but he has given me one day in which to bid farewell to my children."

The Rabbit thought a moment and then told his friend to take heart for he had frequently found a way out of much more formidable complications. The Elephant believed in the assurances of his friend, and they separated after fixing a rendezvous for the next day.

The monster turned up punctually to the moment and found the Rabbit already waiting for him. The Rabbit told him to lie at full length on the ground. When the Tiger was heard bounding through the forest the Rabbit jumped on the Elephant's back and began to cry out at the top of his voice:

"I have just had an elephant for my dinner but I really don't feel equal to a tiger for dessert."

Terrified at such a miracle the King of the Jungle covered eight yards at a bound and vanished in a twinkling into the depths of the forest.

The Tiger and the Tortoise

One evening when the Tortoise was slowly walking up a mountain path she was brusquely ordered out of the way by a Tiger who wished to drink at the river.

"Out of my way, Tortoise! You are only hindering me and you know I can run faster than you!"

"Run faster than I!" exclaimed the Tortoise indignantly; "it's a lie!"

"Will you bet on it?" queried the Tiger.

"Certainly. You see these twelve hills. I bet you I will climb them all before you."

"Done!"

As it was then getting late they agreed to postpone the trial of speed to the next day. The Tortoise, however, was not idle during the night, but called together twelve of her sisters, to whom she gave instructions to take up their stations on the top of each of the twelve hills and to pretend to the Tiger that it was his rival whom he found waiting for him.

Her instructions were carried out to the letter and daybreak found each of the tortoises at her post.

The race began at once. The Tiger started off, covering yards at each bound. When he reached the top of the first hill he looked back in contempt for the Tortoise.

"Where are you, Tortoise?"

"Here I am," replied the first Tortoise. "Don't waste time chattering but get on your way."

Astounded that his competitor had displayed such a fine turn of speed the Tiger resumed the race without a moment's delay. In a few bounds he had reached the next hill, only to find (as he thought) the Tortoise waiting for him with a few mocking words for his slothfulness.

The Tiger lost heart and leapt forward in desperation, but the effort was too much for him. He was soon out of breath and collapsed in a heap long before his goal was in sight.

The fable of the Tiger and the Toad is very similar to the foregoing.

One day the Toad said to the Tiger:

"Will you run a race with me?"

"Don't be a fool," replied the Tiger.

"Come on all the same. I feel myself possessed by an invisible force and I am sure I can beat you."

"Very well then, but what's to be the stake?"

They agreed that the winner should eat the loser. A tortoise who chanced to pass by was selected as judge and performed the office of starter. The Tiger, with his customary astuteness, claimed that he need only touch the starting-post with the end of his tail. The Toad was up to this and promptly caught hold of his rival's tail and refused to be shaken off during the race. When within a few paces of the goal the Tiger suddenly stopped short and the Toad shot over his head. He was greatly chagrined to see the Toad thus arrive before him and complained bitterly to a monkey who had witnessed the contest.

"I saw it all," the monkey said. "The Toad owes his success to a trick. He caught hold of your tail and it was your sudden stop that precipitated him in front of you. Try to get him to run another race with you, and this time be careful to tie a stone to your tail to prevent a repetition of his underhand behaviour."

The Tiger was delighted with this advice and invited the Toad to a second trial of speed, offering his wife as an additional prize.

The monkey induced the Toad to agree and both watched the Tiger start off. He had not gone far, however, before he plunged into a stream which crossed the course. The weight of the stone dragged him down, and in spite of his struggles he perished miserably.

The monkey, tortoise and Toad were highly delighted.

The Toad and the King of Water

In the beginning of things a drought of several months completely dried up a marsh in which a Toad dwelt. By reason of this catastrophe the Toad could not bring up his young, so he decided to make a complaint in person to the King of Water.

To give greater weight to his plea he begged the Fox, the Bear and the Tiger to go with him.

The journey was long and wearisome, but at length the four animals, marching in single file, left behind them the narrow path which leads to heaven, and reached the gate.

A tom-tom was hung there, and the Toad banged it vigorously to announce his presence, while his companions discreetly drew aside.

Hearing the noise, the King of Water sent a genius to find out who the new-comer was.

"It is only a miserable toad," the messenger reported. "What must I do with him?"

The King ordered the cocks to put the intruders to flight, but the Fox flew at them and made a mouthful of them.

The King ordered the dogs to seize and punish the Fox, but then it was the Bear's turn to give them his deadly embrace. The King became more and more angry and ordered his archers to shoot the Bear with poisoned arrows.

With one bound the Tiger laid low the warriors before they could even stretch their bows, and torn by his fangs and claws they soon took to their heels.

The King, seeing himself thus at the end of his resources and tired of war, had the Toad brought into his presence, and inquired the object of his visit.

" I salute thee humbly, Sire," said the Toad, " and would make an urgent supplication before thee. The great heat hath turned the ground to stone, since thou hast forgotten to send rain for many weary months. I can no longer feed my children who are on the point of death through thy neglect."

Touched at the story, the King acknowledged his remissness and at his command a refreshing shower immediately fell upon the earth, which soon revived.

Since that fortunate interview, whenever there is a drought men hear the toad croaking his petition and rain falls without further delay.

It will be noticed in these fables how careful the Moï is to give the Tiger, his dreaded foe, the rôle of the vanquished. They also show signs of education in the habits of the animal world. It is just because the croaking of the toad coincides with a change in the atmosphere that the Moï attributes to that plaintive sound the power to bring down rain.

Is it not equally true that the illustrious chanticleer had only to utter his morning call to cause the sun to rise?

BOOK II
THE CHAM

CHAPTER I

THE CHAM

General characteristics of the Cham—A Mohammedan group—Its place among ancient civilizations—Social life—Dress and ornaments—The calendar—Rites accompanying the construction of a house, a cart, and a junk—Agriculture and industry—Medicines—The use of narcotics by criminals to stupefy their victims.

I HAVE now concluded my investigation of the complex of barbarous peoples who, in spite of the proximity of civilized races, have preserved almost intact the rudimentary instincts and ferocious customs of primitive man. No account of these regions, however, would be complete which omitted all references to the Cham,* a curious Mohammedan people, formerly very powerful, whose conversion to that faith took place during the zenith of their power and prosperity. The traces of this one-time pre-eminence and the Cham themselves are fast disappearing.

The group belongs to the Malayo-Polynesian race, of which the parent stock seems to have inhabited the region of Annam. The Cham were formerly the rulers of the powerful Empire of Champa, which

* Pronounced Tiam, Tiampa. Ch=tia.

occupied, as far as we can judge from the somewhat conflicting and unsatisfactory evidence, the eastern coast-line of Indo-China proper. Marco Polo tells us of the fertility of this region in the thirteenth century. It may even be that this country is the self-same Zabai of which Ptolemy speaks.

Nominally Islam is the official religion of this people who seem to have passed through previous stages of Animism and Brahminism. The ancient faiths were too well established to be uprooted by the Moslem conquerors and the outcome is a strange conglomeration in which the ancestral superstitions frequently profit at the expense of the precepts of the Koran.

The last survivors of this once flourishing empire (in all perhaps 130,000 souls), are now confined to the province of Binh-Thuan in Annam. At the time of its downfall before the rising power of the Annamites many of the conquered preferred exile in Cambodia and Siam rather than humiliation and servitude in the land of their birth.

The opportunity of observing and noting the customs, beliefs, and institutions of the Cham was furnished by the preliminary survey which preceded the construction of the railway from Phantiet to Phanrang. During the whole of this time our party was quartered among this interesting people and had many opportunities of developing friendly, and even intimate, relations.

THE CHAM

We cannot pretend to have been the first to do so, for previous to our arrival two eminent philologists, MM. Aymonier and Cabaton, had made a searching examination of the manuscripts in the possession of the priests and published two singularly exhaustive studies on the subject.*

The Cham have preserved almost unmodified their physical and moral characteristics, largely by means of their law which prohibits intermarriage with any other people. For this reason they exhibit a marked contrast to the Annamites.

The average height of a man is about five feet six inches, that of a woman five feet. The skin is somewhat coarse and varies between a dark brown and a shade of reddish brown such as a European acquires after long exposure in a tropical climate. The auburn or black hair is fine and brittle, while the growth of beard and moustache is more generous than among the Annamites. Partial, or even total, albinism is not uncommon.

The lips and facial outline offer resemblances to those of the European. This is not remarkable, for of all Asiatics the Cham and the Malays exhibit the nearest approach to the Western type.

In spite of a certain tendency to be hollow-backed the women are of fine presence, elegant, and graceful in their movements. Their carriage in walking is particularly remarkable and can be compared with

* *Les Tjames et leurs religions*, by Aymonier. *Nouvelles Recherches sur les Cham*, by A. Cabaton.

that of the Egyptians. The women of both these races habitually carry heavy objects either on their shoulders or heads and can only maintain them in equilibrium thanks to the most perfect ease in their movements.

If the vigour of this race has not deteriorated during the last centuries it is certain that their fertility has diminished. For some time the birthrate has remained stationary. Retrogression is exhibited in other ways also, for although their ancient civilization must have been highly advanced, little trace of it remains in their present low level of intellect. All ambition to renew the glories of the past has long since evaporated. The ruins of many monuments tell of the ancient splendours, but the living representatives are quite content to recount the triumphs without any desire to emulate them. Is it incapacity or merely universal apathy? The indolence of the Cham is notorious. Even the building of their houses they leave to their neighbours the Annamites.

The first time I entered a Cham village I was amazed at the absence of all vegetation. Shade is one of the prime necessities of life in this country, where the fierce rays of the sun pour down pitilessly all day and make it painful, and even dangerous, for a man to be exposed to them without cover. My colleagues, who had been established in the place for some time, soon explained that as long as we remained among the Cham we might as well relinquish vain hopes of finding a house which would not be exposed to the sun.

This inconvenient defect is the outcome of a popular superstition that the shade of a tree exerts a baneful influence over the house beneath it. A somewhat similar belief prevails in Cambodia, where, however, the minister of evil is alleged to be not the shade but the roots of trees which penetrate below a house.

However, the lack of shade was by no means the greatest discomfort we were called on to face. There were many others.

A native habitation comprises as many miniature houses as there are households (and almost even members) in the family. Every girl of marriageable age has a special room. The married members have another, while a third is reserved for the boys who have attained puberty. Naturally, the larger the family the smaller are the separate rooms, and so the apartment assigned to us was usually little more than a box with space for only a small folding-bed, the solitary piece of furniture. These low, thatched huts were scattered about a kind of compound bounded on each side by a flimsy palisade of bamboos secured together by thongs of cane.

The costume of the men consists of a skirt and a very long robe. The women wear a large piece of cloth wrapped round to form a rude skirt. Gay colours are somewhat restricted, white and white striped with red and green being the most popular.

For bodice they have a clinging dark-green tunic open at the throat.

Their taste in jewellery is remarkably restrained. The rich wear silver or gold buttons in their ears. Of the poorer classes some confine their personal embellishment to copper nails and others wear a plait made of coloured threads which falls over their shoulders. We sometimes noticed bracelets on the wrists of some of the girls. This ornament serves to remind its wearer of the temporary vow of chastity which she has taken to guard her against some danger or cure an illness.

Others again wear a necklace of large amber beads from which hangs the Tamrak, a kind of amulet which wards off the powers of evil. This indispensable talisman consists of a small cylinder of lead on which a priest has traced mystic characters with a sharp-pointed instrument.

Both sexes keep their hair long and, like the Annamites, twist it into a knot at the back. The men wear as head-dress either a large turban or sometimes merely a kerchief. Pockets are unknown, but two purses hung from a long girdle provide an excellent substitute.

In early times the Cham princes set up their royal residence and the seat of government in Phanrang. In the seventeenth century their office was still hereditary, but the Court of Hué reserved the right of investiture. In the nineteenth century successive invasions undermined the authority of

THE CHAM

those potentates and all appointments to administrative offices were made by the Annamite conquerors, who made their selection among the local aristocracy.

The Cham of Cambodia are all Mohammedans, but of those of Annam about two-thirds have remained Brahmins. Their countrymen of the later faith call them " Kaphirs " (infidels), and reserve to themselves the title of " Bani " (sons of the faith). Nevertheless, there is perfect toleration between the followers of the two religions. The priests honour with their presence the ritual ceremonies of the group whose beliefs they do not share and neither party attempts to make converts of the adherents of the other.

The calendar of the Cham is partly lunar and partly solar. The beginning and end of each month coincides with a new moon. As in the Hindu calendar, this lunar month has a light half which culminates in the full moon and a dark half which is terminated by the new moon. The duodenary cycle is employed for the purpose of measuring time. This system was invented by the Turks, but the Chinese have been mainly instrumental in securing its adoption throughout the Far East. Each of the twelve years of which it is composed is called by the name of some animal—Rat, Buffalo, Tiger, Hare, Dragon, Snake, Horse, Goat, Monkey, Cock, Dog, Boar.

The year begins in April-May and comprises

twelve lunar months of thirty and twenty-nine days alternatively. They are numbered from one up to ten, but the eleventh and twelfth have special names. Every three years a month is added, and it may well be imagined to what difficulties and disputes this proceeding gives rise in the absence of agreement between the villages.

There are seven days in the week. Their names are borrowed from the Sanscrit and, like ours, represent a planet. Each day has twelve hours, twice the length of ours, of which the first begins at cockcrow. The night consists of five watches.

These are the component parts of the system in which it is quite simple to calculate any date. For example, a document may be dated thus: "Signed, Monday the fourth day of the light half of the fifth month of the year of the Dragon."

It is probable that in early times the Cham computed time by a system similar to that of the ancient Javanese, a people with whom they maintained close political and commercial relations, as witness several alliances between members of the two reigning houses. The Javanese calendar comprised a week of five days, a month of six weeks, a year of ten months, each with its special tutelary deity.

Life among the Cham is greatly complicated by rules of etiquette, of which the most stringent regulate the relations between those of different age and rank. Age is regarded with special reverence and an old man, whatever his social condition, is always addressed

THE CHAM

as Uncle or Grandfather by his juniors in years. An inferior addresses his superior as Elder Brother.

As in Cambodia methods of greeting are various. If a man meets a friend of superior station a due and proper sign of deference is to adjust his girdle or cross the cloth which fulfils the functions of trousers. If he is carrying an umbrella he will hold it forward towards the person he thus wishes to honour. Then a conversation will take place. During the whole time he will take the greatest care to avoid swinging his arms, the most flagrant act of disrespect. To guard against even an unwitting breach of this regulation a well-bred Cham will clasp his hands together, a precaution which prevents any movement of the arms. If a woman desires to address a request to a Mandarin or a European, her preliminary salutation is a complicated manœuvre which recalls the Andjali of the Hindus and cannot be executed without preparation. She takes off the turban which keeps her hair in position, wraps it round her like a shawl, drops on her knees and finally prostrates herself three times in succession at full length on the ground. In the interval between each prostration she rubs her face with her hands.

In India, where etiquette takes a different form, no one should appear in public without an ornament of some kind in the hair; if the head is completely unadorned it signifies either mourning or absolute retirement from the world. This rule seems to be of very ancient origin and to have been kept alive largely by sculpture. It is remarkable that all the statues of divinities in the temples have an ornament of some kind in the hair.

It is not merely the number and variety of the rules of etiquette which distinguish the Cham from other groups of similar culture. They are equally remarkable for the multiplicity of the rites which accompany each act, however insignificant, of their daily life. I can only recount here some of the more important ones which present features of their own.

An accidental fire destroyed the native house which a village chief had placed at our disposal, during the survey in that neighbourhood. We offered to rebuild it on our own lines, with the latest improvements. Far from expressing any gratification at the suggestion he showed the greatest surprise and displeasure and was more than contented with the very modest sum we gave him with which to do the work himself. Little did we imagine the trials in store for us. We were provided with temporary accommodation in a barn, without shade of any sort. The ill-fitting planks let in as much sun as rain and wind, and we were all impatience to see the completion of our future dwelling. Time, however, counts for next to nothing in the Far East, and for nothing at all among the Cham. Within a few days it was patent that a long delay was inevitable and we were soon resigned to the prospect of waiting indefinitely while the rebuilding, impeded by innumerable daily ceremonies, proceeded from stage to stage.

THE CHAM

First of all, a place which is to be hallowed by the performance of so many rites must be enclosed within a light palisade as holy ground. For this purpose dead wood is chosen, for it must never be forgotten that the shade cast by foliage forbodes evil. In this enclosing wall an opening is made to give passage to the divinities of the five cardinal points. Without their help it would be vain for man to enter upon so grave an undertaking.

The area having thus been marked out, the next step is to determine its centre. For this purpose a cord is requisitioned. The spot thus fixed serves as a point by which to find the positions for the columns which are to support the building. A hole is dug to furnish a foundation for the north-east column. Into this the owner throws a magic amulet with the most elaborate precaution. The talisman consists of a sheet of lead on which certain mystic characters are engraved. Only after this solemn consecration is the column fixed in position. The day's work is then concluded. Next day a similar performance accompanies the establishment of a second column. One day one column is more than we can stand, and after every form of persuasion and argument the easy-going architect consents to consecrate the remaining columns on the same day.

Alas! When the framework of the roof is complete religious observance requires that an amulet shall be inserted at every point of contact with the beams of the walls! Then again there is a prolonged and bitter controversy over the choice of thatch. Our Annamite coolies have been foolish enough to collect a supply of bulrushes which are considered to exert a malignant influence! The offending material is immediately burnt and a new delay begins. At length the work is completed and the house stands ready for immediate occupation. Nothing seems to prevent our entry into possession and at daybreak we move across with our baggage and establish ourselves each in his diminutive cabin. Hardly has the unpacking begun than the owner rushes in with hands upraised in horror. In our haste we have unwittingly committed almost every conceivable act of sacrilege!

A cat should have been the first to enter the new abode, and after it the Master, and he alone may declare the building open. There is no help for it. We hastily put back our belongings and tumble the boxes out into the yard. We remain as unwilling spectators of a ceremony which we are assured is positively the last. Our host prostrates himself on the ground at the exact spot which he selects for his own bed. He then rises and intones a chant proper to the occasion, which consists of the recital of all the places to be avoided when selecting a site for a new dwelling.

" I will flee far," says the Holy Canticle, " from the haunts of the White Ant. I will turn aside from the dwelling-places of demons and evil spirits. Sloping places I will shun. I will sound clayey soil. In short I will never be found where evil is to be apprehended."

And the pious architect concludes the last of the rites and leaves us to the place.

Irritated though we were by the interminable proceedings which had postponed our occupation of the promised land, it is only fair to say that at all times we displayed the greatest interest in other ritual ceremonies which involved no personal disadvantages to ourselves. Each day provided us with new matter for investigation and speculation.

Undoubtedly one of the most curious proceedings is the consecration of a cart before its entry into active service. The manufacture of these vehicles is, perhaps, the most flourishing industry of the Cham. Their reputation is almost world-wide and thoroughly deserved. The industry dates from a very early period and was brought into prominence during the fourteenth century by the demand of the Hindu princes for beautiful cars for wedding gifts to their brides. The dedication takes place with the greatest pomp and is not complete without a sacrifice. First the wheelwright sprinkles his new material with holy water, then takes it to the river bank. There he subjects it to a severe scouring, after which it is considered as purified. Next coloured tapers are fixed on the uprights and finally he draws his knife and cuts out the framework.

"Cart," he cries, "woe betide you if ever the fancy take you not to roll your best."

The Cham prefer the banks of a river or the shores of a lake as a site for their settlements. They frequently build whole villages, on huge floating rafts, but the staple industry of these lake-dwelling groups is the building of light boats and racing skiffs. These are made from trees and, as long narrow trunks are indispensable, the favourite medium is the dipterocarpus, which is plentiful in these regions. The tree is felled and then hollowed to its full length, the ends being shaped to a tapering point. To obtain the necessary elasticity the parts are exposed to a wood fire before the moulding process is commenced. Every stage of the proceedings is accompanied by prayers and sacrifices such as we have seen marking the dedication of the wagon.

It is general knowledge that in Cambodia and the region of Laos canoe races figure in all public festivals of importance. These regattas attract a large number of spectators of all nations and the Cham naturally take a conspicuous part.

The boats display quite a high standard of artistic skill. On the inside they are decorated with red lacquer. On the outside they are black and gold. Some idea of the size appears in the fact that they are sometimes built to accommodate fifty paddlers.

Every king, prince, bonze and noble has, or should have, his private boat and liveried crew, for the races proper are preceded by an aquatic procession, when each boat passes before the dais on which is seated the President of the Festivities. Nothing

THE CHAM

could be more elating than the sight of the beautiful rhythmical movements of the paddlers swinging forward with mechanical precision until their foreheads almost touch their knees. These voluntary sailors furnish an example of discipline which might well be followed in high places.

Agriculture among the Cham is limited to the cultivation of a few ricefields and the growth of tobacco, cotton and pea-nuts. Cattle-raising does not include that of cows and pigs, the flesh of which is forbidden by religion. Other industries are bee-keeping, the export of the wax for religious purposes, and the manufacture of torches of resin which find a ready market among the Annamites. I have already mentioned other specialities.

Agriculture, commerce and industry show not the least sign of expansion. The Cham is not ambitious, much less inventive and exhibits no trace of envy of his progressive Annamite conquerors, whose industrious activity is a vivid contrast to the proverbial lethargy of Orientals. Unhappily the indifference of the Cham to material prosperity is a recent development. In the great days of Empire they must have been a very active and intelligent race and even to-day we find relics of their inventive skill among their Medicine Men.

These specialists jealously guard the secret, which has been handed down by tradition, of certain medicines to which Europeans have had recourse on occasion. More than once during our expedition we were glad to invite the good offices of the native herbalists when, prostrated by dysentery, shivering with fever or weakened by anæmia, we had exhausted the resources of our own pharmaceutical arsenal. The native doctors are as skilful as the Chinese in utilizing various simples and are quite familiar with the medicinal properties of certain animal products.

We have known cases in which an unnameable brew, of which the principal constituents were the shells of beetles, the scales of snakes, and the parings of stags' antlers and bullocks' hooves, effected a quicker cure than all our European drugs, for all their scientific names. The pharmacopœia of the Cham is certainly an offshoot of that of the Chinese. It comprises a list of all manner of remedies for moral as well as physical disorders.

Camphor, a substance universally appreciated, appears also among the medicines of the Cham. They use a certain oil which, when impregnated with camphor, acts as an anæsthetic by evaporating and producing a freezing sensation. It forms a kind of liniment and is kept in a small, brightly coloured glass flask, which is stoppered with a cork of wax to prevent evaporation.

Wax is also used to make capsules, about the size of a pigeon's egg, to hold drugs and other medicinal substances which must be kept from contact with the air.

Cholera, which is endemic throughout this region, is treated by taking pills made up of a mixture of sandalwood, the bark of the mangostan, and eaglewood. Eaglewood, of which I shall have much to say later on, is well known as an excellent tonic. Popular superstition endows it with powers so remarkable that a single piece could effect an immediate cure.

Most of the brews or broths are prepared by decoction rather than by infusion and the operation should take place over a slow fire, which makes them more potent. Their effect is extremely violent, and in Europe we should unhesitatingly classify them with the group of remedies popularly known as "horse pills."

Among the most potent I might mention the gall of animals which is often used to produce the effect of an emetic.

At one time the Cham sorcerers used human bile as well as that of animals. This human bile was useless unless taken from a living subject, and consequently murders without number were committed for the purpose of obtaining it. Its reputation as a talisman was universal. It was said that any man who rubbed himself with it became invulnerable. Of course it was inevitable that a warrior should become invincible when he was certain that his victory, thanks to his supernatural protection, was a foregone conclusion. The King himself had no doubts as to the efficacy of this talisman and before going into battle ordered his elephants to be sprayed with it. His special emissaries, who enjoyed the name of *Jalavoi* ("Stealers of human bile"), drew their host of victims from every quarter, and even to-day the memories of their horrid activities evoke a shudder.

Happily those evil days have departed. Human bile is no longer used either for protective or medicinal purposes. It emains only as the subject of legend.

Besides this special and curious emetic the Cham produce the same effect by certain mechanical processes the originality of which merits detailed description.

When a sick man's stomach seems overladen with bile and the medicine man wishes to empty it completely, he stuffs a rag soaked in urine and other evil-smelling substances into the patient's mouth. He rams it down as far as it will go and then quickly withdraws it. Physical aversion and the irritation of the glottis produced by a foreign body immediately provoke a spasm of sickness. No doubt some milder emetic would have been equally successful.

I frequently doctored the Cham and I can bear witness that they make the best of patients. They took ipecacuanha, castor-oil, or sulphate of soda, as if they enjoyed them. When they came again they often brought me a present of a little candle in a curious candlestick made from the banana-plant. I learnt later that it was the custom to bring an offering of some kind in lieu of fee to the native doctors.

Suicide is very uncommon in these regions, where

the means of life are within the reach of all, passions easily mastered, and an easy-going philosophy is practised from the cradle. The few who find life not worth living leave it with the help of opium which they mix with vinegar.

At present the native authorities throughout Indo-China have taken no steps to regulate the manufacture and sale of poisons. It is quite usual for the most virulent of these to be sold publicly in the open market, and it must be admitted that any regulations would probably be ineffective to stop the trade. Nature in Asia has always been lavish with toxic substances. Even if the sale of these were prohibited, anyone could find as many as he wished in the nearest forest. This abundance is undoubtedly responsible for the large and increasing number of murders by poison which distinguish the regions inhabited by the Cham. We ourselves, isolated in the bush, had to take the most elaborate precautions to prevent fatalities of this kind.

On our arrival in the country we were forewarned of the danger by the French resident magistrate of the province. He laid special stress on the risks run by young bachelors who attempted any intimacies with the native girls. The seducer, it appears, is marked out for destruction, even if he has only yielded to the blandishments of the woman. Further, many of the Cham poisons only work slowly and the mischief they cause in the system is frequently taken for disorders which follow anæmia and other illnesses, to which foreigners in this climate are peculiarly liable. One of my colleagues died from an attack of what we believed to be malaria. We all feel now that if an autopsy had been made we should probably have discovered that what we thought was cachexia was the effect of poison.

Besides being familiar with the nature and use of poisons the Cham are also expert in concocting stupefying drugs and narcotics of all kinds. They often poison the air of a room in which a patient is lying by blowing stupefying vapours through hollow canes inserted in the wattled walls. The effect of these fumes is to make the victim sleep more heavily and the criminals take advantage of this circumstance to rob him at their leisure.

I had a vivid personal experience of this diabolical procedure. One evening I arrived with my escort at a house which our coolies had built specially for us and where we were to stay several weeks. The furniture consisted of nothing more than a bamboo bedstead supporting a mattress of cotton wadding. My room was very narrow and the seven cases which contained my instruments and cooking utensils were all the furniture I needed in addition. I told my boy to push two of these cases under the bed in order to save space. We had been marching all day under a tropical sun and I flung myself on the mattress and fell asleep at once. I awoke, according to habit, at about four in the morning and was surprised to feel myself so cramped that I could

THE CHAM 245

hardly move. To add to my astonishment I could not find my matches which I always kept within reach. The case which I had placed to serve as a bedside table had likewise disappeared.

With great effort I rose from bed and stumbling at each step managed to get out of the house. My sole garment was my pyjamas, for my clothes had followed the matches. It was still dark and I soon collided with an obstacle which proved on investigation to be one of the cases. I was somewhat alarmed and called for my servants. No one answered. A feeling of overpowering drowsiness overcame me and I had just time to get back to my bed before I fell asleep again. When morning came my orderly came in to announce that six out of the seven boxes were scattered about the outskirts of our camp. Locks had been forced and all my papers, instruments, photographic plates and prints, and wallets ruthlessly thrown out after obvious examination. It was plain that the burglars had been hunting for bank-notes. Fortunately I had no money in the cash-box. I had left the few thousand piastres which constituted our reserve with a colleague, so the total haul did not amount to more than two silver bangles and a few gewgaws, which together were not worth more than ten piastres.

As for the seventh case, it contained the whole of our supplies, and its disappearance left us with nothing but the impressions of our journey to breakfast on

That evening, while clearing the thickets quite

six kilometres from our camp, our coolies came upon the missing case. It was almost intact. Only one box had been opened and it bore upon its label a sketch of the sucking-pig it contained. As swine's flesh is abhorred by the Cham I can only conclude that we owed the recovery of our portable larder to that happy chance.

Two years later a second attempt of the same kind and not less audacious was perpetrated upon me. I was at Hanoi, residing in a house situated in a narrow avenue and next to the barracks. It was at the beginning of the rainy season and a violent storm was raging. I was sleeping on the first floor, and one of my Tonkinese orderlies, a hardy young bachelor, stationed himself at the bottom of the stairs to guard me. I had allowed another to bring his family into the house and the family, including its real members, friends and acquaintances, turned out to comprise eleven persons. In return for this concession they arranged to mount guard in turn. It will be acknowledged that I was thus not alone in the desert !

It must have been about midnight and I was dozing lightly (being prevented from sleeping by feverishness), when I suddenly noticed that my reading-lamp outside the mosquito-net was lit. It occurred to me that I could not have been so foolish as to leave it lit and I distinctly remembered putting out the light when I got into bed. I sat up to rouse my senses and heard a slight noise in the next room.

I was out of bed in a moment just in time to catch a parcel of clothing which was evidently thrown at me to trip me up. By the light from the reading-lamp I distinctly saw a man perfectly naked, his body shining as if he had just had a bath in oil. I remembered in a flash that the Annamite robber always take this precaution to make capture more difficult. Before I could snatch my revolver the burglar had displayed his ape-like agility by leaping through the window and vanishing in the darkness.

I called up my men, but they only told me they had heard nothing. I confess with shame I lost my temper. Suspecting those whom I had so imprudently harboured of complicity in the plot I hunted from the house all except my usual staff. I enjoyed such consolation as was afforded by the sight of the silhouettes of the defaulting watchmen cowering in the pelting rain. Any remorse I experienced quickly vanished when I made inquiries later !

CHAPTER II

SOCIAL AND FAMILY LIFE

Traces of the matriarchal system in the conception of the family—The " Karoh "—Circumcision—Precautions against seduction—Rites incidental to betrothal, marriage, birth and infancy.

IT is well known that the ancient matriarchal system of government and ownership still flourishes among certain peoples who inhabit the peninsula of the Ganges and some groups of Malayo-Polynesian origin. In this system man belongs to an inferior order of creation. All political and social authority is exercised by woman and she alone can possess and inherit. This veritable triumph of feminism might have been expected to produce results far more disastrous than has been the case. Proof that life under such circumstances can be both possible and tolerable is furnished by the history of the Malays of the Negri Sambilan (British Malaysia), which is little more than a monotonous record of good fortune and prosperity.

The system is frequently accompanied by the institution of polyandry in which the husbands

SOCIAL AND FAMILY LIFE

cohabit in turn with the common wife who has herself selected them.

Now the institutions of both the Cham and the Cambodians show traces of descent from an earlier organization of which the matriarchal system was the distinguishing feature. On no other hypothesis can we account for some striking facts. Family is traced through the mother. The children take her name, adopt her religion if they are the issue of a mixed marriage, and remain her property in case of divorce. Inheritance descends in the female line alone. A woman is the principal figure in many of the domestic ceremonies and she retains at all times the right to select her husband.

The time at which girls pass from infancy to puberty (when they are at once considered of marriageable age) is celebrated by a curious ceremony called the "Karoh," which is doubtless derived from that precept of the Koran which prohibits a repudiated or divorced woman from entering upon a new union until after a retirement extending over three menstrual periods. The festival lasts two days and the proceedings are under the personal supervision of the Ong Gru (High Priest) himself, who is assisted by a number of acolytes.

Two huts of boughs and leaves are constructed specially for the occasion. One is destined to serve as dormitory to the girls of the village whose puberty is to be officially recognized. The other is to accommodate the numerous audience which always gathers to witness the accomplishment of the rite.

At the first sign of daybreak the young neophytes advance in a group towards the High Priest. Each wears her gayest robes and her most precious jewels. Her hair falling freely on her shoulders is crowned with a mitre. One by one they bow reverentially before the officiating minister who places on their lips a grain of salt, offers a cup of pure water, and then cuts a piece of hair from their foreheads. This last action signifies that the girls' reputation is unsullied. If the contrary is demonstrated by ocular proof the piece of hair will be taken not from the forehead but from the back of the neck. This constitutes, both among the Cham and the Cambodians, a mark of infamy.

A one-year-old baby, carried in the arms of an old man, is the object of the same rites.

The girls thus initiated now retire to the place assigned to them, obviously to carry out the semblance of withdrawal from the world. During their absence the priests take a hearty meal, the remains of which are distributed to the faithful. About midday the girls return, this time with their hair twisted into a knot on their necks, a patent indication that the age of marriage has been reached. Relations and friends join in offering them gifts to celebrate the happy event. A generous feast follows to which are invited all who have taken any part in the proceedings, and shortly after the girls enter into their new sphere.

Photo by] [A. Cabaton.

Royal Elephants in Cambodia.

Photo by]   A Buddhist Procession carrying Offerings to a Distant Pagoda.   [*Henri Maitre.*

The High Priests say that the "Karoh" is in essence a symbol. The moon, a feminine divinity, attains her full perfection only at the fifteenth day. In the same way the "Karoh" must be celebrated as nearly as possible in a girl's fifteenth year when her development is complete.

Up to the time of her consecration in this manner a girl is "taboo," and all sexual relations with her are strictly prohibited.

The Cambodians have very similar rites and regulations. Before attaining the age of marriage a girl is regarded as one of the spouses of Indra, the King of the Gods, and in virtue of this exalted station no man dare cultivate any intimate relations with her. Immediately on the occurrence of her first menstruation she "enters into the shade," that is, takes refuge under her mosquito-net and withdraws from the world altogether for a period which varies between five and a hundred days. As long as the sun shines the recluse may not even leave her couch, but occasionally an eclipse procures her a temporary release from her gaol. No man may approach her, for she must not be exposed to the temptation of looking at a male. Her diet is strictly prescribed, fish and meat being prohibited, and in any case she is restricted to one meal a day, taken between sunrise and midday, after the manner of the bonzes.

This compulsory seclusion is a terrible hardship, for an open-air life is almost a necessity in these tropical climates where the heat is overpowering. It is not to be wondered at, therefore, that the termination of the imprisonment is an occasion for great rejoicing. "Leaving the shade," as this fête is called, is frequently marked by the lacquering of the girl's teeth, an operation which is accompanied with all manner of rites and is preceded by a special dedicatory ceremony.

Regulations which seem to aim at secluding girls at the time they attain puberty are not peculiar to Indo-China. Thus the Vaï of Liberia cloister their girls at the age of ten in a place called "Sandy," which is hidden away in the depths of a great forest. The recluses are considered dead to their family who are not allowed to see them. Their only visitors are a few old women, their only occupations minor domestic duties and initiation into the mysteries of marriage. If a betrothal is arranged during this period the girl is liberated on the appearance of the first signs of puberty.

If we are to believe legend (and legend is often worthy of belief), both in Denmark and Siberia the same period in a girl's life is preceded by a similar retirement. Frazer cites several instances which dispel all doubt on the subject.

The rite of circumcision, or rather, the rite of simulated circumcision, among the Cham Bani only takes place when the boys are in their fifteenth year. This ceremony is, in fact, purely symbolical. Armed with a wooden knife the officiating priest makes a pretence of performing the act after which he gives the novice his ceremonial name, which is always taken from the Arabic calendar and is sure to be either Ali, Ibrahim, or Mahomet. The acquisition of this religious surname does not prevent a boy from using his unredeemed name in ordinary life.

The ceremony known as the "Entry into Religion" should take place at about the age of five, but in practice it is always reserved until the age of puberty though never delayed until after marriage. It will be remembered that the custom of postponing circumcision characterized the Persians also.

The Cham have a saying that you might as well leave an elephant among the sugar canes as leave a man alone with a girl. The proposition may be sweeping but receives enough illustration to make it plausible.

However that may be, it must be remembered that no sexual relationships are prohibited except those which do not sooner or later contemplate marriage. If a girl is seduced and the consequences of her action begin to make themselves evident she is at once put under arrest. Her ankles are secured by thongs of buffalo hide; with these marks of ignominy she appears before the Council of Notables. There she is adjured to reveal the author of her undoing. If she gives the name of the seducer he is compelled to marry her and pay a fine by way of compensation to her parents. This fine is the "Price of Shame" and invariably substantial. If, however, the girl refuses to divulge the name of her seducer a sentence of fifty strokes with a cane is passed, an extremely heavy penalty. Before the punishment is actually inflicted a hole is dug in the ground and the sufferer made to lie at full length with her stomach in it. This is a precaution to prevent an abortion.

As soon as a girl has found the man of her choice her parents pay an official visit to those of her fortunate husband-designate. They take with them two cakes and some betel. If the young man tastes this it is a sign that he accepts betrothal and an engagement follows.

A curious custom in this country is that the consummation of the marriage does not coincide with its celebration. To do so would be to court the malevolence of the powers of evil! Cohabitation is the first step in the proceedings. In this way the new household saves all wedding expenses and it is by no means infrequent that the children are old enough to take part in the festivities by the day fixed for the official celebration of the nuptials.

The marriage takes place in the evening in a hut specially built for the occasion. Hand in hand the happy pair walk on mats from their own dwelling to the place appointed for the fête. Indeed it is a most important part of the rites that their feet shall not come into contact with the bare ground. Their garments are of white cotton and unhemmed, resembling in this respect the mourning clothes worn by the Annamites. The girl enters the house,

SOCIAL AND FAMILY LIFE 255

leaving her partner on the threshold where stands the priest who is to bless their union.

A dialogue ensues between the minister and the man.

"Prince Ali," asks the former, "what are your gifts to the Princess Fatima, your future spouse?"

"O Lord Mahomet, I bring her a silver ring, two talismans for her neck, a necklace of amber, a fertile rice-field, and two bullocks trained to the plough."

With these words the husband gives the ring to the priest who blesses it and hands it to his two acolytes, who bear it away to place on the finger of the bride.

She, invisible behind the door of the house, receives the two messengers who question her on her desires. If she gives her consent to the marriage she is immediately led to her husband who escorts her in solemn procession to their new home. Before entering, however, the man throws three betel leaves on the ground and crushes them one after another with his foot.

A white cloth is thrown over the nuptial couch and the married pair take their places side by side upon it. The deacons join their hands and sprinkle holy water over them. Next several candles are lit, the pair receive official benediction, and at length find themselves alone.

The rites, however, are not yet concluded, for the woman gravely rolls up a quid of betel which she puts into the mouth of her husband. In return he takes off part of his clothing to make a covering for her. They then leave the house and fall at the feet of the priests and their parents. Their friends seize an early opportunity of proclaiming in a loud voice the gifts they offer, while a secretary draws up the list to prevent misunderstanding.

The proceedings terminate with a monster banquet. The man's family provide the meat and drinks while the woman's are responsible for the rice and cakes.

In Cambodia the Cham allow a disappointed suitor to prevail over the opposition of his loved one's family by executing the following mock manœuvres.

He waits until nightfall and seizing the moment when the girl's door is open to make his entry into the house, clasps her in his arms and throws about them both a shawl brought for the purpose.

After this elaborate pretence of rape the family have no choice but to withdraw their opposition and allow the match to proceed. They never fail, however, to exact vengeance from the mock ravisher in the shape of fearful abuse and a more or less substantial fine.

The women make very faithful wives, so much so that cases of adultery are rare. Normally this crime is punishable with death, but in practice the sentence is always commuted to a fine, sometimes accompanied by whipping.

Besides, every facility is afforded for the dissolution

SOCIAL AND FAMILY LIFE

of the union on the ground of incompatibility of temperament. Divorce is easy. The woman's right to select her husband is paired with the right to get rid of him at will or change him for another. In this case she herself keeps the family dwelling and the lion's share of the property.

Although the religion of Mahomet permits the possession of four wives, in practice the Cham have insufficient means to provide for more than one. Accordingly, polygamy is exceptional, the expense being prohibitive.

Certain prohibitions are too remarkable to be passed over in silence.

Both the Brahminist and the Mussulman Cham abstain from sexual relations on Mondays, as being the day of the week on which Allah was born.

During pregnancy the women take the greatest care to avoid a certain kind of Javanese banana for fear of giving birth to a monster which will one day turn and torment them.

The rites accompanying birth are materially the same as those of the Moï. There is the same "Accouchement at the Fire," to use the expression in vogue in the country. It means that a fire is kindled by the woman's couch from the beginning of the accouchement to the time she is allowed to leave her bed, seven days after the birth. This fire is kept carefully guarded by the matrons with a "ring" of cotton thread. They also leave a huge lighted candle at the side to ward off evil spirits.

When the mother is about again the midwife puts out the fire and plants an iron stake in the middle of the ashes. These she collects with the greatest care and bears them off with religious fervour to deposit at a fork of the nearest road in the vicinity. They form a little heap on the top of which she places a stone. Then she lays a quid of betel on this improvised altar.

I was extremely curious for a long time as to the meaning of these pious erections which I saw at every cross-road, but no one dared nor cared to give me any information. Those whom I interrogated took refuge in evasion and turned the conversation. I might have remained for ever in ignorance had not the Annamites proved more communicative some time later. I then learned that in popular superstition cross-roads are the favourite haunts of spirits, souls in torment, ghosts, and other beings whose influence is baneful.

The Cham are extremely fond of their children and spare no pains to keep them amused. Indeed, their affection goes the length of leaving them in complete ignorance of soap and water, an omission for which the babies are duly grateful. It is especially gratifying to the benevolent spirits if the mother smears her child's face with a mixture of flour and saffron a substance the yellow colour of which meets with the particular approval of the deities whose own visages are of that colour if we are to credit tradition. On the other hand, the mother who has been visited by a bad dream covers her baby with soot to hide it from evil spirits.

The natural consequence of these precautions is that the young Cham, like the young Moï, grow up in a condition of filth which is aggravated by the onslaught of mosquitoes and the appearance of innumerable sores. Further they are extremely liable to gastro-enteritis due to their parents' reprehensible practice of stuffing them with rice until their small stomachs are stretched taut like a drum.

Throughout the Far East the kiss is replaced by a kind of snort applied to the back of the neck just behind the ear. The children are particularly fond of this type of demonstration for they burst into shouts of laughter whenever their mothers relieve their maternal feelings in this manner. If the child grows up in spite of his parents' apprehensions, at about the age of six months he receives a name which is considered to sum up his prospects in life. Thus a fine chubby boy will be called Peace, Amber or Gold. A small, weakly girl will receive the name of Discord, Pillage or Bat. But suppose this last child survives the early years and her infantile disorders, at about the age of twelve her name of reproach is exchanged for one of more happy meaning for she has passed the age at which the spirits are allowed to exercise a baneful influence. In spite of this mode of rehabilitation, however, the parents usually forget to change the name and her old soubriquet clings to her through life. This at all events is some explanation for the curious fact that in searching the historical records of the Cham we are always coming across kings rejoicing in the unfortunate titles of "Typhus the Third," and "Cholera the Fourth."

It will be remembered that the Aryans considered the name as forming part of a man's nature. The Hindus, too, believe that it exercises a profound influence over the destinies of its bearer. For example, the Laws of Manu enjoin that a man shall not marry a woman who bears the name of a serpent, a barbarous race, a slave, or any ugly object.

Among the Cham of Cambodia every child undergoes the operation known as "Molot," the "Haircutting," a rite which has much in common with the "Tonsuring" of the Brahminist Hindus and the non-Mussulman natives of Cambodia. It even bears some resemblance to the ceremony of Christian baptism as it was observed in the days of the early Church under the name given to it by the Early Fathers of "Regeneration of the Soul." Both centre round the rite of purification with holy water and both show the neophyte in that same robe of spotless white which is the symbol of the pure life on which he enters.

A Hindu legend relates that Siva himself instituted this ceremony when he baptized his grandson, the child of Genesa. It took place on the holy mountain of Keylasa in the centre of a marvellous island inhabited by spirits, and secured from the intrusion of mortals by a great lake filled with a liquid on which nothing could float.

An odd day and year is chosen for the celebration of the rite. If the novice is of illustrious parentage a wooden erection is put up and painted to resemble the legendary Mount Keylasa. Two paths are made leading to the top and bordered with shrubs. The one faces to the East and is used by the minor officials, the other facing the West is destined for the presiding priest only.

Some of the deacons now play on archaic instruments such as castanets of bronze, and a novel feature of the orchestra is a kettle-drum with an ingenious contrivance by which each side is struck alternately with a stone ball.

The child, dressed in a long white robe studded with small pieces of metal, advances towards the priest who shaves the crown of his head and lays the hair removed on a snow-white linen cloth. Then priest and neophyte ascend the path to the top of the imitation Keylasa where a large circular basin awaits them. The youth, with a cotton crown on his head, is at once sprinkled with holy water and baptized while some children carefully wipe his feet and march round him holding torches. This circumambulation is repeated nineteen times in honour of the novice's nineteen souls. Throughout the East many souls are accredited to every human being. Of these one alone is deemed immortal. The vital soul resides in the navel, the supreme soul in the bosom.

The young Cham only receives the minimum of education. The priests teach the boys the first principles of reading and writing. In the first lessons the pupils learn by heart the letters of the alphabet, each letter representing, according to Hindu belief, one of the divinities which make their dwelling-place in the human body. After the alphabet come the names of the animals which symbolize the years of the duodenary cycle. The remuneration of the teachers consists of a present of eggs and a bottle of spirits and is due at the beginning of the first lesson. The Cham, however, are not apt pupils, being incorrigibly lazy and it is quite a triumph if a woman knows the elements of housekeeping. When we tried to make laundresses of some of the women in our escort we discovered the depths of their ignorance and stupidity. The articles we sent to be washed came back as dirty as when they went, for the sole idea of washing was to beat the object a certain number of times against a stone. The number of times was a fixed quantity beyond which the laundress refused to go, even if the dirt remained unshaken!

But if the domestic education of the women is neglected what shall be said of their moral education which is practically non-existent? Here, as elsewhere in the Far East, a woman is regarded as requiring nothing more than a knowledge of etiquette and her instruction is complete when she can recite by heart all the rules which govern social intercourse and constitute good manners. Some of these rules seem nothing less than comic to the European.

For example, to laugh in public as a sign of pleasure is strictly forbidden, but it is the height of good form to yawn when bored. When the flax is being gathered in it is proper to pretend to be drunk, for the plant is thereby encouraged to preserve its inebriating qualities.

When a domestic utensil, such as a cooking-pot, becomes broken with use the good housewife will do nothing so ill-advised as to throw it away. Good breeding as well as respect, which is due to inanimate objects just as much as to living persons, exact that the faithful servant shall be hung on the piles on which the house stands and in due time be graciously abandoned to a sudden flood. Hence the enormous number of utensils of all descriptions which are to be seen in the rivers of Cambodia and other countries inhabited by the Cham.

Lessons in etiquette, which are obligatory on both boys and girls, are varied most pleasantly with games of all kinds. Of these perhaps the most popular are the foot races which are organized for children of all ages. The competitors are handicapped according to their years and intense is the excitement when the signal is given to start. The prizes awarded to the winners are generally bananas or mangoes, whichever is in season. When the sugar cane is ripe the children are very fond of a game which is played in this wise.

A stick of sugar cane is put on the ground. The player takes a knife and his task is to cut the stalk into five pieces in three strokes. If he is a skilled performer he makes the second cut in such a way that two of the pieces lie close enough together to be slashed through with the final stroke. The rules forbid the player to use his hands to arrange the pieces so that the second stroke requires no little skill.

If the canes cannot be obtained from the paternal field recourse must be had to the shops, and then a contest ensues in which each child tries to avoid being left to pay the bill. To settle this thorny point lots are drawn, for the first comers have a great advantage. The fortunate player on whom the lot falls has the right of selecting the largest stalk from the dealer's stock, taking care that the bottom section is of normal form. He now balances the cane before him, and with one slash of his knife cuts it in two before it has had time to fall. He is entitled to keep the part he has cut off and if he is skilful it will be a large one. The second player now takes the rest of the stick and performs the same operation. The others follow in turn, the various sections are compared and the owner of the shortest piece has the honour of paying for all after which they devour the booty with the solemnity of a public ceremony.

The children pick up a smattering of musical knowledge and never lose an opportunity of performing on their fathers' gongs. Sometimes they play together and occasionally attain the height of a recognizable melody when the instruments are of much the same pitch and the touch of the artist is light. Children of a more serious disposition are initiated into the mysteries of chess, a game which is played all the world over. The Cham chessman is very similar to ours and the board has also sixty-four squares. The castle, however, is replaced by a general, the bishops by canoes, and the pawns by fishes. The object of each player is to put the opposing king in check and the means adopted are virtually the same as in our game.

CHAPTER III

RITES AND SUPERSTITIONS

The beginnings of Islam in Indo-China—Rites which accompany initiation into the priestly caste—The gods of the Cham—Temples—Resemblance between the architecture of the Cham and that of the Kmer—Phallic rites—A visit to a royal sepulchre.

THE date of the introduction of Islam into Indo-China has never been more than approximately fixed. The better opinion is that it made its way into the country in the twelfth century through the medium of Persian or Arab traders. However that may be, the new faith maintained itself more or less in its primitive purity among the Cham, thanks largely to the zeal of the Malays who had proved ready converts and migrated into Indo-China, and more especially Cambodia, in large numbers from the fourteenth century onwards. In Annam, on the other hand, Islam was speedily blended with Hinduism to form a compound in which the original ingredients almost defied recognition.

Among the Mohammedan Cham, known as the Cham Bani, the head of the priestly caste is called " Pô Gru " or " Ong Gru," titles the sense of which may be rendered by "Leader of the Faithful." He is selected from the Imôns, the priesthood who are assisted in the discharge of their ceremonial duties by various religious officials of lower rank.

The rank of a priest is indicated by the length of the scarlet and gold tassels on his turban. Otherwise there is no distinction in the costume which consists of a white sarong, a white shirt fastened with yellow glass buttons and a white girdle also ornamented with tassels. The crook is a long rattan stalk carried in the hand. The High Priest's crook is distinguished by having its roots plaited together to form a kind of basket.

Few of the priests read Arabic and that with difficulty, while the surahs they recite by heart bear only a distant resemblance to the Koran. The very word "Koran" is unfamiliar. It is usually referred to as "The Book of Islam," or "The Book of Praise," or the "Treatise of the Faith."

In Annam the Ramadan lasts only three days, though the priests observe the fast for the full prescribed month.

On the evening before the fast begins each priest makes his way to the mosque and takes up his station in the building with his impedimenta. He is careful not to forget his minimum of necessaries. His first act is to spread out with meticulous care the mat which is to serve him for a bed. At one end of this he places a cube of lacquered wood, his pillow. Next he solemnly unrols the palm leaves on which the sacred lines have been engraved with some sharp instrument. Then he hangs his string of amber beads on the wall. As earthly indulgences are not entirely forbidden to him, he takes good care to bring his cigarettes and the apparatus for preparing betel and tea.

As long as the fast lasts he is prohibited from leaving the building, so the two vessels containing water for the nine liturgical ablutions are set up under the porch just within reach. These ablutions are a very serious part of the business, for it is absolutely essential that no part of the ceremony should be omitted, even in forgetfulness.

First he washes his hands, spraying the water up to his elbows, then his mouth, nostrils, forehead, and finally his feet as far as the ankles. Woe to him if he forgets to recite his five daily prayers or his nightly salaam, religious exercises which he usually consigns to oblivion at other times! The meticulous observance of the rites during these four weeks is a guarantee of sanctity and the redemption of sins, past, present and prospective.

Of these sins the commonest are breaches of the multifarious regulations, affecting both the Kaphir and Bani priests, prohibiting the consumption of certain specified foods. That sins of this character should be distressingly frequent is hardly surprising when we remember that each month, and even each day of the month, has its particular prohibition. Thus stews, hashes, hare and poultry are strictly forbidden on Mondays in the second month. All foods containing oil and dark-coloured meat may not be touched on Thursdays in the fifth month. Prohibitions so strict and comprehensive show the road to certain transgression in a country where in the nature of things there can be little variety of diet.

Historians have noted in all peoples, whatever the degree of civilization that has been attained, the prevalence of the idea that some intermediary is necessary to establish communication between man and his God. Thus, in Egypt of the Pharaohs, the King was considered the son of God, and as such the proper medium through which his subjects should address their deity. This sacred office of the King was recognized by the deity himself. On certain appointed days the statue of the god made some conventional sign to indicate his approval and assent. We have the evidence of bas-reliefs in the temples to show that this fiction was still maintained in the days of the Roman Empire. At a subsequent period the sacred function was delegated to a special priestly caste; under the later Empire we find the High Priests of Amon at Thebes usurping the royal authority in its entirety.

Professor Foucart, in his "History of Religions,"* shows that the origin of the sacerdotal caste is to be sought in remote antiquity. Man has always experienced the need of a privileged class, set apart for the purpose of ensuring the observance of

* See Bibliography at end.

certain religious rites and securing their transmission from generation to generation in their primitive purity. These rites, which are usually simple in character and in essentials common to all religions, are generally accompanied by mystic phrases, the sum of which constitutes Ritual. As the phrases are often high-sounding and impressive, historians have been tempted to attribute to them a meaning which is not warranted in fact. In most cases the words used do nothing more than define the character of the ceremonial act which they accompany. But as the essence of Magic is the endowment of a simple phrase or object with an ulterior mystical significance it is not surprising that the ritual-makers should spare no pains to produce an illusion in the minds of the worshippers. Their obvious motive is to exploit, in the interest of their own class, a science which results in material advantages.

The education of the priests is not confined to the study of the secret language but extends to a knowledge of the special objects used in religious ceremonies. Consequently a period of initiation, a phenomenon noticed in all ages and among all races, is regarded as essential for aspirants to the priestly ranks. The rites which mark this period of initiation are substantially similar among all races. They are directed in the main towards the purification of the neophyte from the sins inherent to the secular state and to set the stamp of legality on his adoption of the religious life. In general, they consist of a rite of separation to mark the abandonment of old ties, a rite of purification proper, and rites of adoption into the new association. From this it is easy to see why ceremonies of this kind always enshrine the metaphor of a death to the old life and a re-birth in the new one. Whether we turn to the Shamans of Siberia, the Lamas of Thibet, the Brahmins of India, the Bonzes of Cambodia, the Padjaos of the Cham, we find the essence of the ceremony identical, however diversified the details may be.

All those familiar with the practice of the Roman Catholic Church know that among certain of the Orders the ceremony of entry or taking the veil includes the Burial Service followed by a hymn of triumph to hail the resurrection of the new spirit reclaimed from the world. In other religions the procedure is a heavy sleep from which the novice awakes to find himself consecrated by Heaven.

The rudiments of this idea are found in the rites which mark the ordination of a Padjao among the Kaphir Cham. A Padjao is not so much a priestess as a prophetess in whom resides the power of foretelling the future and also of protecting from all evil when the Spirit—or rather the "Transport," to adopt the professional phrase used by her class—takes her.

Properly speaking the Padjao does not "take vows," but rather devotes herself to strict celibacy. If she is married when the heavenly call comes to her her husband must leave her at once. The observance of continence, apparent if not actual, is obligatory, and any breach of this rule would be visited by the Spirits with the most condign punishment affecting both the transgressor and her accomplice.

According to a certain priest of Phanrang, "Padjao" means "Princess," and the modern priestesses perform the functions which formerly devolved on the ladies of royal blood who filled religious offices in ancient Champa. On the other hand, "Padjand" in old Javanese, means "Moonlight," and in this connection it is significant that the Cham identify with the moon one of their most highly venerated divinities, the "Celestial Padjao." However this may be, the ordination of these women in Annam is marked by some very curious ceremonies. The novice is selected by the Priestess herself when, feeling herself advancing in years, the choice of a successor becomes an urgent matter. The fortunate object of her selection receives the name of "Happiness of the Human Race." She falls on her knees before her spiritual mother and offers her two eggs, a cup of spirits and some betel, a sign of her dutiful submission. The recipient of these gifts now takes off her girdle and passes it round the head of her newly appointed assistant who is bound henceforth to appear in this form of turban at every public ceremony. Then they both swallow three grains of rice and salt, symbols of plenty. The novice next falls into a sleep or trance, during which her soul departs to the moon

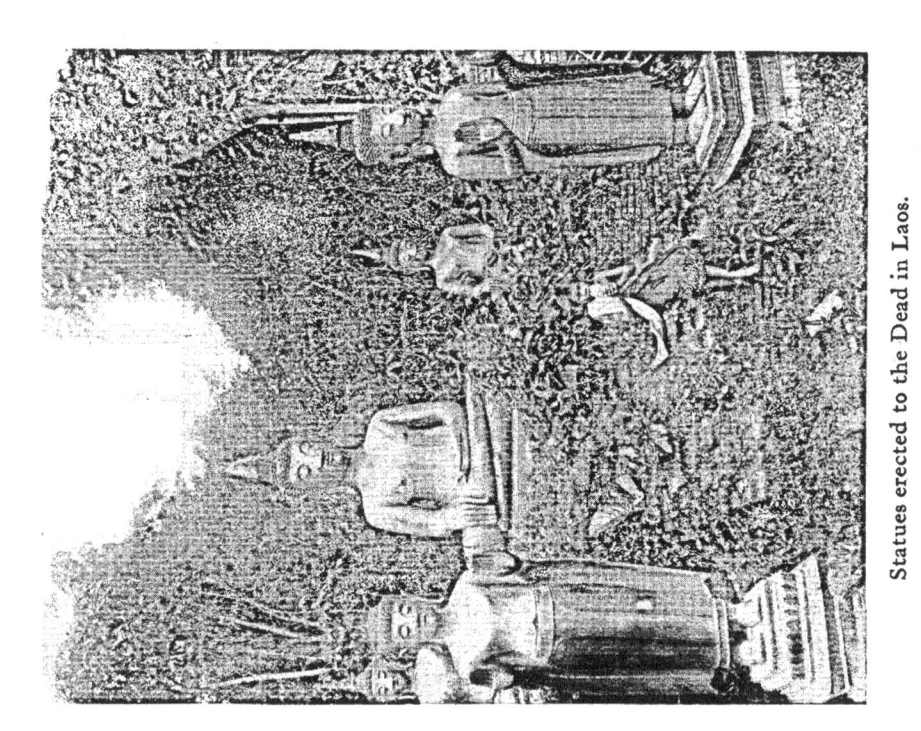

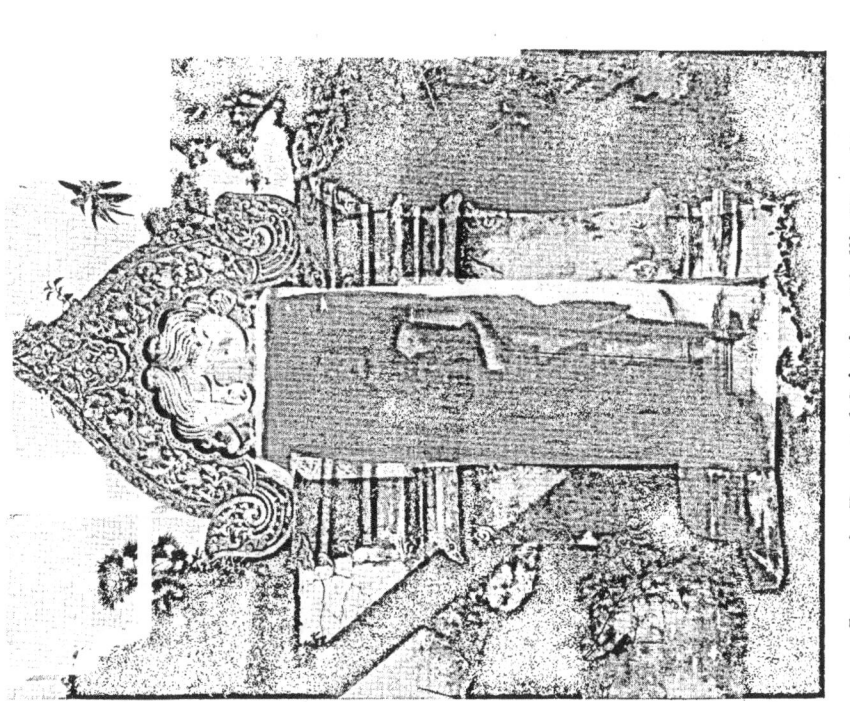

Image of a Departed Saint in a Phallic Temple.

Statues erected to the Dead in Laos.

[*To face p.* 272.

Shrine of a Laotian Priest.

The Interior of the Shrine.

RITES AND SUPERSTITIONS

to be consecrated by the great " Celestial Padjao," who will reveal to her all the mysteries of life and the secrets of mortals. This trance is, of course, the counterpart of the symbolic death and resurrection which we have seen to be characteristic of the change from the earthly to the heavenly life.

During this ceremony, which is called the " Deification of the Padjao," the Faithful sacrifice a black kid and burn eaglewood the odour of which is supposed to be particularly agreeable to the dwellers in the Heavens.

Priestess and novice next indulge in a religious dance known as the " Tania." In their left hands they wave a scarlet scarf while holding a fan in their right. Then taking a betel leaf the priestess passes it through the flame of a candle and offers it to her who is thenceforward to share her office. It must not be imagined, however, that the novice secures her entry into the priestly caste by this ceremony. Her admission is temporary and is only confirmed when, after a novitiate of a year, the Gods indicate their consent to delegate their powers to her. A second ordination is thus necessary which must be attended by all those who were present at the first. If, however, some of the original spectators have died in the meantime the rites are satisfied if they are represented by members of their families of the same sex.

On the evening before this second ceremony

all those who are to take part in it must take the bath of purification.

As the approval of the Celestial Padjao is by no means a foregone conclusion her answer is awaited by the priestess with some trepidation. With a view to securing her favourable regard the latter brings an offering in a basket on which she sets up two lighted candles. These candles are the medium through which the divine will is to be revealed. If they go out or burn with a smoky flame this is a clear indication to the novice to abandon her hopes and return to her old life. In that case a successor to her will be found in due time. But if the candles burn up brightly the year's apprenticeship has been judged sufficient to qualify her for divine approval.

A person whose assistance is indispensable to the Padjao is the "Meûdoun," an individual who does not belong to the priestly caste but who is in constant touch with the deities by virtue of his office. The period of initiation is short and is occupied by learning to perform on the drum and reciting liturgical phrases. The "Meûdoun" is appointed by his predecessor and enters upon his duties immediately. His services are requisitioned when exorcisms, incantations or divinations are on foot.

Among the Cham of Cambodia another variety of ceremonies marks the ordination of their Prophetess. In the first place, the social status enjoyed by that official is not as high as in Annam. She seems to inspire a kind of awe rather than any sentiment of veneration. Here the rites of initiation savour of Demonology.

The requirements of time and place are satisfied by a clear moonlight night and a deserted ant-heap in the depths of the forest. The prospective Prophetess appears and with one sweep with a sword severs a cock in twain from its head to its tail. Then, totally naked, she executes a frenzied dance, accompanied by 'weird incantations before her victim until the mystic moment when, thanks to the powers of magic and the veil of night, the severed halves join together and the resurrected fowl utters a pæan of victory!

Priestesses of all these regions have this in common, that they dress either in white or in black and red. The flesh of swine and lizards is absolutely forbidden, no mean hardship in a portion of the globe where the lizard is regarded as a great delicacy.

It is to be observed that, contrary to the practice prevailing among most semi-barbarous peoples, the Cham allow young and middle-aged women to perform religious functions. The age of twenty is, in fact, the normal time for entering the sacerdotal caste. This is all the more remarkable because it has frequently been demonstrated that among primitive races women are not admitted to the privileges of men until after the menopause.

The Pantheon of the Cham Bani consists of the " Heroes of Civilization " to whom they ascribe the foundation and development of their three ancient capitals. Thus Pô Oulah, or Allah the Mighty, made his residence during the eleventh century in the town of Bal Sri Banôy. It is more than likely that this potentate was the actual conqueror who first brought Islam into Indo-China.

Pô Klong Garaı is said to have founded the second capital, Bal-Hangov, the "City of Pine Trees," the reputed traces of which have been discovered near Hué. Finally Pô Binôsuor shed the lustre of his name on Bal Angouai, the ruins of which are still visible at Cha Bàn in the province of Binh Dinh. Some philologists associate this city with the ancient town of Balonga mentioned by Ptolemy. For this last ruler, however, whose great achievement was the repulse of the Annamite invasion, the Cham have substituted the name of Pô Ramé, a prince of no great fame, who seems to have been a kind of adventurer who sprang into importance by marrying a princess of royal blood.

It need hardly be said that these great heroes are credited with all manner of marvellous exploits. The supernatural even enters into their birth, for they are supposed to have been born of virgin mothers, a detail which enhances their resemblance to the Brahminic divinities. In this connection it may be observed that the members of the Hindu Trinity, Brahma, Vishnu and Siva, with their "Saktis," or wives, Umâ, Lasmî and Kali, are universally confused with the native deities of the Cham either under their own or substituted names. For example, Pô Inö Nögar, the Black Lady, the Queen of Women, is none other than ancient Bhagavati, the sakti of Siva.

The Pantheon of the Kaphir Cham is no less nondescript. At its head stand out three masculine divinities. The first is Pô Amö, Lord of Creation, who bears a close resemblance to Brahma. The second, Pô Yâta, is only an emanation of Pô Amö and reigns over the Vault of Heaven. The third is Pô Allah, an incorporeal deity whose sanctuary is at Mecca and who has been borrowed from the pantheon of the Cham Bani.

Then follows a certain number of female divinities, among whom Pô Inö Nögar of the Cham Bani appears as Pô Yang Inö Nögar Taha, the Great Mother-Goddess of the Kingdom who is endowed with authority over the others. This venerable matron, born, it is said, from a wave of the sea, married no less than ninety-seven husbands. Her offspring, however, amounted to no more than thirty-eight daughters, a poor compliment to the prolific powers of her spouses.

These girls remained virgins all their lives and showed the effects of their enforced celibacy in their sour tempers. This unpleasant characteristic, however, has made them objects of peculiar veneration to the natives whose utilitarian morals teach them to neglect the deities reputed to be amiable and concentrate all their fervour on those considered evilly disposed towards man.

In addition to housing these disagreeable virgins, the Heavens are also the abode of a young queen who can grant or withhold all human joys. Her name is Padjao Yang and she personifies the Moon, the faithful minister of Pô Adityak, the Sun. When the Sun passes before Padjao Yang she shows her good breeding and training by bowing to the ground before her Master, a mark of respect which produces the phenomenon of eclipse. One characteristic which this immortal person shares with her mortal sisters is worthy of remark. She is never more than thirty years old! This figure has been selected probably because thirty is the average number of days in a lunar month. It need hardly be said that she never complains of this burden of youth. Some of the more gallant Cham go further, and seeing her sometimes arrayed in a diaphanous halo, swear that her age never exceeds that of her robe! How many of those same mortal sisters would like to say the same!

The temples in which the ritualistic ceremonies of the Cham take place differ according to the observances of the various sects. Thus the mosques of the Cham Bani are narrow huts which could hardly accommodate a single family. It is doubtful whether more than a dozen are to be found in the whole of Annam. They invariably face west, the direction of Mecca, and for furniture and accessories contain a few mats for the use of the worshippers, a drum to call them to prayer and a pulpit which never seems

RITES AND SUPERSTITIONS 279

to be occupied. On the very holiest of holy days strips of white cloth are hung over this pulpit and spread over the floor. On Fridays is held the general service of prayer, which, however, is usually but sparsely attended. The Koran requires a quorum of forty, but in practice that figure is seldom reached. At the conclusion of this ceremony wine and spirits are freely circulated among the worshippers though these liquids are taboo to the true Mussulman.

The hut-temples of the Siva-worshippers among the Kaphir Cham are not more elaborate. The chief object to be seen in one of these is the " Mukha-Linga," a piece of stone cut to resemble the male organ of generation but adorned with the face of the god Siva, which is made more lifelike by a dressing of coloured plaster. On special occasions this curious object is dressed up in a scarlet mantle. A stone receptacle for holy water and a few other utensils complete the necessary accessories.

These temples, however, are not the only outward and visible signs of religious life among the Cham. A certain number of ancient monuments, which both Annamites and Europeans erroneously call towers, but which are in fact exclusively devoted to religious uses, are carefully preserved. These constructions are always to be found on hills or at other conspicuous points dominating the surrounding country. The choice of the site is not without significance. It is a matter of universal knowledge that most races attach a sacred character to heights.

For example, Mount Sinai and Mount Tabor are mentioned as holy mountains in the Bible. The temple of Delphi stood on a hill. The Acropolis looks over Athens, and the Celts always selected some prominent spot as the scene of their sacrifices.

The best preserved of the temples which date from the days when the kingdom of the Champa stood at its apogee is only a few miles distant from Phanrang. It was built early in the fourteenth century and was consecrated to Pô Klong Garai. I had plenty of opportunity to examine the ruins carefully, for with the sacrilegious indifference of Europeans we had erected on them the lofty mast which was essential to our geodetical operations.

They consisted of a principal building with three annexes. All four faced east and were made of brick. As we made our way into the sanctuary for the first time, through the opening which served for sole entrance and exit, we were greeted by a nauseating smell and the clapping of innumerable wings. The place was literally infested with bats, and, in addition, was pitch dark, so that a torch was a prime necessity.

The interior was not what might have been expected from inspection of the exterior. As access to light and air was only provided by the one narrow doorway, it is not difficult to imagine how the sanctuary had become the favourite resort of all the bats in the district.

A stone altar stood against the back wall. The

upper surface was slightly concave to enable liquids to run off. On one of its sides was a " Mukha-Linga " with black beard and whiskers, which contrasted strangely with the pallor of the face. In the vestibule, with a necklace round its throat was a " Nandi," the White Bull of Siva, which the Cham call " Kapila." He it is who bears away the dead on his back to Keylasa, of which he is the guardian. According to the Hindus the " Nandi " is also Siva's favourite mount and frequently their identities blend in the figure of a Hermit with the body of a man and the head of a bull.

The Samaritans also favoured animal-headed deities. It will be remembered that Thartac had a donkey's head and Anubis that of a dog. Other analogies between various early religious systems readily suggest themselves.

Thus the Babylonian Ishtar stood for the principle of fecundity and must be compared with the goddess Kali, the sakti of Siva, who is also known as " Yomi," the " Fertile Womb."

The Assyrians worshipped another Ishtar, a highly formidable goddess, who always appears in her statues armed with some murderous weapon. This characteristic of cruelty is equally prominent in Kali, the goddess of Blood, Lust and Death, whose statues always represent her grimacing and repulsive with a necklace and bracelets of human skulls and bones.

The doorway of the temple is formed of three granite monoliths of which the two uprights are covered with inscriptions. Above is a bas-relief on a kind of sculptured lintel, representing Siva dancing. It is remarkably well-preserved. The god has six arms. The lowest pair grasp a trident, as is usual in statues of Siva, and a lotus-bloom, which is more generally associated with Vishnu. The middle pair brandish a scimitar and a dagger. The other pair are clasped behind the god's head.

Four small stone elephants complete the accessories of the sanctuary. They represent the wild elephants which, so legend says, entered the temple while it was being built.

There is a broad general resemblance between the temples of the Cham and those of the Kmer who also professed the Brahminic religion. The Kmer also selected rising ground with a wide sweep of view as the site for their sacred edifices. Great care was taken that the main façade should face towards the east. The interior consisted of a single hall with an entrance sometimes so low that it was necessary to stoop to get in. The walls were innocent of all decoration and became damp and clammy in the darkness. The outside walls and especially the doorway, however, were the objects of considerable artistic effort. The doorway in particular was usually surmounted by a lintel with figures of the gods and their distinctive symbols. Thus Vishnu is represented astride of Garuda, the parrot-headed god, Brahma rides on geese and Indra a three-headed elephant. The dancing Siva, with a multitude of arms disposed halo-wise around his head, is one of the commonest figures. I remember seeing one on the façade of the Temple of Pô Klong Garai.

The architecture of the Javanese also furnishes some equally remarkable resemblances.

I have already remarked that the Siva-worshipping Cham, like their Hindu co-religionists, have adopted the symbol of a linga to represent that deity. It is worthy of note in this connection that the Egyptians represented their god Osiris in the form of a phallus, the equivalent of a linga. This phallus-worship made its way into Greece, and especially Babylon where the earliest inscriptions are found engraved on large clay phalli.

Phallus-worship, transformed into linga-worship, was introduced into the Far East by the Hindus. Traces of it have been found in Java. In spite of the distance, Japan also welcomed it along with many other foreign cults but to-day it only remains a tradition in that country, though there are some Japanese villages where huge phalli, made of bamboo covered with canvas, figure in the local processions. At the top of these weird structures is a small opening from which urchins make a pretence of haranguing the crowd.

Barth considers the origin of linga-worship to be wrapped in obscurity. We know that phallic rites were part of the religions of the Veda but that there was no actual phallus-worship.

Some say it came from the west, probably Greece, but it is at least as likely that the Hindus evolved this particular symbolism themselves. However that may be, it is certain that the cult made its appearance simultaneously with Siva-worship.

The linga is often represented in conjunction with the yoni, the female organ and the symbol of Devi, wife of Siva.

It should be said at once that these objects are treated symbolically, not realistically. The linga is a simple cone, the yoni a triangular prism. This abstract treatment is said by some to be the outcome of a protest against idolatry, in proof of which they point to the fact that Vishnu and ⸨Lasmî his wife are represented respectively by a fossil-shell, the Calagrama, and a plant of the sweet-basil species, the Tulosi. It should be added that Hindu art is remarkable for its freedom from suggestiveness and that, in whatever guise the mystery of life is symbolized, the form selected is one which never provokes indecent ideas.

The Kaphir Cham of Phantiet and Phanry have another cult of the same kind, the worship of the yoni in another form. This rite is the introduction into some cavity, the hollow of a tree perhaps, or the fissure of a rock or the burrow of an animal, of a large rudely carved wooden cylinder. The worshipper recites the wish on the fulfilment of which his hopes are set while pouring spirits on the cylinder. He makes his prayer to Pô Yang Dari, the Shameless Goddess who can cure children of all diseases.

The primitive conception which underlies all this symbolism must, of course, be traced to the belief in imitative magic, which endows the performance of a ritualistic act with the power of inducing other beings or objects to imitate that act. It is thus quite natural that the idea of fecundity, the word being taken in its widest sense, should be closely associated with every phase and form of phallus-worship.

It is a thousand pities that from the beginning of the nineteenth century the spread of pharisaical prudery has prevented even those best qualified by long residence among uncivilized races from probing into questions concerning sex and publishing the results of their researches. The explorers of the eighteenth century were not so hampered, and their observations, from which the veil of priggish reticence is withdrawn, furnish us with much valuable information on a department of human activity which is of surpassing interest and importance to the ethnographer.

The Kmer took their architecture from the Hindus. There is an obvious resemblance between the religious edifices of the two peoples and in addition both built their temples in naturally secluded places, a preference which is amply explained by the nature of a religion which endows its deities with so formidable a character that only priests may approach them. The rank and file of worshippers have to be content with following the sacrifices with their thoughts. They congregate in the outer paved courts of the temples and make themselves shelters of bamboos and leaves. In some places asylums for ailing pilgrims are built in the immediate neighbourhood of the temples. These hospices are under the charge of monks who care for the stricken wayfarers.

Of the slight differences which distinguish the buildings of the two peoples the most noticeable is the treatment of the roof. The Kmer roof is a kind of ogival dome recalling the edifices of the Arabs, while the Hindus crown their quadrangular pyramids with a four-sided cone.

The artistic skill of the Kmer has mainly been lavished on pyramids, sacred pools and rock-surfaces, many of which are entirely covered with figures of gods. There are also many towers which serve as shrines for images of the deities. It will be remembered that the stupas of the Hindus are devoted to a similar use.

The temples face east, an arrangement which is explained by the fact that the services usually take place early in the morning on that side of the building which receives a maximum of sun. On the other hand certain temples devoted to the worship of the Gods of the Lower Regions face to the west, for the reason that the rites are always celebrated at sunset.

The statuary of the Cham seems to owe much both to the Kmer and the Hindus. One fact, indeed, is incontestable, that the human type represented is clearly the Aryan, whereas the Cham artists spent all their lives among men of a totally different type. It is plain that they did not take their own people for their models. The explanation can only be that the Cham imported their art of sculpture just as they imported their religion. Another remarkable fact is that in their statues of gods and prophets the figures are almost destitute of clothing, while their kings and heroes are always represented in gorgeous apparel. In this connection it may be remembered that the prophets of one of the two principal sects of the Jainists call themselves the " Digambara," which means " They who are clothed in space."

The usual type of headdress is conical or cylindrical in shape. The lobes of the ears are elongated and pierced with holes from which earrings are hung. The feet are always bare. The figures of women show them as of the same type as the men, and their hair is dressed in similar fashion. The upper half of the body is uncovered, exposing their breasts which are full and perfect in shape. The lower half is concealed by a kind of skirt secured at the waist by a girdle with fringes which sweep to their feet. Their ears, neck, legs and arms are adorned with jewels.

These main features are found reproduced in the few antique statues still to be found among the Cham.

I have a lively recollection of one occasion on which, so I was told, I was the first European to enter a certain temple. No experience in my varied life has left a more indelible impression on my memory. The Mission was engaged in scientific operations between Phantiet and Phanry, the ancient home of the Cham, and our headquarters consisted of a number of rude huts in the very heart of the forest.

One day I received a visit from the headman of a neighbouring village, a diminutive individual with a face the colour of a dead leaf. I had previously rendered him some service by treating him for severe ophthalmia and he now proposed to show his gratitude by revealing to me the whereabouts of a ruined temple which was so concealed in the forest as hitherto to defy discovery by Europeans. He told me I should find two statues, in excellent preservation, of kings who had been raised to the rank of deities by their subjects. Also I was to have every opportunity of sketching and taking photographs.

The temple was not more than thirty miles distant, so my expedition was duly announced as a mere excursion for pleasure. We set out, accompanied by two young natives, my usual companions in my private wanderings, who had charge of the photographic and other apparatus as well as our arms and provisions. Our journey was without incident, for my kind guide gave me the fullest instructions as to the route to the Temple of Song Sui.

Statue of an Ancient King of Cambodia.  Statue of an Ancient Queen of Cambodia.

An Old Cham Temple in a Cambodian Forest.

[*To face p.* 288

The House of a Cham Aristocrat.

A Cottage Home in Cambodia.

[*To face p* 289.

RITES AND SUPERSTITIONS

This remarkable sanctuary is the tomb of an ancient king of the Cham and the object of a very popular pilgrimage at certain seasons of the year. It consists of three separate pavilions in a large enclosure which is divided into two halves, one higher than the other. The lower half is used by the general public while the upper is reserved for the family of any worshipper who desires to make a sacrificial offering.

The statue of the King is in the central building. It is cut from a single block of granite and coloured to show a robe of red and gold. On the King's head is a fez to which a golden helmet is added on special occasions. The neck and the ears are pierced with holes from which necklaces and earrings are suspended. The eyebrows meet above the nose, the moustaches are twisted upwards and the eyes are half-closed.

The door of the central pavilion is of beaten iron, hand-forged. Of the two other pavilions one alone remains, a picturesque ruin. The other has completely disappeared in the undergrowth, a few stones remaining to mark the site. In the survivor there is a statue of one of the King's two wives standing between two elaborate steles. The Queen's hair is arranged in the shape of a cone, a fashion which is typical of the statues of the Kmer. The nails are stained red, and all the fingers (except the middle one), and also the thumb, are covered with rings.

A balustrade, very similar to those which decorate

European tombs, runs round behind this pavilion. In this enclosure an unhappy black goat is chained up, destined to decapitation at the precise moment when the sacrifice is consummated. The floor is made of stone with a narrow trench through which the blood is drained off.

Having exhibited the resemblances between this temple and those of the Kmer I propose to suggest other resemblances, not less striking, between it and some of the ancient Egyptian tombs.

The royal steles of the Egyptians are of a fairly regular outline, gently rounded at the top and usually semicircular. As is well known, their purpose was to hand down to posterity the identity and genealogy of a particular Pharaoh. The monarch's statue, on the other hand, was the actual living image of the departed, for it was universally believed that the dead man's double returned to make its abode in his form. It is even possible that the first idea of statuary had its origin in this conception of a magical reanimation.

The deceased was always represented in his robes of state (however scanty) and seated on the throne. Food was set on a small table within his reach. The figure was dressed, covered with jewels and smothered in perfumes. The nails were coloured with henna and the eyes blackened. Every step in the proceedings was accompanied by formal chanting.

In the case of royal statues these ceremonies were observed up to the twelfth dynasty. They then fell into desuetude and it became customary merely to paint up the statue with clothes, jewels and other accoutrements in as realistic a manner as possible. In the British Museum there are three large wooden statues, taken from royal tombs of the thirteenth century, which are remarkable illustrations of this process of evolution in statuary.

It is to this process of evolution, due to a change of ideas, that we must ascribe the gradual disappearance of the belief that the soul of the deceased returned to dwell in his statue, and also of the equally primitive belief that the purpose and meaning of offering a sacrifice was to furnish the deceased with food in his new existence.

I was extremely interested in my visit with its valuable discoveries, and it may readily be imagined that I was in great haste to return to camp and develop my plates. My guide announced that he knew a route which would save us many miles. The morning passed uneventfully enough. On many occasions we crossed the tracks of elephants, but I was not to be moved from my purpose. Hunting was out of fashion that day. We were too bent on getting home.

To be ready for any emergency I gave one of my rifles to the Cham chief who was a good shot. Some alligators were sunning themselves on the sandy banks of a stream. We broke in upon their siesta without hesitation and without apology.

My companion informed me that we should pass

through a certain village and that, at the rate at which we were then marching, we should reach it before nightfall. However, our two boys, less accustomed to forced marching than their elders, began to show signs of distress. I could see them shifting from one shoulder to the other the bamboo-pole from which our impedimenta was slung and they soon began to complain of the thorns in the path which lacerated their feet. The two boys were quite young, the elder being perhaps sixteen. They had been attached to the Mission for more than six months, a long period for natives, who dislike regular occupation and are ever in search of change. I had a peculiar affection for these two. They were indefatigable servants and remarkably docile and even-tempered.

Their complaints seemed reasonable enough and to relieve them the chief and I shouldered the bamboo-pole. We set off again but soon put a large and growing distance between ourselves and the younger generation lagging behind. Meanwhile the sun was hastening towards his western bed. At one time the loiterers seemed to have put on a spurt, but the effort exhausted itself and they fell behind once more. At a bend of the path we decided to wait until the boys came up. We kept ourselves carefully out of sight lest the vision of our halt should inspire them to a similar indulgence.

Some minutes passed, but no one appeared. Had the rascals given up the attempt to follow us or had they lost their way? I ran back to the bend in the path. The route by which we had come stretched away in a straight line for miles, but no human being was in sight.

Our coolies had fled!

The mask-like countenance of my companion betrayed neither surprise nor any other emotion. The truants were not of his faith nor did they hail from his village. They were but vulgar Annamites, at best a race of sneaking hucksterers. His sympathies were evidently confined to the faithful of his own parish.

I confess I was irritated by his obvious indifference. To my knowledge the forest through which we had passed was infested with tigers and the stunted leafless trees were the most illusory refuge from the brutes. I had an uncomfortable premonition that our pleasure-party, so happily begun, was entering the realms of tragedy.

In the course of our three years' residence in southern Annam no less than twelve natives had been devoured by tigers. Several of the victims were attached to the Mission, and on more than one occasion I had been the hapless witness of their horrible sufferings.

On one occasion a coolie suddenly vanished through the wicker-work floor of our hut, which was built on piles quite nine-feet high. The tiger, however, had climbed on to a baulk of timber which was lying on the ground below and using this as a platform had succeeded in catching hold of one end of his victim's waist-cord which happened to be hanging through the interstices of the floor. The beast gave a violent tug and dragged the hapless coolie through the floor. The man, taken by surprise, was helpless and fell, an unresisting prey, into the tiger's jaws.

I feel considerable diffidence in telling a story which I myself should not have believed had the tragedy not occurred before my very eyes.

On another occasion one of my colleagues and myself were taking our evening meal, waited on by a Cham boy about twelve years old. It was shortly after seven, I think, and the rain was falling in torrents. All at once we heard a shriek proceeding from the direction of the kitchen and in a moment the boy entered, white with terror.

"The Tiger," he could hardly get the words out, "seized hold of my coat." He showed us a huge rent in the flimsy material which covered his trembling body. Outside it was pitch dark. We had no lamps and it seemed highly risky to venture forth with so undesirable a neighbour watching us. We quickly set about protecting ourselves by barricading the entrance to the room with a palisade of wattles. The real mystery was how the beast had made its way into the enclosure, guarded as it was by a solid fence made of baulks of timber and forming a veritable blockhouse. An hour later we heard the stamping of hoofs, violent kicks and terror-stricken neighing. Then silence. About midnight our light went out.

It would have been madness to go to the kitchen to fetch another, so we found ourselves condemned to wait in the darkness, listening for every sound and our nerves on edge. Needless to say, sleep was impossible. At dawn we ventured out. Everything was in confusion. Our horses had broken loose and stampeded over the fence. One of them lay disembowelled before us and half its hindquarters had disappeared. On the face of the embankment on which our house was elevated, immediately before the door of the room where we had been sitting, were the traces of a tiger's paws clearly visible in the clay.

The boy had not been mistaken. He had indeed been seized by the beast and owed his safety to his worn and tattered clothing. The marks of teeth and claws on some of the baulks of the palisade showed us that the visitor had climbed over. We learnt one lesson from this experience. Our camp, with its solid rampart ten feet high, was only an illusory protection against a really determined man-eater!

All these horrible recollections—and many others which can find no place here, this not being a story of adventure—flashed through my mind in the space of a few seconds.

Meanwhile time was flying and night came down on us unheralded by twilight as in Europe. Our search was all in vain and no answer came to our repeated shouts. The coolies had gone.

It was not until late at night and after much

struggling that we reached the village. In spite of the friendly light thrown by a torch I remained all night a prey to the most vivid hallucinations. Time after time I watched a huge tiger spring out of the darkness with the corpse of one of the missing boys in his jaws.

Two days later the elder of the two came into the village. He was shivering with fever and dared not present himself before me, so I went to see him. Ghastly was the story he had to unfold. Just before the bend in the path which I have mentioned the two boys had been unable to go further and had sat down. When we were out of sight they had attempted to continue their journey, but before they had advanced a few yards a huge tiger had sprung upon the younger, while the elder had remained dumb with astonishment and terror. Helpless with fear and weariness the survivor had wandered in the forest and at last, in sheer desperation, had climbed into a tree expecting at every moment to share the fate of his luckless companion.

The Cham chief, who listened to this harrowing story with an air of indifference and barely concealed scorn, at length delivered himself of an aphorism:

" Fear claims far more victims than courage."

CHAPTER IV

RITES AND SUPERSTITIONS (*continued*)

Agrarian rites—Tabooed ricefields—Secret ploughing—Sleeping rice—Various uses of eaglewood—How the Cham procure it—Public festivals and holy days.

OF all the races which inhabit Indo-China the Cham come easily first for the variety and individuality of their agrarian rites. There is practically no difference between the Bani and Kaphir in this respect. Both peoples recognize three kinds of sacred ricefields in which no manner of work may be carried on without the accompaniment of a special ritual. If, in the course of ploughing a ricefield, excessive fatigue has been occasioned to either man or beast, sufficient to cause illness, the field becomes taboo, " Hamu Tabung." The evil eye has been cast upon it, and no remedy exists but to sell the contaminated place at no matter what sacrifice. It need hardly be said that the only possible purchasers are the few Annamite Christians who are scattered throughout these regions. The Buddhist Annamites shun such a spot as if it were plague-stricken. The cause of the mischance is supposed to be the presence of some ancient burial-ground, the existence of which was not suspected.

Every village has its two or three sacred ricefields the "Hamu Canrauv," which are invariably the first to be ploughed. As a rule they are the property of the local aristocracy. The owner with his wife, who plays the principal part in the ceremony, goes to the field in question, either in the evening or at dawn. They lay down a mat at one corner and on it place two eggs, a cup of spirits and three betel leaves, which the wife offers as a sacrifice to Pô Olwah Tak Alâ, the great Lord of the Underworld, begging him to accept them. To set a good example, husband and wife share the good things between them while making three furrows round the field. After this ceremony ploughing and sowing may proceed in the ordinary manner.

There are also fields where cultivation is forbidden, the "Hamû Klaik Lavâ." To speak more accurately the interdict only extends to open cultivation and the tabooed area is ploughed and worked in secret. These operations are accomplished in the following manner. With the first signs of day the husband and wife go to the field and after making three furrows in silence return home. When morning comes they walk to the place and profess the greatest astonishment that the work of ploughing has already begun. "Who is the kindly Spirit," they exclaim, " who has worked for us while we slept ? " Without loss of time they run back to their house to fetch suitable offerings.

So great a marvel as a field which cultivates itself is worthy to be consecrated with a sacrifice. Accordingly they first bury five pieces of betel in the ground and throw a handful of rice into the three magic furrows, after which plough and bullocks are sprinkled with holy water and the remaining operations may be carried out without further concealment.

A sacrifice is offered as soon as the stalks have emerged from the ground and are tall enough " to hide the doves." Another marks the moment of flowering, and a third, the most important, celebrates the time of harvest. On this last occasion the owner cuts off the heads of three of the stalks and wraps them up in a cloth. The next step is to pass them through the smoke of a fire in which several pieces of eaglewood are burning. These ears are the first-fruits offered to the goddess Pô Nögar, and they are afterwards hung in the owner's house until the next sowing time comes round. The same field will then be sown from the rice thus gathered.

For " unconsecrated " ricefields the ritual is less complicated. When the harvesting is due the oldest woman of the group is selected to cut three tufts, which she sets with much pomp against the bank which borders the field and harangues the grain as yet ungathered in the following terms :

" Follow the example you see here before you and you will be worthy of a place in my barns." After this address harvesting proceeds without interruption.

When the grain is safely gathered in, the Cham believe that it sleeps all day and only awakes at night. It would be the height of desecration and imprudence to disturb its slumbers, and consequently we soon learnt the futility of asking our hosts for paddy in the daytime. We were invariably informed that we must wait until night. It was only at a late hour that the owner would consent to open the door of his barn and give us what we wanted.

There was a very curious rite, fallen into desuetude since our occupation in 1888, which accompanied the gathering of the precious essence known as eaglewood or aloe-wood. This substance is mentioned in the Bible, the Egyptian papyri, and by many Greek, Hindu and Arab writers. It seems to have been used extensively for embalming the dead, as also for combining with camphor to make a kind of incense burnt in the temples. It appears under different names, "ahalot" in Hebrew, "aghäluhy" in Arabic, "ἀγάλλοχον" in Greek, "agaru" in Sanscrit. The Cham call it "galao." Portuguese explorers, who seem to have been the first to discover its commercial value, used the Arabic name and translated it "pao de Aguila." In Latin this becomes "lignum aquilae," and so, in modern tongues, "eaglewood," or "agalwood," "adlerholz," and "bois d'aigle."

This essence has attracted the attention of travellers of all nations owing to its various properties, and was formerly a commercial product of great importance among the Cham. It is found all over this region, which seems to have been the land of its origin, for it is never met with further north than the thirteenth or fourteenth degree of latitude.

Botanists are not yet agreed as to the class of trees from which it is produced. The most up-to-date investigators assert that it is produced by diseases due to malnutrition in certain trees such as the *aquilaria secundaria*, *aloexylum agallochum*, and *aquilaria agallocha*, all of the family of the *aquilarinæa*. It is an aromatic substance with a slightly resinous odour and bitter to the taste.

The natives distinguish three varieties, according to their commercial value. The first quality, which is almost impossible to find to-day, commanded a price of no less than fifty-four pounds a kilogramme. The medium quality was worth sixteen pounds for the same quantity, and the cheapest quality was worth rather more than one pound a kilogramme.

The variety of uses to which this accommodating substance can be put is astonishing, though it is not suitable for cabinet-making.

It is largely used for incense. When thrown into a fire it melts like wax and gives off an odour which is supposed to be particularly pleasing to the Gods. Certain other of its properties are no less useful to man, who values more material favours. Thus, for example, it has very great value as a safeguard against dysentery, which is prevalent throughout Indo-China. No Mandarin in all this region ventures forth on a journey without having a supply of this indispensable medicine with him.

Of course, the oriental imagination is not content to confine the virtues of this substance to those which have been demonstrated by actual experience. The supernatural is bound to appear somewhere, and accordingly all kinds of magical powers are also attributed to it. Thus every person who bears this talisman will never succumb, however long he may be deprived of food. On the contrary, his body will no longer be subjected to earthly necessities but will enter on a state of divinity which requires no sustenance. The Mandarins have every reason to appreciate this arrangement, especially at the time of their presentation at the Imperial Court at Hué. Etiquette exacts that until the Sovereign actually enters the throne-room they must remain quite motionless, and they sometimes find themselves compelled to stand for hours without stirring!

With properties so invaluable as this, it is hardly to be wondered at that eaglewood figured largely in the gifts presented by the sovereign of Annam to the Emperor of China by way of tribute every three years. To ensure a sufficient supply, all trade in this substance, whether for home or export, was strictly prohibited, but the prohibition was removed after our occupation, when the obligation of tribute was suspended and finally annulled.

According to Masoudi, the celebrated Arab writer, eaglewood has a celestial origin.

" After the Fall, when Adam had been driven from Heaven by the angel, he fled to Mount Rahoun in the island of Ceylon. Before leaving Paradise, however, he contrived to snatch some leaves from the trees and sewed them together to make a garment. To his astonishment they shrivelled up immediately and the winds scattered them to every corner of India. It is said, but of the truth God alone can judge, that these remnants of our first father's vestment gave birth to all the perfumes of Asia, and, among them, to eaglewood."

Other legends of Hindu origin say that the aloes tree grew in an earthly paradise and that fragments of it were swept over the face of the globe by a series of floods.

It is also said that the tree originally grew only on the tops of inaccessible mountains where fearful monsters or wild beasts guarded it from the greedy hands of man.

However that may be, it is certain that at the present time the public is not interested in the origin of this substance so much as its exploitation for commercial purposes. An industry formerly so flourishing should be systematically revived, if only for its prospective financial importance.

Balap, where the members of our mission remained for some time, is celebrated as the residence of Pô Galao, the " Lord of the Eaglewood," on whom devolved in former times the duty of supervising the gathering of the precious substance. His associates were sixteen men of the same village and a certain number of the "Raglaï" Moi, a group living in the neighbourhood whose keen sense of smell is vital to success. A good nose is of far greater importance than good sight, for eaglewood exhales a characteristic odour which has to be detected from among the various smells of the virgin forest. Indeed the task of finding the tree is beset with difficulties. The undergrowth is so thick, the vegetation so hardy and rampant, that progress can only be made by clearing a path with knife and hatchet. The decaying vegetation is a prolific source of fevers. It is easily understood that with so many perils ahead the expedition never sets out without a preliminary sacrifice to the deities who can assure or withhold success. Of these deities the most important to appease are the four tutelary divinities of the valley of Phanrang. To earn their goodwill it is necessary to build a special barn for the sacrifice and make offerings of a goat, cooked rice, eggs and spirits.

As soon as the expedition starts the searchers are bound by a religious law of silence. Should any member of the party speak it would be almost certain that the wood would lose its perfume, and therefore all its value.

Of course, an occasional direction to the "Raglaï" Moï is unavoidable, and for this purpose the Cham make use of certain brief vivid expressions. For example, if they wish to indicate an axe they say "the wood-pecker." When they want to speak of fire they say "the red."

For a long time it was believed that this conven-

RITES AND SUPERSTITIONS 305

tional language was a form of religious speech, somewhat similar to the " Bhasa Hantu," or language of the Spirit, employed by the Malays. Further research, however, has proved that these expressions are confined to a few detached words borrowed from the Raglaï dialect and used by the Cham to communicate with them alone.

The women who remain behind in the villages are strictly forbidden to quarrel amongst themselves while their husbands are away looking for eaglewood. A breach of this regulation would mean that the men would run grave risk of being attacked by tigers or bitten by serpents. The cynical, however, assert that even this evil possibility is insufficient to preserve harmony in the village!

While I was at Malam near Phantiet I was present at the annual festival of the Cham Bani of that village. The ceremony is known as " Raja," a name which is also applied to the priestess who officiates.

On reaching the courtyard of the compound to which I was invited I observed a large hut and several sheds ornamented with branches of trees on which sheets of coarse cotton were spread. The sheds served to accommodate the many guests who, like myself, had accepted the invitation to be present at the festival. The hut was devoted to the ceremonies of ancestor-worship, which were that day celebrated.

This building faced the east. On entering I immediately noticed at the back of the room a kind of trough serving as an altar. From the ceiling hung paper figures of boats, carts, animals and various domestic objects. In the middle of the room, suspended from the two principal beams, was a swing with its seat covered with brightly-coloured materials, which took on a strangely gay and barbaric aspect under the lights of many little candles.

The native orchestra comprised a flute, a stringed instrument with some resemblance to a guitar, gongs and tambourines. The conductor, who seemed to be the principal performer, also improvised on a flat drum, timing his melodious drone to fill the intervals when the priestess was resting.

The latter, clothed in a long white robe and with a wreath of flowers in her hair, joined with an assistant priest in the steps of a saraband. Together they gave vent to their feelings in dancing, singing, prayers, imprecations, tears, grinding of teeth and hypnotic ecstasies, all with the object of appeasing the shades of the ancestors. Suddenly the priestess seated herself on the swing in the narrow passage left between the candles. She swung herself slowly to and fro, running her hands up and down the supporting ropes and droning through endless prayers. When she had finished the priest followed her example and went through the same rigmarole. So curious was the scene that I could not resist the malevolent idea of taking a photograph and without reflection I fired a piece of magnesium ribbon.

Woe to me for my impatience! In the confusion which followed the flash both I and my camera were almost upset. I had purposely given the company no notice of my intention in order to avoid the " posing " which self-conscious sitters cannot avoid. The Faithful, in their amazement, had taken the sudden apparition as an emanation of the Gods themselves. Something more than explanations was necessary to allay the general alarm, and it was only after a generous distribution of tobacco that I was able to restore some measure of harmony.

The religious celebrations lasted three days, interspersed with feasts and other diversions, notably an acrobatic display by a performer who roused his audience to a frenzy of enthusiasm. At the beginning of each feast a priest called all the deities by name and executed the movements of a dance in their honour. These evolutions are an invitation to the divinities to take their place in the celebrations.

At dawn on the second day the priestess filled with cakes and fruit a toy boat hollowed out of the trunk of a banana-tree by some ingenious artisan. In this frail canoe a rag monkey was placed, squatting on its haunches in a very grotesque position. The boat was meant to commemorate the vessel which in former days came from China every three years to fetch the tribute exacted from a vassal state.

After this the roysterers fell upon the improvised temple and hacked it to pieces amongst general rejoicings.

The next day, by way of applying the closure to the festivities, the whole crowd, headed by the priest and priestess, marched to a neighbouring canal, taking the symbolical boat with them. While the orchestra poured forth an unmelodious symphony the lilliputian vessel was entrusted to the waters, in which it speedily filled and disappeared.

There are strong resemblances between this Cham ceremony and the celebrations in India which mark the changes of the monsoon. In this latter country travellers find the same gaily bedecked sheds, the same rude figures cut out of paper, and the same swing scene. The Hindus regard the backward and forward movement of the swing as a symbol of the movements of the seasons.

Most of the rites which obtain among the Cham, in fact, recall the ritual observances of the Vedic and Brahminic religions, of which the following are among the most characteristic features.

The place selected for the crowning act of sacrifice, "Devayajana," is always an open space, whether at a cross-roads or in an enclosure. The improvised temple is made of branches or clods of earth and is invariably destroyed by the worshippers after the solemn ceremony is over.

Each sacrifice is regarded as the conclusion of a treaty between the gods and mortals. The value of the offering is in proportion to the extent of the favours desired. Most sacrifices are for heat or rain, two necessaries of life without which neither health nor prosperity is possible.

The officiating priest and his bodyguard of acolytes are housed and fed at the expense of the "Yajamana,"

RITES AND SUPERSTITIONS

the individual for whose ultimate benefit the benevolence of the gods is solicited. I ought to add that the previous life and blamelessness of this person have nothing to do with the efficacy of the sacrifice. On the contrary, the only thing that matters is the exact, punctilious observance of the rite itself.

It is plain that intellect plays little part in these religious ceremonies. Throughout, each act is designed to fire the imagination and arouse the emotions, rather than carry conviction.

It is equally certain that rites of undoubted Dravidian origin are to be observed among the Chain. The common denominator of all the religions of India is the worship of divinities personifying the earth or the elements, generally in the shape of a woman, and almost always considered malevolent.

Horrible sacrifices are offered to appease them, and the religious ceremonies usually terminate in the most abandoned orgies. The presiding priest, or "Devil Dancer," after a series of frantic contortions, falls to the ground in a hypnotic trance, during which the incoherent expressions that fall from his lips are greedily noted and repeated by the Faithful, who regard them as the words of Divinity itself.

For a last example there are certain fêtes, such as the "Durgapuja" in Bengal, marked by buffoonery and pantomime, in which the worshippers conclude the ceremonies by carrying a statue of the goddess in procession to the river banks, and casting it into the waters to the strains of an ear-shattering orchestra.

CHAPTER V

RITES AND SUPERSTITIONS (*continued*)

Burial rites—Philology—Legends and fables.

THE exorcisms of the "Padjao" directed towards expelling disease from the bodies of the Cham are too similar to those of the Moï sorceress to merit description, which would be little more than repetition.

On the other hand, the burial rites of the Kaphir Cham are highly characteristic.

Children who die before the age of puberty, and therefore not initiated into the full rights and mysteries of manhood, are buried in the earth, while adults of both sexes are cremated. The reason for this distinction is not far to seek. The adults are regarded as a class set apart with its own complex of funeral rites and observances. Further, those who die while still of tender years die in innocence and need no such purification from their sins as is implied in the practice of submitting the bodies of their elders to the scourge of fire.

After death the spirits of the little ones are supposed to dwell in the bodies of rats, and their memory is perpetuated from time to time by ceremonies in which the head of the family, clad in a new robe for the occasions, makes offerings, waves his hands in the air to imitate the movements of a bird, performs certain mystical passes, and puts a red flower in a bronze vase.

The burial rites which are still practised by the Kaphir Cham of Phanrang and Phanry serve as excellent comments on the duties of the priest in case of the death of any inhabitant of a village.

The fundamental notion on which all the observances are based is that the soul of the deceased must have a new body in which it may take refuge after the loss of its earthly dwelling-place. All the ceremonies are designed to create this new body. It is universally agreed that rice alone can operate the necessary transformation, and as the rice must be of the finest quality procurable, each family preserves the best stalks from the harvest and lays them up in anticipation of a death.

When the dread moment arrives the selected grains are mixed in a bowl into which a gold ring, symbol of immortality, has been dropped. The priest now glues a few grains together with melted wax to form a soft round ball, which is introduced under the dead man's tongue. A few mystical passes, and the soul leaves its old shell for the new ætherial body thus called into existence. The next and last step is to give the soul its necessary directions. These depend upon the manner of life of the deceased. Virtuous men are sent to the sun, women against whom there is no reproach to the moon. If the credit and debit items of a man's moral account balance out he is dispatched to the planets. The wicked are dispersed among the clouds, as are also the poor and lowly, an inequitable disposition worthy of a theocracy!

The actual ceremony of cremation follows after a period which is determined by the state of the corpse and the financial position of the deceased's family. From the moment of death to the cremation custom exacts that all visitors to the family should be housed and fed at the expense of the relations. These visitors come to keep the deceased company and pretend to entertain him by their wit and conversation. They also cheer up the relations and do their best to keep sorrow at a convenient distance.

The family build a special shed under which the corpse is laid, after having been dressed in eight robes, one over the other. Thus swathed in white linen the body looks exactly like a package with the head, covered with a thin veil, emerging from one end. It is strictly forbidden to offer any nourishment to the deceased before he leaves his own house. The bed on which the corpse is laid is turned towards the south and surmounted by a kind of canopy from which hang birds cut out of paper. It seems that the function of this winged escort is to conduct the soul to its future home. Clumps of hemp and various foods are strewn around the bier and the walls of the shed are hung with martial trophies.

Three times a day the priestess prepares a meal

Photo by] [A. Cabaton.
Cremation in Cambodia : The Head of the Procession.

Photo by] [A Cabaton.
A Catafalque upon which several Bodies are being carried away for Cremation.

Photo by]   *[A. Cabato*

The Hearse and Bearers at an Annamese Funeral.

Photo by]   *[A. Cabaton.*

The Altar of his Ancestors which accompanies the Deceased.

for the deceased. An orchestra plays from morning to night almost without intermission. It is soon plain that this lying-in-state, so far from being a rite of mourning, is more like a festival. The guests consume enormous quantities of food and drink, and only the unfortunate relations are under ban to refrain from meat until after the cremation.

When at length the great day arrives the priests construct a catafalque adorned with paper figures, the mourners line up in procession behind, and all proceed to the appointed place. Every villager dons his white scarf—white being the colour of mourning—brandishes a spear, sword, or flag, and joins in the cortège. The bearers perform the most remarkable evolutions with the body, carrying it now feet first, now head first, or turning it round and round in order to confuse the spirit and prevent it from finding its way back. This essential object is also secured by a priest, known on these occasions as " Pô Damoeun," " Lord of Sorrow," who remains in the house of the deceased, shuts himself in, and calls on every object, animate and inanimate, to prevent the soul from entering and molesting the living.

When the funeral procession is within a hundred yards from the exit from the village a priest takes a spade and marks out the spot destined for the funeral pyre. Wood is brought and piled up and the corpse is stripped of its wrappings and offered its last meal. As soon as the flames break out the clothes of the deceased are thrown into them. Now comes the moment, marked by the passage of the soul to the life beyond, when the living send gifts to their dead relations. Each man writes his list of presents on a slip of paper and then burns it. The list is exhaustive, including such homely and necessary articles as a pipe, spittoon and the inevitable receptacle for betel and lime. Even underclothing and small change are not forgotten. During the progress of the conflagration the spectators joke and chatter together, leaving the serious business of desolation to the hired mourners, who weep aloud and tear their hair. At the conclusion of the ceremony the frontal bone of the deceased is carefully broken in nine pieces, which are collected in a metal box, the "klong," a special kind of urn. Every man provides himself with one of these receptacles in anticipation of his own death, but the usual practice is to conceal it in some place known only to his family, as it is not altogether pleasant to be perpetually reminded of the terror to come.

The fragments of bone are now subjected to a long and tedious process of purification, after which they are buried at the foot of a tree, which is carefully noted, as being only a temporary depository. For the next seven years on each anniversary the family dig up the box, carry it back to their house, and offer sacrifices in its honour. After the seventh year the interment is permanent. A spot is chosen near to the best of the family ricefields, trees are planted round it, and a tombstone is erected.

RITES AND SUPERSTITIONS 315

Sometimes the rites require that for the first interment the "klong" of a man and a woman must be used together. It follows that in small families where many years may elapse between the deaths of its members the first "klong" runs a great risk of exceeding its seven compulsory years of waiting before reaching its final resting-place.

The direction in which the urn is placed varies with the sex of the deceased. The "klong" of a woman points to the west, that of a man to the east.

I have described these rites at some length on account of their intrinsic interest, but it would be illuminating to compare them with similar ceremonies obtaining among other groups.

The Man Quan Trang, or "white-breeched" Man of Tonkin, bury the hair and portions of the nails and bones in a different place from that of the corpse itself. The reason for this is that these fragments are considered the abode of the Material Soul and the Vital Spirits.

The Bouriates of Siberia bury some of the bones of their priests at the foot of a tree.

The Egyptians made a set speech to their dead, in which they gave directions for the guidance of the soul to the distant regions, and enumerated a list of necessary articles to accompany it. The recitation of these articles dispensed with the necessity of furnishing them. The will was thus considered as good as the deed.

Lastly the funeral rites I have described find analogies among the Laotians and the peoples of Cambodia. Here also a death is celebrated as a happy event, as being merely a step to a new existence far more blessed than the life on earth. The face of the corpse is covered with a mask in gold leaf which is moulded to the features, and the process of decomposition is retarded by the introduction of mercury. The catafalque is large or small according to the social position of the deceased. A king, for example, has a regular monument known as the "Mén." A Minister of State or a High Priest is honoured with a rather smaller edifice, while those of humble estate have to be content with a simple pyramid. A large white cloth is hung over the catafalque, of which the opening is guarded by a small figure in the mask of a monkey. This is "Yéac," a subject of Couvera, the God of Riches, whose statue adorns every place where a mystical transformation is to be accomplished. The quaint figure holds in its hand a reel of white cotton, of which one end is secured to the coffin and which will guide the soul after it has left the body. The torch which fires the funeral pyre is lit at a brasier which contains the sacred embers which must never be extinguished. When cremation is complete the bones are collected into a box made of precious metal, which is buried under a tower, the height of which varies with the wealth of the deceased.

All these rites, however much they vary among

themselves in detail, seem to be based on the same popular ideas of the significance of death.

Like ourselves, the Cham write from left to right. Their alphabet varies in different regions. In Cambodia it comprises four vowels, two diphthongs, and twenty-nine consonants. In Annam there are five short vowels, five long vowels, and four diphthongs. Both of these alphabets have two special signs which correspond to the "Anusvara" and "Visarga" of Sanscrit. There are also certain signs usually employed in conjunction with the vowels which influence their pronunciation. With the exception of the figures 4 and 0 the numerals are only a modified form of the letters.

The popular pen is a short bamboo cut to a point and manipulated like a paint-brush. The European pen is, however, coming into fashion with the progress of Western ideas.

In Cambodia manuscripts are written in a beautiful free hand on paper of Western form and manufacture. On the other hand, the Cham of Annam use sheets of rice-paper of tremendous size imported from China. Occasionally the traveller meets with inscriptions made with a needle on palm-leaves.

The priests of Annam employ a hieratic writing, which they call "Akhar Rik," especially for such purposes as engraving magical inscriptions on amulets.

A secret system and an abbreviated system are also used when occasion requires.

A curious feature of their books is that the authors display a tendency to coin new words from Sanscrit or Arabic roots even when the idea expressed in those roots has only the remotest similarity to the meaning they wish the word to convey.

The Cham Bani of Phanrang are the proud possessors of the manuscript of a Bible, the text of which has been modified in many places by Mohammedan influence. The truth of this will be demonstrated from the examples translated by Father Durand.

"This Book tells the story of the beginnings of Earth and Heaven. . . . The creation of the Sun God and the Moon Goddess. The Lord Uwlwah —Allah—then created the Pô Adam and the woman Hawā, whom he took from the man's side. . . Their children numbered nine and ninety, an equal (!) number of boys and girls. They died in the Kingdom of Judah."

Then follow the story of the flood, the lives of Abraham and David, without conspicuous discrepancies.

"The son of Nabi Dalawat—Daoud, David—(the Cham have no final d) was called the Nabi Suleiman —Solomon. Allah commanded him to build the Caabah—temple—and gave him a mountain of gold and silver. Suleiman covered the walls of his Caabah with these precious metals and it became wondrously beautiful. He was appointed Chief of the Priests

RITES AND SUPERSTITIONS 319

therein. . . . Then Nabi Esā—Issa, Jesus—was born in the country of Baitelem and him Allah took to himself. . . . Then Mohammat—Mahomet—for forty years decreed all the Doctrine in the Kingdom of Makah—Mecca—and died in the Kingdom of Madjanah—Medina. . . . Then Adam and Hawā produced the seven Royalties. The sum of these seven epochs gives the total of 7306 years to the cyclic year of the Tiger. . . .

" That is all. . . ."

The Cham, like the Kmer, have taken little trouble over the composition of their legends and fables.

Apart from certain legends which by internal evidence and local flavour can only be regarded as having originated among the Cham, all the others are more or less successful adaptations of Hindu tales. In almost all countries, and conspicuously in the Far East, popular fancy fastens and feeds on the fabulous, or, at least, incredibly romantic, adventures of the ancient Kings. It is at least true to say that these adventures furnish a canvas on which imagination has worked wondrous pictures.

The origin of the special tight-fitting costume worn by the Cham women is explained on this wise.

In the darkness of the Past a Cham Prince named Hon Hoï declared war on a Laotian Princess, whose ricefields he coveted. In accordance with the customs of the women of her race, the Princess, Diep Lieu, was arrayed in nothing more than a scanty covering of bamboo fibres. The barbarity and ignorance of her subjects was incredible. All buying and selling went on by night, and in the darkness it was impossible to determine the quality of the wares displayed except by their fine smell. The Prince had no difficulty in overwhelming her forces and making her his prisoner. But she found favour in his sight, and within a short time she exchanged captivity for freedom and honour as his wife. The Prince, however, was shocked at the summary attire of his betrothed and for the wedding-day he gave her a costume of his own making. This was a kind of sack, at the top of which was a narrow hole for the head to come through. The Cham also honour the thesis that imitation is the sincerest form of flattery, so the women adopted this new mode with avidity, and it has survived all the attacks of time and feminine caprice.

A legend has gathered round each of the kings who has been raised to the ranks of divinity by the Cham. Pô Klong Garai was born of a Virgin Mother, Pô Sah Ineu, who rose alive from the waves. Though hardly yet a woman she conceived her son while sipping water from a stream which flowed through a rock. The child was smitten with the horror of leprosy from birth. While he rested near a rock, a dragon emerged from a cavern, licked the sores caused by the fell disease, and the child was immediately cured. From that day he felt himself endowed with matchless celestial powers. On one occasion, when about to make a distant journey, and at a loss for a receptacle in which to carry water he saw a pumpkin.

At the first touch of his hand the fruit broke its stalk and offered its services as a gourd. When this magician became King he built several dams in the valley of Phanrang and turned an arid desert into a fertile plain. So great were his services to his people that finally the gods rewarded him by calling him to be one of themselves.

Hardly less humble in origin than this prince was Pô Romé. He also was born of a Virgin Mother, whom the family drove from their doors in horror at the alleged crime. Nature, too, was not more kindly to the tiny bastard, who had neither arms nor legs and rolled over the ground like a cocoa-nut (a peculiarity from which he soon took that name). In spite of his deformity, however, the reigning sovereign praised him to his mother and appointed him to guard the cattle. Destiny was watching over him and a Dragon soon appeared to tell him of all the glories the future had in store. Warned of the approaching miracle by the court astrologers, the King set himself to win the regard of one who might one day prove a formidable rival to himself. He finally decided to abdicate in the young man's favour and added to his benefits by giving him the hand of his daughter in marriage and two other wives of the second and third degree. But Cocoa-nut was not happy even with his three wives. Hardly had he ascended the throne than he lost his crown through the artifices of his second wife. This lady was the daughter of the King of Annam who coveted his neighbour's lands and was not above treachery to secure them. At this time the tutelary deity of the Cham was shut up in the trunk of a tree, known as the "Kraik," and so long as this tree was alive no misfortune could befall the race beneath its ægis. The second wife, adopting the counsel of her evil father, pretended to be smitten with a grave malady. She refused all cures and asserted that her only hope was the destruction of the Kraik. Cocoa-nut, who had a strong affection for this wife, had her carefully examined by the four most eminent medicine-men of his kingdom. All four agreed that the illness was a sham, and all four paid for their truthfulness with their heads. Meanwhile the lady's condition seemed to go from bad to worse, and the King decided to fell with his own hand the tree on which hung the destinies of his people. Streams of blood flowed from the smitten trunk and soaked the ground around. The King had not long to wait for retribution. Betrayed by his treacherous spouse, his kingdom was wrested from him and he was hacked in pieces by his triumphant foe. His incisors alone were restored to his first wife that she might pay the honour due to his remains. The ex-Cocoa-nut, become Pô Romé, now dwells among the Gods, but even there, it seems, his domestic tribulations have pursued him, and he is often glad, when distracted by the factious quarrels of his womenfolk, to get away from his palace and leave it to them.

The Cham have a certain partiality for songs and lyrical poems not destitute of taste and feeling have acquired popularity among them. A romance which the girls of Phanrang sing on their fishing expeditions is as follows :

" Do you go forth to set sail, my Lord, that you look at the leaves for the direction of the wind ? Ibrahim, my soul of gold . . . hard would it be if you left me. . . .

" Pity your little sister fair as gold itself ! Do not leave her, like an orphan, to wander in the forests where fear and danger lurk. . . .

" You will stay ! Oh joy ! Life will be naught but play and laughter and walks together, hand in hand ! "

Finally, there is the skeleton, not much more, of a literature. Here are some extracts from a bedside book which all girls are supposed to study before making their own homes.

" Liver and Bile of thy mother, approach, my child, and learn what a woman should know.

" When thou speakest with thy husband, let thy tone above all be modest.

" Strive not to appear superior or even as his equal, for the man it is who should lead the woman.

" My child, the boat will not leave its moorings if the stake is solid and secure ! In a family the husband is the keystone of the structure !

" The honour he gains goes to the credit of his wife.

" My daughter, ever remember that the happiness of a household lies in the hands of the wife. She must not waste the goods he entrusts to her.

" Waste not then the least trifle. See that every door has always its bolt. . . . Follow these precepts and wert thou as hideous as an ape thou shalt keep the love of thy husband, for thy presence shall be more profitable to him than a bar of gold, were it the height of a cocoa-nut tree. "

Of such homely advice consists the very ancient manuscript which Moura translated and which escaped the wreck in which all the others were lost.

I expect modern young ladies will find these mother's words somewhat out of date. But what European husband would not occasionally envy the Cham so perfect a partner?

THE END

BIBLIOGRAPHY

I HAVE kept the scientific side of my researches in the background in this book, but the curious may consult the following works with advantage:

AYMONIER, E., "Les Tjames et leurs Religions." Paris, Leroux, 1891; "Légendes historiques des Chams," in *Excursions et Reconnaissances*, No. 32, 1890.

BARTH, "Les Religions de l'Inde." Paris, Fichbacher, 1879.

BARTHÉLÉMY, DE, "Au pays Moï." Paris, Plon Nourrit, 1903.

BERNARD, DR. NOËL, "Les Khas, peuple inculte du Laos," in *Bulletin de géographie historique et descriptive*, 1904.

BERGAIGNE, A., "L'Ancien Royaume du Champa dans l'Indochine," in *Journal Asiatique*. Paris, 1886.

CABATON, ANTOINE, "Nouvelles recherches sur les Chams." Paris, Leroux, 1901; "Notes sur les sources européennes de l'histoire de l'Indochine," in *Bulletin de la Commission Archéologique de l'Indochine*, 1911; "Les Malais et l'avenir de leur langue," in *Revue du Monde Musulman*. Paris, 1908; "Les Chams musulmans de l'Indochine," in *Revue du Monde Musulman*. Paris, 1907.

CADIÈRE, LE PÈRE, "Croyances et dictons populaires de la vallée du Nguon Son," in *Bulletin de l'École Française d'Extrême Orient*. Hanoi, Schneider, 1902.

CRAWLEY, E., "The Mystic Rose." London, Macmillan, 1902.

Cremazy, "Le droit coutumier de l'Extrême Orient à travers les ages." Conférence faite à l'École Coloniale en 1909.
Cumont, Franz, "Les Religions Orientales dans le paganisme romain." Paris, Leroux, 1907.
Cupet, Commandant. See Pavie.
Diguet, Le Colonel E., "Les montagnards du Tonkin." Paris, Challamel, 1908.
Doudart de Lagrée. See Garnier.
Dourisboure, Le Père, "Les sauvages Bahnars." Paris, Téqui, 1904.
Dulaure, J. A., "Les divinités génératrices, ou du culte du Phallus chez les Anciens et les Modernes." Paris, 1805. A new edition by the Société du Mercure de France. Paris, 1905.
Durand, Le Père, "Les Moï du Song Phang," in *B. G. D. H.* Paris, 1900; "Les Chams Banis," in *B. E. F. E. O.* Hanoi, 1903; "Notes sur les Chams," in *B. E. F. E. O.* Hanoi, 1905; "Les Archives des derniers Rois Chams," in *B. E. F. E. O.* Hanoi, 1907.
Fillastre, Le Père Adrien, "Bois d'aigle et bois d'aloès," in *Revue Indochinoise.* Hanoi, 1905.
Finot, Louis, "La Religion des Chams d'après les monuments," in *B. E. F. E. O.* Hanoi, 1901. Cours d'Histoire et de Philologie Indochinoises professé au Collège de France, 1908.
Foucart, George, "Histoire des Religions et Méthode Comparative." Paris, Picard, 1912.
Frazer, "The Golden Bough." London, Macmillan, 1900.
Garnier, F., "Voyage d'exploration en l'Indochine." Paris, Hachette, 1873.
Gennep, Arnold van, "Religions, Mœurs et Légendes." Paris, Mercure de France, 4 vols. 1908 à 1911; "Mythes et Légendes d'Australie." Paris, Guilmoto, 1908; "Les Rites de Passage." Paris, E. Nourry, 1909.

HAVELOCK, ELLIS, " Studies in Sexual Psychology."
HOLBÉ, T. V., " Les poisons Moï et recherches sur le Cai voi-voi." Montpellier, Serre et Roumegous, 1905.
HUTEREAU, A., " Notes sur la vie familiale et juridique de quelques populations du Congo Belge," in *Annales du Musée du Congo Belge.* Brussels, 1909.
JOYCE, T. A., " Notes ethnographiques sur les peuples communément appelés Bakuba, ainsi que sur les peuplades apparentées Les Busongo," in *Annales du Musée du Congo Belge.* Brussels, 1911.
KEANE, A. H., " On the Relations of the Indo-Chinese and Inter-Oceanic races and languages," in the *Journal of the Anthropological Institute of Great Britain and Ireland.* London, 1880.
KEMLIN, LE P., " Les rites agraires des Reungao," in *B. E. F. E. O.* Hanoi, 1910; " Au pays Jaraï," in *Missions Catholiques.* Paris, 1909.
LANDES, A., " Légende djarai sur l'origine du sabre sacré par le Roi du Feu," in *Revue Indochinoise.* Hanoi, 1904.
LEFÈVRE, PONTALIS, " Notes sur l'écriture des Khas," in *L'Anthropologie.* Paris, 1892; " Notes sur quelques populations du Nord de l'Indochine," in *Journal Asiatique.* Paris, 1892.
LEMIRE, CH., " Les anciens monuments des Kiams en Annam et au Tonkin," in *L'Anthropologie.* Paris.
LETOURNEAU, CH., " La littérature synthétique des premiers âges," in *Bulletin de la Société d'Anthropologie.* Paris, 1894.
MAITRE, H., " Les régions Moï du Sud Indochinois." Paris, Plon, 1909; " Les jungles Moï." Paris, E. Larose, 1912.
MALGLAIVE, CAP. DE. See Pavie.
MASPERO, " Le Royaume de Champa," in Toung-Pao. 1910 à 1912.
MOURA, J., " Le Royaume du Cambodge." Paris, Leroux, 1883.
NEIS, DR. P., " Explorations chez les Sauvages de

BIBLIOGRAPHY

l'Indochine," in *Bulletin de la Société de Géographie*. Paris, 1883.

PAVIE, AUGUSTE, " Mission Pavie en l'Indochine, 1879-1895." Paris, E. Leroux, 1901 à 1911 ; 6 vols. (See Cupet and Malglaive, in collaboration.)

REINACH, SALOMON. " Cultes, Mythes et Religions." Paris. E. Leroux.

RIEDEL, J. G. F., " Prohibitieve Teekens en Tatuage— vormen op het ecland." Batavia, 1907.

SAINTYVES, P., " Les Vierges Mères et les naissances miraculeuses." Paris, E. Nourry, 1908.

SÉBILLOT, P., " Le Folklore de France." Paris, Guilmoto, 1905.

SKEAT, W. W., " Some records of Malay magic." Singapore, 1898.

TORDAY, E. See Joyce, in collaboration.

TOURNIER, COLONEL, " Notice sur le Laos Français." Hanoi, 1900.

ZABOROSKI, " Les Tsiams. Origine et caractère," in *Revue Scientifique*. Paris, série IV.; " De la circoncision des garçons et de l'excision des filles comme pratiques d'initiation," in *Bulletin de la Société d'Anthropologie*. Paris. 1894.

X., " Notes analytiques sur les collections ethnographiques du Musée du Congo, publiées sous la direction du Musée. Tome I., fascicule II. La Religion." Bruxelles, 1906.

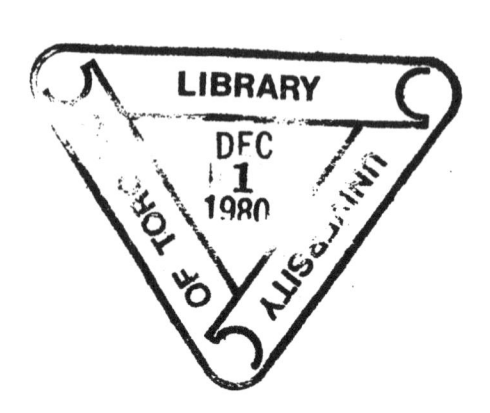

**PLEASE DO NOT REMOVE
CARDS OR SLIPS FROM THIS POCKET**

UNIVERSITY OF TORONTO LIBRARY

GN   Baudesson, Henry
635   Indo-China and its primi-
I6D3813 tive people

2 JUN '94